Training Teachers

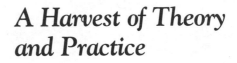

A Harvest of Theory and Practice

Margie Carter
Deb Curtis

Redleaf Press
a division of Resources for Child Caring

Published by:
Redleaf Press
a division of Resources for Child Caring
450 N. Syndicate, Suite 5
St. Paul, MN 55104

Distributed by:
Gryphon House
P.O. Box 207
Beltsville, MD 20704-0207

Library of Congress Cataloging-in-Publication Data
Carter, Margie.
    Training teachers : a harvest of theory and practice /
Margie Carter, Deb Curtis.
        p.   cm.
    Includes bibliographical references and index.
    ISBN 0-934140-82-0 : $32.95
    1. Teachers—Training of.   2. Adult learning.   3. Learning.
Psychology of.   I. Curtis, Debbie.   II. Title.
LB1707.C37   1994
370'.71—dc20

                                              94-38144   CIP

This book was set in Minion and Futura typefaces by Peregrine Graphics Services, St. Paul, Minnesota. It is printed on Glatfelter B-05 paper. A special lay-flat binding called otabinding was chosen to make the book easier to use. Printed by Versa Press Inc., East Peoria, Illinois.

PERMISSIONS

The following publishers have generously given permission to use extended quotations from copyrighted works. (p. xi) The excerpt from *The Education of Little Tree* by Forrest Carter, published by The University of New Mexico Press, is reprinted by arrangement with Eleanor Friede Books, Inc. © 1976 by Forrest Carter. All Rights Reserved. (pp. xi, xii, 88, 89, 160, 161) *The Hundred Languages of Children: The Reggio Emilia Approach to Early Childhood Education* © 1993 by Ablex Publishing. Reprinted with Permission. (pp. 6, 10) Brooks, Jacqueline Grennon (1990) "Teachers and Students: Constructivists Forging New Connections," *Educational Leadership*, 47, 5:69. Reprinted with permission of the Association for Supervision and Curriculum Development © 1990 by ASCD. All Rights Reserved. (pp. 9, 65, 67, 77) *Helping Others Learn to Teach: Some Principles and Techniques for Inservice Educators* © 1979 Lilian Katz. Reprinted with Permission. (pp. 12, 13, 97) B. Spodek (March 1975) "Early Childhood Education and Teacher Education: A Search for Consistency" and E. Jones and L. Derman-Sparks (January 1992) "Meeting the Challenges of Diversity," *Young Children* © NAEYC. Reprinted by Permission. (pp. 10, 18, 162, 206) E. Jones *Growing Teachers: Partnerships in Staff Development* © 1993 NAEYC. Reprinted with Permission. (pp. 23, 79) Reprinted by permission of the publisher from Wasserman, Selma, *Serious Players in the Primary Classroom* (New York: Teachers College Press © 1990 by Teachers College, Columbia University. All rights reserved). (p. 36, 243) Reprinted with permission from Diane Trister Dodge, *A Guide for Supervisors and Trainers on Implementing the Creative Curriculum for Early Childhood* © 1993 by Teaching Strategies, Inc., P.O. Box 42243, Washington, DC 20015, p. 16. (p. 58) E. Prescott (April 1979) "The Physical Environment—A Powerful Regulator of Experience." Reprinted with permission from Exchange Press, Inc., P.O. Box 2890, Redmond, WA 98073. (p. 71) "Playing Is My Job," *Thrust for Educational Leadership* © 1990 Elizabeth Jones. Reprinted with Permission. (pp. 93-94) *More Talks with Teachers* © 1984 Lilian Katz. Reprinted with Permission. (p. 11, 70) M. Schwebel and J. Raph, *Piaget in the Classroom* © 1973 by Basic Books Inc. Reprinted with permission of Basic Books, a division of HarperCollins Publishers Inc. (pp. 77, 87) M. C. Bateson. *Composing a Life* © 1990 Grove/Atlantic, Inc. Reprinted with Permission. (p. 77) Lilian Katz, (February 1990) "On Teaching." Reprinted with permission. (p. 94, 100) Excerpted from Delpit, Lisa D., "The Silenced Dialogue: Power and Pedagogy in Educating Other People's Children," *Harvard Educational Review*, 58:3, pp. 280-298 © 1988 by the President and Fellows of Harvard College. All Rights Reserved. (p. 110) "Culture as a Process" © 1991 Carol Brunson Phillips. Reprinted with Permission. (p. 113) D. Sawyer and H. Green. *Nesa Activities Handbook for Native and Multicultural Classrooms* © 1990. Reprinted with Permission. (pp. 100, 101) M. Randall. *Walking to the Edge* © 1991 South End Press. Reprinted with Permission. (p. 123) H. Ginott. *Teacher and Child: A Book for Parents and Teachers* © 1993 Collier Books. Reprinted with Permission. (p. 123) *Goals of Anti-Bias Curriculum* © 1991 Louise Derman-Sparks. Reprinted with Permission. (p.161) David Weikart and Clay Shouse "What Years of Inservice Training Have Taught Us" © 1993 High/Scope Resource. Reprinted with Permission. (p. 162) E. Jones and M. Carter (October 1990) "The Teacher as Observer, the Director as Role Model." Reprinted with permission from Exchange Press, Inc., P.O. Box 2890, Redmond, WA 98073. (p. 164) *National Child Care Staffing Study. Who Cares? Child Care Teachers and the Quality of Care in America* © 1988 Marcy Whitebook. Reprinted with Permission. (p. 71, 87, 88) Reprinted by permission of the publisher from Jones, Elizabeth, and Reynolds, Gretchen, *The Play's the Thing* (New York: Teachers College Press © 1992 by Teachers College, Columbia University. All rights reserved). (p. 183, 193–194) M. Hohmann, B. Banet, and D. Weikart. *Young Children in Action* © 1979 High/Scope Press. Reprinted with Permission. (p. 197–198) B. Bos *Before the Basics: Creating Conversations with Children* © 1983. Reprinted with Permission. (app. B) "Profile of Adult Abilities" © 1988 Jane Meade-Roberts. Reprinted with Permission. (app. B) "If the Shoe Fits: A Worthy Wages Fairy Tale" © Marcy Whitebook and Jim Morin.

Contents

Acknowledgments

Our heartfelt thanks to the colleagues, teachers, children, friends and family members who shared your thinking, time, expertise and excitement with us. You have taught, inspired and supported us such that writing this book was quite a treat. Special appreciation goes to: Ann Pelo, Betty Jones, Bonnie and Roger Neugebauer, Casey Bloom, Charlotte Jahn, Chris Beahler, Deovanna, Eileen Nelson, Elliott Bronstein, Jason, Jeanne Hunt, Jim Greenman, Joan Newcomb, Kristin Sampson, Lonnie Bloom, Louise Derman-Sparks, Maralyn Thomas-Schier, Marilyn Jacobson, Myrna Cannon, Nanette Cordon, Randi Solinsky, Red & Black Books Collective, Wayne Reinhardt, Wendy Harris, Ronna Hammer, Worthy Wage Campaign activists, and Child Care Resources.

Dedication

Elliott Bronstein

For Jerome Jackson *(January 29, 1950–May 16, 1993)*

*whose work with young children reflected
the ideas in this book.*

Foreword

ELIZABETH JONES

$\mathcal{R}$eading this book, my first reaction was that I wish I'd written it. My second reaction was that I'm grateful that the group of those committed to active learning for adults keeps growing, and is represented here by two such articulate, thoughtful practitioners as Margie and Deb. They combine broad experience in teacher training and supervision with a lively capacity for collaborative play with ideas. They've credited me with "reinforcing our own playful dispositions" as we have reflected together on teaching—inventing, experimenting, critiquing, arguing, and delighting in the process.

To support active learning, the teacher must play with the possibilities—planning and then letting go—as learners contribute their own ideas in response to teaching strategies like those offered in this book. To let go, a teacher must have confidence that there are more good ideas where those came from, and that many of them will come from the learners. Margie and Deb actively practice this with adult learners. "The having of wonderful ideas," Eleanor Duckworth has written in her book of that name (Teachers College Press, 1987, p. 1), "is what I consider the essence of intellectual development. And I consider it the essence of pedagogy to give (the learner) the occasion to have his wonderful ideas and to let him feel good about himself for having them."

Teachers of young children aren't often treated as intellectuals—autonomous thinkers capable of significant decision making. But teachers in their classroom must continually make decisions, collaborating with other adults and with children to craft a learning environment. In a developmentally appropriate classroom, teachers respect children as thinkers and choosers, enabling them to practice these skills as the foundation for the rest of their lives. Adults are unlikely to respect children unless they experience respect for themselves, and that is the philosophy underlying this book.

In a changing society, people need to be able to make wise choices and moral decisions. In a society founded on the democratic vision but fraught with injustice, people need to take stands on behalf of change. And so how we teach is more important than what we teach; do we model conformity, or action on behalf of the vision? Margie and Deb are clearly on the side of taking action, challenging teachers to engage in critical thinking and offering them tools with which to do so.

This is, above all, a collection of teaching tools and learning strategies. As a teacher of adults, one could use this book and never have to invent any more new strategies oneself. Since I wrote *Teaching Adults* (NAEYC, 1986), readers have continued to write me to ask for more ideas. Here they are, ideas in profusion—and they are offered by the authors not as canned curriculum but as examples of the process of teacher invention and as challenges to invent for oneself. The book's beautifully organized structure provides frequent guideposts and road signs to keep reminding the reader of the route and the goal: Here's a good idea we've tried, and this is *why* we use it.

Margie and Deb are great at metaphor, and this one is my favorite:

> Someone once described going into the 21st Century as akin to living in permanent white water. Child care teachers know this feeling well and, depending on their disposition, put their energies into damming the waters, ferociously paddling to keep up, or actively scanning for the optimal balance between challenge and safety. Helping teachers cultivate a disposition to expect continuous change and challenge enhances their responsiveness to classroom dynamics and sustains their ability to ride out the continual demands and frustrations of their job.

As the mother of a white water kayaker, I have found this book an exhilarating paddle.

Introduction

$\mathcal{T}$his book is for anyone responsible for staff development or for those interested in training as the next step in their career path. At first glance, you may not find the recipes you are looking for. These pages contain a bounty of thought-provoking ideas and strategies—ones that again and again have been useful in our twenty-some years of training teachers. But rather than listing step-by-step instructions for tried-and-true recipes, we offer a fresh look and descriptions of the ingredients for effective teaching. We encourage you to look in your own garden and cupboard of experiences for the seeds that will lead to your own harvest.

Writing this book is a response to the critical need we see for overhauling the approach to training early childhood teachers. Each week our jobs take us to programs that provide direct care and education for children. We see programs where staff turnover is alarmingly high and the workforce increasingly inexperienced and lacking in understandings of child development. We often see classrooms that are either out of control and in chaos or under tight control with a rigid structure and curriculum that is developmentally inappropriate. In these classrooms, principles of cultural relevancy and anti-bias practices are either missing or mistakenly applied. Many times, education coordinators and program directors are overwhelmed with a multitude of responsibilities and lack the time and preparation to effectively coach staff into deeper understandings and improved job performance.

As part-time college instructors and consultants active in the National Association for the Education of Young Children (NAEYC), local AEYC affiliates, and professional development efforts of resource and referral agencies (R&R's), we see delivery systems for teacher training that are haphazard, uncoordinated, or inappropriately compartmentalized. Child guidance and curriculum methods classes tend to be taught as topics separate from child development; at best producing effective classroom technicians, not responsive child development practioners. In-service training programs at conferences, R&R's, or program sites offer a smorgasbord of seminars and workshops. These programs, however, lack a consistent theoretical framework from which teachers in training can develop their knowledge and practice.

Most disturbing to us is the fact that few teacher training programs, including those promoting Piaget and developmental education, use a pedagogy that parallels what we want teachers to do with young children. Ignoring, if not defying, the research and implications of constructivist theory, it appears teacher educators believe that all adults are at the stage of formal operations. They teach to one learning style that revolves around lectures, reading, memorization, and imitation. No wonder we see teachers perpetuating the cycle of inappropriate practices!

You will find this book reflects a very different approach. We teach teachers in ways consistent with how we want them to teach the children in their care. This

In the field of education, as in many others, good theory—I boldly say—has come mostly as a harvest, a reflection of successful practice. Harvested from past practice, theory in turn can, then, bring new practical guidance.

David Hawkins, *The Hundred Languages of Children*[1]

Gramma said when you come on something good, first thing to do is share it with whoever you can; that way, the good spreads out where no telling it will go. Which is right.

Forrest Carter, *The Education of Little Tree*[2]

is not only a matter of modeling, but also a reflection of our understandings of adult learning theory after evaluating what has and hasn't been effective in our years of work as program directors, college instructors, on-site trainers, and consultants.

In truth, we never set out to write a book. There are any number of valuable ones already available to early childhood educators. We discovered, however, that many of these are undiscovered or underutilized by those working in teacher training programs. Believing these little-used resources could help teachers and teacher educators improve their practice, we began building training strategies around them.

For instance, as we enthusiastically studied new books, such as *The Hundred Languages of Children: The Reggio Emilia Approach to Early Childhood Education* (Ablex, 1993), we found ourselves substituting the word "adults" for "children" in thinking about this approach to education. Though our ideas are certainly not original or unique, feedback from educators about our training methods has included praise for our innovative and uncommon strategies. High enrollment in our Staff Development and Training of Teacher Trainer classes and scores of requests for presentations and consultations convinced us we could make a further contribution by writing the story of our efforts to put theory into practice.

The thinking of two of our mentors—Lilian Katz and Elizabeth (Betty) Jones—is woven into our training practices and the pages of this book. Katz's *fostering dispositions* is a central goal in our work with teachers. She also has taught us to think in terms of *teacher developmental stages*. Jones has written extensively on applying Piaget to adult learning practices and has inspired us to create specific training strategies aimed at helping teachers *construct* their knowledge. Our focus of training teachers to assume new roles has been greatly influenced by our dialogues with Jones. Her emphasis and writing about the importance of play for children has reinforced our own playful dispositions. Playing—with objects, ideas, and peers—not only makes learning more fun, it provides opportunities for consolidating understandings, *constructing knowledge*, for adults as well as children.

A word about our use of terms in this book. We are aware that the term "trainer" is not favored by some, given its association with behaviorism and animal training. When we use the term, we have more in mind those who train gymnasts, vocalists, or mothers giving birth—a coach who watches, listens, and shares observations, skills, and resources. As trainers we may, from time to time, focus on form or techniques, but our primary attention is on the adult learning process itself and strategies that will empower a teacher to be autonomous and thoughtful in planning and responding to the daily delights and challenges children offer.

HOW TO USE THIS BOOK

From a writer's point of view, there is always a logic to how a book is organized, with chapters to be read sequentially. Yet as busy readers ourselves, we know all too well that typically readers scan a book, looking for things of interest and seldom read from front to back. This awareness has influenced our decisions about what to put where in these pages. We think you'll get the most out of the book if you read it from front to back, but we've created each section to stand alone in case you choose otherwise. This means that a few of the ideas that are the foundation of our approach to training are repeated so that each chapter can be understood independently.

Our hope is that the reader will want to understand the theoretical framework that guides our approach to training. We've organized these chapters sequentially to represent the process we use in planning a training. This should enable you not only to develop an understanding of that process, but also adapt it to your own needs.

Section 1 provides an overview of the context for adult learning, suggesting the different ways of learning and knowing and theoretical considerations of developmental education. These chapters chart our journey in understanding and applying these concepts, with a preview of the new emphasis we now have in our teacher education practice—training for constructing knowledge, dispositions, new roles, and embracing diversity.

Section 2 lays out the landscape of a training practice built on constructivism and introduces you to a collection of tools we've gathered to inform and enhance our teacher education. We constantly return to these to sharpen our thinking and planning. On any given topic, we ask ourselves which tool might be useful. For instance, if we are planning a training on child guidance, is there a strategy using childhood memories that might be effective? Are there representations or metaphors that might expand thinking on this topic? What role plays could enhance skills? These pages are full of sample strategies with reduced forms and charts that are available complete in the appendices, with permission for you to reproduce as needed.

Sections 3 and 4 return to considerations of dispositions and roles for effective teaching and training for culturally sensitive and anti-bias practices, offering further food for thought after the reader has tasted multiple examples of how we plan training strategies with these considerations in mind.

Section 5 gets down to the nitty-gritty business of planning workshops and working in staff development as a program supervisor. Here you'll find practical examples of applying a developmental, inclusive approach to teacher training.

Section 6 offers perhaps the best holistic snapshot of our approach to training with a consistent group of teachers. It outlines how to use the project approach for teacher training on child-centered curriculum practices in the form of an ongoing college class or focused in-service training program on site.

Finally, in **Section 7** we discuss the invisible life of a trainer—all the behind-the-scenes things you need to be effective, including how to develop professional networks, where to find useful resources, and tips on how to stay organized while on the go.

At the end of the book are several supplemental sections. The glossary includes definitions of frequently used terms; and the notes and references section includes notes for each chapter. We've also included an annotated list of recommended resources and appendices with forms and other training material you may want to copy.

Unlike many books that offer specific teaching strategies, we have intentionally not formatted ours as a recipe with goals, objectives, materials, and steps listed. Rather, our strategies are described in a narrative, nudging the reader to imagine the possibilities, trying to foster divergent, rather than convergent, thinking. We have highlighted paragraphs that are specific training strategies to help you easily spot them, and in many cases we have cross-referenced related strategies throughout the book.

Whether you are a methodical or whimsical reader, the organization of this book should work for you. There are places for the eye to rest, space to add your own notes, and a binding that allows the book to become a workbook as you set about training teachers while juggling a busy work life. Let us hear how you use *Training Teachers* and the things you discover about yourself and the teachers you work with. You can write to us in care of the publisher. Remember, everything worth taking seriously is worth having fun with.

Section 1

Changing Our Approach to Teacher Education

CHAPTER 1: CONTEXT FOR ADULT LEARNING
CHAPTER 2: NEW EMPHASIS FOR TEACHER EDUCATION

$\mathcal{L}$ooking in on a typical early childhood staff meeting, workshop, or college classroom, you are likely to see teacher training approached in what Brazilian educator Paulo Freire calls the *banking method*: the expert attempts to transfer and deposit rules and requirements and their skill and knowledge into the minds of those present.[1] The content of these sessions focuses on predetermined standards, step-by-step techniques and prescribed curriculum models. Both the content and method of these trainings reinforce the notion that to become a good teacher of young children, all you must do is learn the information and master the techniques. We alternately find this thinking puzzling, humorous, and outrageous.

Most early childhood educators have a working knowledge of learning theory. We know children learn best when they are provided opportunities to pursue their interests, make choices, actively manipulate materials, and interact with others. Research underpinning adult learning theory has uncovered a similar set of factors. Why then do adult classrooms and in-service meetings, particularly those training teachers, reflect so little of this? Do we teach adults so differently because they have the ability to think more abstractly, use more sophisticated knowledge to communicate, and sit still for longer periods of time?

Here we pose the same questions that we ask about teaching children: just because adults are compliant or polite enough to let us teach them that way, does that mean the teaching method serves their interests well? Are they really learning at their full capacity under this method?

We see the work of teacher educators as either maintaining the whole system of education in this country, or setting about to change it. The training we provide teachers can ensure conformity and preserve the status quo, or it can create new ways of thinking and teaching that lead to significant social change. Whatever methods are used to educate teachers will surely be duplicated in their work with children. We can turn out clones and robots who do as they are told, or we can foster a love of learning, produce critical thinkers, and develop creative, socially responsible citizens.

Our teacher training practice has changed dramatically as we've come to understand the learning process. We've found that when our primary focus is on covering the regulations, standards, or curriculum content, we create self-illusions

about what people will learn from us. In fact, it's the approach we use and the interactions we have that will impact learning far beyond any particular topic at hand.

In training teachers we must continually remind ourselves to model what we're inclined to preach. For instance, if we want teachers to focus more on the children than the curriculum projects or academic lessons of their classrooms, we too must keep the emphasis on our students rather than the curriculum to be covered. If we want teachers to provide opportunities for children to explore and make their own discoveries, these possibilities must be provided for them as adults. Our experience, as well as study of adult learning theory, has convinced us that more learning will result.

With the continually changing world children are growing into, teachers must help children *in*quire more than they *ac*quire. What kind of teacher training will enable this to happen? How can we develop people who trust and respect themselves as much as some unknown expert? Is there a way to foster collaboration and a desire for diversity, rather than limit ourselves to one viewpoint or way of doing things? Teacher education has to address these questions. And our teacher training methods need to model how this is done.

This section offers a brief overview of the ideas and approaches that shape our teacher training practice. First we consider learning styles and teacher developmental stages and suggest their implications for training approaches. In Chapter 2, we summarize why constructivism is our guiding theoretical framework and end with a review of other areas of emphasis for us—training for dispositions, new roles, and embracing diversity.

We will come back to these ideas again and again in subsequent sections, offering numerous examples of actual strategies we use and further discussion of the theory, philosophy, and methodology they represent. It is our hope that this process will become second nature to you—as it has to us.

Chapter 1
Context for Adult Learning

A View of How Adults (and Children) Learn

1. Under optimal conditions of safety and challenge, human beings are inherently curious, intrinsically motivated, self-directed learners.
2. Knowledge is constructed by the learner through action on the environment and interaction with peers.
3. The construction of knowledge involves narrative and socio-emotional, as well as logical, connections. Knowing is embedded in collectively shared meanings and depends on validation in significant relationships.
4. Active, self-expressive learning is necessarily a social process; it should take place in, and contribute to, a democratic community of critical thinkers.
5. Learning takes place in the context of social/political realities. In a diverse society, members of groups with unequal access to power often internalize oppression and fail to develop an effective voice. Education is never neutral; it can be designed to maintain or to change the status quo.

Elizabeth Jones, *Growing Teachers: Partnerships in Staff Development*[2]

Having lived more years in the world, adults bring to the learning process a complex web of experiences, knowledge, skills, and mindsets regarding themselves, the teacher, and the topic at hand. This includes such things as their learning styles, childhood experiences (family of origin issues), cultural influences, and their own developmental stages. Many come with unexamined values and a lack of self-awareness, while others have a strong sense of identity and are quite articulate about it. Some are new to their work with children and others have been at it a long time. In training teachers we need to discover who they are and what they bring to the learning setting.

Adult learners bring their individual backgrounds to our training settings, and they also come representing a larger social and political context. The dynamics of power and privilege in our society always seep into our classrooms, impacting not only the individuals, but the functioning of the group as a whole. Those of the dominant culture with access to power may or may not be aware of their privilege or of behaviors and systems that prevent those without this access from developing an effective voice. We keep this in mind as we plan what we will do, anticipating differing needs, styles, and contributions teachers bring to a learning arena.

LEARNING STYLES

Thanks to the work and writing of a number of researchers, the recognition that there are diverse ways in which people learn is increasingly popular. There are various methods used to categorize and explain different learning styles, each with its own emphasis and formulation. Some adult educators have developed self-assessment tools to determine someone's learning style, such as visual, auditory, or kinesthetic. We have found it helpful to keep abreast of the literature in

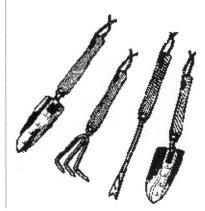

this area and to play around with training strategies that allow for different kinds of learning.

Of particular interest to us have been the work of Mary Belenky and her colleagues in *Women's Ways of Knowing: The Development of Self, Voice, and Mind* (Basic Books, 1986) and Howard Gardner in *Frames of Mind: The Theory of Multiple Intelligences* (Basic Books, 1983). These publications address the kinds of learners we often find in early childhood programs.

Because early childhood teachers are predominantly female, we suspect that there is a strong correlation between the stages of knowing for women that Belenky and colleagues discovered, and the adult learners in our profession. These authors describe five stages that women experience in their developmental process of coming to be confident, competent learners. Their findings certainly parallel much of what we've seen in the child care providers with whom we work.

1. Silence
This stage is characterized by little awareness of intellectual capabilities. Learners have only begun to think about thinking; they do best with very concrete information.

2. Received Knowledge
Many learners stay in this stage with strong faith in authority and someone else's definition of "the right way" of doing things. They are typically buffeted by change and do not see themselves as growing and learning.

3. Subjective Knowledge
The shift to this stage is often characterized by someone who listened to the learner in contrast to failed male authority. As learners begin to value their own experience, they typically go through a period of passionate rejection of science and a stubborn immunity to the perspectives of others.

4. Procedural Knowledge
Those in this stage have become more objective and are seeking out the points of views of others. They are becoming analytical and reflective and looking for truths below the surface.

5. Constructed Knowledge
This stage represents an integration of feeling and thinking, with a growing tolerance for contradiction and ambiguity. Those who have developed to this stage are able to live with compromise. The authors describe these women as thriving on complexity and contradiction. Question posing is central to these learners' thinking process. In fact, they don't try to answer questions, but rather pose new ones. They are careful listeners and learn from relating personal experience to theories and ideas from experts.

Knowing that a group of teachers might represent any number of these developmental stages or *ways of knowing* when they come to a training, we try to plan accordingly. Of course we are eager to see them move to the stages of procedural and constructed knowledge, but many are primarily functioning at the received knowledge stage, if not the one of silence. This means they need concrete suggestions and specific regulations. Thus, to address these learners we frame our ideas about the open-ended nature of teaching as a set of guidelines to be learned, simultaneously giving them practice in self-reflection and analysis through our specific training activities. By providing multiple opportunities to work together and hear the experiences and ideas of other participants, we also provide for those who have developed other ways of knowing.

Howard Gardner describes this in terms of the *kinds of intelligences.* He outlines the kind of education most of us have experienced, one which uses and values only verbal/linguistic and logical/mathematical learning. Gardner describes the many other kinds of intelligences people bring to learning settings and, though we sometimes hear reference to these regarding children's needs, these ways of learning or knowing are rarely acknowledged in efforts to educate adults.

1. Intrapersonal intelligence
Learners come to understand things through individual projects, research, and reflection.

2. Interpersonal intelligence
These are social-minded people who learn best when they collaborate with others to answer questions, solve problems, and create representations of their understandings.

3. Musical intelligence
Rhythm and musical patterns are a means for these learners to develop understandings on most subjects.

4. Spatial intelligence
In putting together their understandings about things, these learners need to manipulate diverse media.

5. Kinesthetic intelligence
Moving around, touching, and dramatizing are often a means for these learners to translate the understandings their bodies develop into more traditional modes such as reading and writing.

Though they may have some technical differences, the terms learning styles, ways of knowing, and kinds of intelligence have merged and become interchangeable in our work as they seek to expand how we think about and provide for learners. In any workshop we offer, participants have the opportunity to see things written down, hear ideas in a variety of ways from a variety of people, and move around and try things out (using methods such as props, case studies, and role plays). Throughout this book, we've included strategies that provide for the different approaches to learning teachers bring to our training.

TEACHER DEVELOPMENTAL STAGES

Teachers come to us with varying degrees of experience, knowledge, and skills in working with children and in being a learner themselves. In a typical "banking" or transfer-of-information approach to education, most college courses pay little attention to developmental stages or learning styles of students. To the extent that teacher stages of development are considered, the education program is arranged to begin with basic introductory level 101 courses and move students sequentially towards more advanced classes. This has some use in addressing different levels of knowledge, but it is misleading for both the teacher and student. There is rarely a complete match between a student's acquired knowledge and the content of a course, let alone among all the students who make up a class. Furthermore, this sequential, compartmentalized approach to teacher training doesn't reflect the reality of what teachers are faced with in a classroom of children.

If teachers are to set up class-rooms where inquiry is encour-aged, then they must be educated in ways that encourage inquiry. The willingness and the compe-tence of the teacher to seek and find meaning through direct expe-rience and reflection influences how she or he will structure and mediate that learning environment.

Jacqueline Grennon Brooks,
"Teachers and Students:
Constructivists Forging
New Connections"[4]

Similar problems exist in staff meetings and workshop settings. Rarely do we hear reference to the developmental level supervisors or trainers presume teachers represent. We wonder how much they consider this aspect in their planning. Most often workshop leaders put all their effort into gathering a clear presentation of their ideas and experiences on a topic. If they think about the possible range of participant experience in their training, they tend to address their presentation to "those somewhere in the middle." Trainers who believe that their students are at a beginning "basic competency" level, usually concentrate on providing teaching techniques and curriculum recipes, neglecting to offer a process for thinking about children and continual reflection on their own understandings of teaching and learning.

Even when teachers are new to the job, seem naive, off-track, or inappropri-ate, they need to be respected. Though as teacher trainers we may be called the ex-pert, we should base our training on a belief that teacher learning will come more from what they know than from what we know. Our role should be to create a set-ting and activities for participants to examine and name what they know. We help them connect what they already know, and their emerging questions, to the larger framework of the core Early Childhood Education (ECE) knowledge or the stan-dards and practices that need to be considered. As teachers wrestle with the com-plexities and disequilibrium that comes with integrating new knowledge and skills, we support them with feedback and opportunities to practice and reflect.

We know that effective teaching requires continual analysis, adjustment, refl-ecting, and refocusing. This leads us to believe that even teachers in "the survival stage" need to have reflection and critical thinking reinforced. From the begin-ning, teachers survive better when they recognize the complexities of teaching rather than having the impression they have only to master content and tech-niques to be successful. Even as we convey beginning baseline knowledge, we em-phasize metacognition—an awareness of how this little piece fits in the bigger picture of teaching and learning.

Eleanor Duckworth reminds us that central to the job of teachers is asking learners to explain their own thinking.[3] Making thoughts clear for others helps people gain greater clarity for themselves. Students experience the powerful feel-ing of having their ideas taken seriously, rather than simply parroting what the teacher says. When teachers experience this feeling in their own education, they come to recognize the importance of providing it in their classrooms with children.

IMPLICATIONS FOR TRAINING APPROACHES

As we've learned about differing styles and ways of knowing, we've realized we needed training strategies to uncover how, who, and where teachers are in their learning process. These strategies reveal what our focus should be as the training progresses, and help us connect what teachers already know to the larger frame-work of ideas we are pursuing. We remind ourselves that there will be divergent approaches, experiences, and familiarity with the topic, whether the participants are brand-new teacher aides in a preschool, those with a CDA or community col-lege associate degree, or teachers with a graduate degree. Ultimately, the way we plan for each of these groups is not all that different because we bring a variety of activities for teachers to choose from. What *is* different is how we respond to the knowledge and experiences different participants bring to the training.

A general picture of a training we offer in a class or at a conference for 20 to 30 participants might look like the following.

We begin with an activity that asks participants to consider their own experience. This might be done through any number of the activities described in Section 2, such as childhood memories or a short simulated experience. As we debrief this opening exercise, asking for some of the themes teachers uncovered in the activity, we list on a chart what people say, providing for both the visual and auditory learners. Looking over the list, we point out how much they already know about learning environments, affirming the experience and resources that exists among them. Mentally, we note anyone who has seemed hesitant to speak in either the small group opening activity or the large group debriefing. These participants may be taking notes, attentively listening, or gazing blankly out the window. When we begin a more active exercise, they might be given the instruction cards to lead it off.

As we offer an overview of the key elements on the topic at hand, we refer to examples of this already listed on the chart from their opening activity. In presenting an overview, we typically make use of visual aids or props to represent the key elements. These can be passed around and become the basis of forming small groups for the next activity. In this way we continue to provide for diverse experiences and ways of learning.

The bulk of any class or workshop we offer is spent in small group activities with choices for participants and opportunities to pursue their interests and learning styles. Typically, we may offer case studies to discuss, a manipulative or sorting game of regulations or checklist information, a scavenger hunt or "search and find" activity, and a resource table with books and handouts to look over.

With this approach, a respectful place for learning is provided for all involved, from the silenced and inexperienced learners to the advanced thinkers. We believe that people will learn as much from each other as they will from the trainer. Inexperienced teachers benefit from hearing the experienced, while experienced teachers solidify their understandings as they share them with others. This process repeatedly reinforces valuable dispositions toward learning and teaching.

Coming to understand the role of backgrounds, experiences, and learning styles, all of our training now incorporates these basic assumptions:

1. Participants bring their own knowledge, experiences, and learning styles to any training session.

2. Existing knowledge and experiences are the source of new learning.
   • to help children learn, we give them concrete materials and experiences to explore and reflect upon.
   • with adults, the concrete materials and experiences we focus on are their own daily lives, ideas, understandings, and values to explore and reflect upon through a variety of learning activities.

3. From the outset, training should help teachers find their own voices and foster reflection and problem solving. Our role as teachers of adults is to help with the naming of their understandings and offer concrete activities that relate these to a larger body of ECE knowledge.

4. Each training requires a variety of activities to address the different learning styles and intelligences of the participants.

These assumptions have served us well and become a touchstone as we continue to refine our interactions and facilitation skills. When training a group of teachers, we continually analyze what they bring us, adjust our activities, reflect on their responses, and refocus our next steps accordingly. This is the very process we think those teachers need to master in order to provide for the learning needs of the children in their care.

Chapter 2
New Emphasis for Teacher Education

Some in-service educators are especially intent on getting something accomplished for the children, and seem to construe the situation as "getting to the kids through the teachers." If you want to help children (and no doubt you do), then do so directly. Try not to "use" teachers. Instead, focus on helping the teachers as persons worthy of your concern and caring in their own right. Try to define your role as someone who helps and works with teachers for their own sakes. When we do that wholeheartedly and well, the children they work with will stand to benefit, also.

Lilian Katz, *Helping Others Learn to Teach: Some Principles and Techniques for Inservice Educators*[5]

Over the last decade, with several key publications by the NAEYC[6] and the Council for Early Childhood Professional Recognition,[7] our profession has clearly identified a core knowledge base, the key content areas for early childhood teacher education and professional development. Most teacher educators and staff trainers have been teachers of children themselves and want to pass on what they know: how children learn and how to teach them. This body of knowledge, quite practically, is what our profession has been researching, accumulating, and promoting in a big way. But while we have been expanding this knowledge and advocating this practice with children, our profession has neglected to give adequate attention to the parallel practice of helping teachers learn this core knowledge.

In our own efforts to develop an effective teacher training practice, we've come to believe that as critical as acquiring core ECE knowledge is for teachers, it is not adequate in and of itself. Of equal importance to teachers is understanding the process of learning, for themselves as well as for children. Thus, the emphasis in our training has shifted. Teachers need to understand the complexities and forces that impact their roles, getting past the urge for quick fixes and recipes. We want to help them find joy in the challenge of this work and develop a desire to continue growing and learning themselves. A primary goal for all of our training is to provide teachers with a framework for examining the events of their classrooms, their reactions, and needs for further professional development. We offer strategies to sustain them through the disequilibrium and ongoing research that working with children requires.

The following is a sketch of the "big ideas" and passions that shape our new emphasis in teacher education. This overview will familiarize you with the ideas and terms found throughout this book. These are the underlying principles of our planning and ongoing dialogue with teachers. We believe they are the foundation of effective teacher training, reinforcing the notion that teaching involves a lifelong process of study and reflection, rather than practicing a set of techniques or curriculum activities. A fuller discussion of each of these ideas is found in subsequent chapters, after you see them in action in the numerous training strategies of Section 2.

TRAINING FOR CONSTRUCTING KNOWLEDGE

In teaching adults, as well as children, most of us have a body of ideas to unlearn as well as learn. We have to disregard the idea that lecturing people is the best way to get them to learn. Commonly, supervisors and trainers tell teachers what we think they need to know. We give them regulations, basic concepts, demonstrations, techniques, and curriculum models to follow, thinking this will help them understand how to be a good teacher. Simultaneously, however, the content of our

Developmentally appropriate practice in early childhood education is also a good model for effective practice in teacher education. Adult learners, like children, need to play—that is, they need to take initiative, make choices among possibilities, act and interact. And, as adults, they need to engage in reflection and dialogue about their experience. They do need baseline social knowledge—training—to get started, to know how to behave, but then they need continuing opportunity to make intellectual and moral judgments, to observe children's behavior, and to put their experience into words that are taken seriously by other adults, both peers and teacher educators. I believe that this process should characterize both college classes and inservice experiences. In both settings, learners should be doing more talking than their instructors do, and their talk should be based in their concrete experience.

Elizabeth Jones, *Growing Teachers: Partnerships in Staff Development*[8]

Constructivism reminds us that order exists only in the minds of people, so when we as teachers impose our order on students, we rob them of the opportunity to create knowledge and understanding themselves.

Jacqueline Grennon Brooks, "Teachers and Students: Constructivists Forging New Connections"[9]

message to teachers is to use a very different pedagogy with children: Set up an interesting learning environment, offer choices, and provide engaging, open-ended materials and activities to help them learn through play.

The allegiance to this approach with children is rooted in the theory of *constructivism* first associated with the work of Jean Piaget. Years of closely watching children in preschools has helped us understand more clearly the concept of "constructing knowledge" and what parallel experiences for adults might look like. Children naturally explore, reflect, and consolidate their understandings at whatever level they are functioning. Watching four-year-old Deovonna at the easel illuminates this process.

> For days Deovonna has been pouring and stirring water in containers at the water table. Frances, her teacher, sees this interest and arranges for her to discover something new at the easel as she pursues this. Today, Frances sets out only red and blue paint. Going to the easel Deovonna takes a brush and makes a few strokes of red on her paper. Next she uses the blue to paint a few letters in her name. Putting the brush again in the red paint and sweeping it across the paper she exclaims, "Look, it's changing!" Frances responds, "You mix it, it changes." Deovonna begins pouring the red paint into the blue and stirring it with her brush. She calls her understanding out to Frances, "It changes to red-blue." Then, the moment of new understanding, as she bursts out with, "Look, now it's changing to purple!"

Frances could have taught Deovonna that red and blue make purple, but this would have robbed Deovonna of the discovery process. It would have limited the possibility of her constructing the broader, more useful understanding of the infinite variations of colors available through the combination of basic elements. In addition, the opportunity to reinforce some basic dispositions toward learning would have been missed: being observant and curious, taking initiative and risks, feeling you can solve problems, valuing your own ideas and discoveries, and searching out new information.

Discovery and invention are not just for children. Piaget's theories and the long-standing research on constructivism is applicable to adults as well.[10] Teachers must invent their own way of teaching. To effectively understand this, they need a constructivist approach in their own education. We began experimenting with activities to provide adults the opportunity to explore, invent, and discover in ways similar to children's learning.

Finding the work of Eleanor Duckworth was a leap forward for us. Her book, *The Having of Wonderful Ideas and Other Essays on Teaching and Learning* (Teachers College Press, 1987), offered us a glimpse of adult constructivism in action. Reading and taking classes from Elizabeth Jones gave us further exposure. We began to shape our training to provide teachers multiple opportunities to connect new ideas to things they already know, steadily constructing what they understand about children, how they develop, and what they need from adults and a learning environment.

Constructivism is not only effective for a teacher's learning, but also models a pedagogy that is vital for children. Recognizing the learning that happens for them in constructivist-oriented activities, teachers are more likely to provide them for children. Throughout this book you'll see evidence of our enthusiasm for creating exercises that get teachers hooked on actively relating their own experience to a larger body of ideas and providing parallel activities for children with whom they work.

TRAINING FOR DISPOSITIONS

During a meeting with a group of child care directors, we were interested to hear one of them comment, "I try and try to help my staff be more responsive to the children. We have a really clear staff manual and we have trainings on the subject. I'm always reminding them of what they need to do. It seems like some people were born to work with children while others just don't get it, no matter how much training you give them."

We've held the same sentiments over our years of observing teachers. Some, even with very little education, seem to know just what children need and like. Others with years of training and experience stay focused on checklists and curriculum projects more than they pay attention to children. We've seen two teachers with similar educational backgrounds and experiences, one who fits the description of "born to work with children," while the other "never seems to get it." So what's going on here?

Revisiting the writing of Lilian Katz on the subject of "worthwhile dispositions for effective teaching" helped us to analyze what we were seeing and ultimately led us to rethink our approach to teacher training.[13] Katz defines dispositions as "relatively stable habits of mind" and as "tendencies to respond to one's experiences or to given situations in certain ways." As we thought about our observations of teachers, the differences we noticed seemed based on their "habits of mind" rather than their knowledge or skills. Some who could describe aspects of child development could still not apply this to their work. They lacked the disposition of being curious about children and the unfolding events of their classroom. Instead, they were focused on trying to apply the rules and techniques they learned in their training, perhaps akin to trying to change a tire without noticing which car had the flat. We realized these teachers needed some new mindsets, not more techniques.

We believe that the way we attend to learning for teachers influences their dispositions toward children's learning. A centerpiece of our work now is training to cultivate certain dispositions. Through analyzing our observations and the stories others tell about teachers, we've defined what seem to be "core dispositions" for master teachers in the early childhood profession. We design training to foster and strengthen these dispositions, not only through the ideas and information we present, but in the way we structure training activities. Further discussion and examples of this are found in Chapter 9.

TRAINING FOR NEW ROLES

As the world grows more complex, social, political, and technological realities demand creative, multifaceted, critical thinkers to help transform and improve the quality of our lives. We need individuals who will take risks, try new ideas, and use failure as a learning experience and try again—rather than seeing it as a personal indictment. Our country's approach to education does not reflect these understandings.

School systems and early childhood programs promote prescriptive objectives, standardized measurements, and a limited focus on basic skills. Teachers see

Thoughts are our way of connecting things up for ourselves. If others tell us about the connections they have made, we can only understand them to the extent that we do the work of making these connections ourselves.

Eleanor Duckworth, The Having of Wonderful Ideas and Other Essays on Teaching and Learning [11]

So what is the role of teaching, if knowledge must be constructed by each individual? In my view, there are two aspects to teaching. The first is to put the teachers into contact with phenomena related to the area to be studied—the real thing, not books or lectures about it—and to help them notice what is interesting; to engage them so they will continue to think and wonder about it. The second is to have the students try to explain the sense they are making, and instead of explaining things to students, to try to understand their sense.

Eleanor Duckworth, The Having of Wonderful Ideas and Other Essays on Teaching and Learning [12]

Just as educational programs for young children can be analyzed for their ideological base, so can teacher training programs.

Bernard Spodek, "Early Childhood Education and Teacher Education: A Search for Consistency"[14]

their role as giving information, testing for memorization, maintaining discipline, and determining who will advance and who will fail. In preschool and Head Start programs, getting children ready for kindergarten is of utmost concern and results in an earlier and earlier focus on academic instruction.

What will get children truly ready for school and academic and social success are opportunities to experience themselves as successful actors involved in learning. Beyond learning the rules and behaviors required by "school culture," they need multiple opportunities to explore, experiment, investigate, invent, and evaluate their actions. Children need repeated experiences with collaboration and problem solving. They must learn coping skills that don't require them to abandon their identity or motivation to pursue their interests. For teachers to provide for these more significant educational experiences, they must rethink their roles, planning processes, and interactions for the classroom.

Because the only educational experience most teachers have had is a traditional academic one, they have a large barrier to creating something different. It seems the traditional view of a teacher's role is permanently etched in their minds. Even when teachers begin to question the banking method of education and want to provide for such things as critical thinking and problem solving, they still have powerful images of school and teachers to overcome.

Because of this, our training places an emphasis on examining and redefining the role of the teacher. We stress that if significant educational experiences are to be provided for children, their teachers will need to invent new roles for themselves. Our training strategies examine the possible roles a teacher might assume in given situations, and then practice the reflection and behaviors they imply. We discuss this in more detail and offer examples of these strategies in Chapter 10.

TRAINING FOR EMBRACING DIVERSITY

In no other area of early childhood education is the use of critical thinking, reflection, and responsive approaches more necessary than when working with and conveying ideas about diversity. For teacher educators, considerations of diversity are a natural extension of paying attention to who our students are and using teaching strategies relevant to them. This involves an awareness of how people from different backgrounds may experience educational settings, how familiar or comfortable they may be with "the school culture," and the ways in which differences of race, gender, and class may impact group dynamics.

We pay attention to the power and influence of the social and political context in which our training occurs in order to be sensitive to the learning needs of our students. Knowing that preschool teachers and child care providers are a predominantly female, underpaid, undervalued workforce, we draw parallels about their learning process from the accounts of people who have been marginalized by the culture and pedagogy of our schools. Some of these are powerfully described in works such as Mike Rose's *Lives on the Boundary* (The Free Press, 1989); Antonia Darder's *Culture and Power in the Classroom* (Bergin & Garvey, 1991); Jonathan Kozol's *Savage Inequalities* (Harper Collins, 1991); and Lisa Delpit's "The Silenced Dialogue: Power and Pedagogy in Educating Other People's Children" (*Harvard Education Review*, 1988, vol. 58, no. 3).

As we strive to ensure our practices are inclusive, we invite the teachers we train to do the same. We are not only modeling how to incorporate considerations of diversity into the work of teaching, but offering guiding principles and strategies for working with diverse populations of children and their families. By including training strategies that highlight different values and approaches to child rearing, and by designing activities to bring diverse perspectives to the forefront, we are giving both a direct and indirect message to teachers. Our training tells them: remember there are many cultural outlooks and lifestyles, some of them visible and vocal, others less so; pay attention to the assumptions you make; include representations of all walks of life in the environment and activities you plan; model and foster respect for and excitement about the ways in which people are alike and different.

For us, embracing diversity is an ongoing process of learning, risk taking, and inquiry. We have few answers, but we bring passion and commitment to this process, integrating our questions and emerging understandings into all of our training. Embracing diversity requires that we continually examine our own practices for cultural relevancy and bias, and that we work to confront and eliminate the bias of the institutions we work for. This is, of course, the practice we want teachers to develop in their programs. The chapters in Section 4 provide an extensive discussion of how we view training for culturally sensitive and anti-bias practices, with examples of specific strategies we use in our work with teachers.

PLANTING THE SEED

With the above elements as the emphasis in all of our training, we feel more able to help teachers to become autonomous, responsive planners and problem solvers in their classrooms. Our task as trainers is to help them develop a methodology for composing their role as a teacher as we foster a set of effective teaching dispositions and coach them in consolidating their knowledge and skills. Ultimately this approach is what Elizabeth Jones terms, "a growth model, rather than an engineering model."[16] What it boils down to is trusting teachers to take responsibility for their own learning and growth. Acknowledging the risks involved, this is what we hope they will do for children and we must do for them.

The fact that one approach to teacher education is being advocated generally by funding agencies and certification agencies in the United States today, and that this approach represents control interests, has many educational and political implications.

Bernard Spodek, "Early Childhood Education and Teacher Education: A Search for Consistency"[15]

Section 2

Tools for the Harvest

In today's world teachers are put in positions where they are responsible for a group of young children about whom they have little experience or educational background. Most teachers are trained on-site, with little time or encouragement to observe the interests and developmental pursuits of children as a basis of planning for them. Those who receive training in college or workshop settings usually experience the banking method of education in full force. Constructivism, if referred to at all, is a theoretical consideration, not an applied practice.

Learning to be a teacher is full of complexity. It involves more than the memorization and imitation that most classrooms suggest. Reading or being lectured to are not enough for teachers to develop into reflective, critical thinking practitioners. Real understanding comes from direct experiences with materials and with ideas. It comes with time for discussion and reflection where new ideas and skills are integrated. If teacher educators have the goal of making classrooms better for children, the means to this goal is improving the educational experience of the teachers themselves.

Chapter 3
Landscaping for Constructivism

Clarifying our theoretical framework for teacher education was an important step in starting to change our training practice. The ideas made sense to us but still our eyes would squint, straining to see what this pedagogy might look like in a training setting with adults. If teachers are to construct their own knowledge, what should we be doing to help them? What tools can we offer to help them cultivate their understandings?

As we came to realize the importance of a constructivist approach to teacher training, we struggled with how to do it. We scoured libraries and bookstores for any resources we could find on developmental education and adult learning. We invented and tried new approaches, observed, analyzed, and compared ideas and experiences with colleagues. Two years into experimenting with applications of constructivist theory to teacher training, we discovered a description of constructivist classes by Jacqueline Brooks that paralleled the approach we had been developing.

- Experiences are structured around one or two primary concepts—big ideas—rather than a long list of objectives.
- Big ideas are explored, not covered, in the natural and spontaneous context of the student's own thinking.
- The student's point of view is explored, misconceptions are uncovered, and inconsistencies between their notions and new data are confronted.
- The teacher restructures plans to allow more exploration, add complexity, and help students negotiate disequilibrium.[1]

Brooks' description offers a glimpse of education quite different from the banking method, one toward an improved pedagogy for teacher education. And as we study Freire and his banking method more closely, we understand that it is reflection on one's experience, not just the experience itself, which aids the construction of knowledge. Without the opportunity to analyze one's experience in the context of a larger framework, new understandings are seldom consolidated.

We began experimenting with activities to provide adults the opportunity to explore, invent, and discover in ways similar to children's learning. Knowing that children's learning comes mostly from direct experiences with objects, we sought out materials that would give adults direct experiences with ideas. Because we found it awkward and ineffective to have adults pretend they were children, we reached for things that would challenge teachers at their own level—opportunities to translate knowledge from one domain to another, familiar children's activities with adult content, word games, and collaborative projects. Keeping in mind the need to provide for diverse learning styles, family backgrounds, and cultural

frameworks, we tested different strategies on ourselves to enhance our own learning about teacher training.

For example, we explored metaphors for our work and roles with teachers. If trainers are "growing teachers," how do the elements of gardening—seeds, dirt, water, sun, fertilizer, and weed maintenance—translate to our work?[2] With this kind of experimentation, we clarified and defined the basic elements of our training methodology as a set of five examinations.

WHAT'S THE BIG IDEA?

It is characteristic of an adult educator to put all one's efforts into planning a presentation. Some do this because they are nervous they will run out of things to say before the session has ended. Others try to cover everything about a topic they think students should know. The underlying assumption seems to be that people will learn from the teacher if he or she gives a clear presentation and answers all the questions.

In these situations it is usually the trainer who has done most of the learning. By planning a presentation, a teacher is reframing and consolidating their own ideas and experiences. This leads to deeper understandings for the trainer, but not necessarily the participants. Because we want to focus more on the participants' learning rather than our own expertise, we rarely deliver presentations. Rather, we choose one or two big ideas to develop activities around, giving our students the experience of reframing and consolidating *their* knowledge. There's a temptation to squeeze in as many ideas as possible, but experience has shown us that more learning happens when participants can focus on a concept or two, using interactive experiences to sort through their understandings.

To select the big ideas, we draw on the core knowledge of the ECE profession and our years of experience in the field. For us, this involves information about *what we hope to see* and *what we hope not to see*. Over time we've consolidated a framework of five examinations to explore nearly any content topic of the core knowledge. These encompass the factors influencing most child development and ECE situations. As a set of examinations to consider, these become a ready method by which we explore the big ideas of our profession's core knowledge.

- *Examining our own filters*
  What experiences and conditioning do we bring to the teaching situation?

- *Examining the environment*
  How is environment influencing or prescribing the context?

- *Examining child development*
  What indicators are operating here?

- *Examining issues of cultural sensitivity and inclusiveness*
  What assumptions, biases, or limiting factors are at work?

- *Examining teacher roles and strategies*
  How can we be more responsive and skillful?

There are any number of excellent professional resources available in choosing a couple of big ideas to explore on a topic. For example, in planning a training on learning environments, we either brainstorm a list of what we hope to see and hope not to see in classrooms, or consult trustworthy resources such as those of

Five Examinations Framework

- Examining oneself
- Examining the environment
- Examining child development
- Examining issues of diversity
- Examining roles and strategies

NAEYC or Diane Trister Dodge.[3] We choose one or two ideas from our list as the foundation for the activities and discussion we are planning.

For the topic of learning environments, we might choose to pursue the following big ideas:

- the organization and aesthetics of the environment have a tremendous influence on children's ability to engage in self-directed learning;
- the arrangement of the environment can foster continual discovery and engagement, classification and social skills, or it can serve to defeat these; and
- opportunities for social interaction and living with conflict must be structured into the environment.

With a decision about the big ideas to be explored, we move on to structuring our training. Initially, we worried about not offering a presentation during our classes and workshops. We know the prevailing attitude is that teachers need much information and we better make sure we give it to them. But while telling teachers our knowledge and presenting a list of techniques may mean they *hear* the information, without time and encouragement to explore concepts, they have trouble putting them into practice. We find teachers are much more successful at practical application when we focus training sessions around one or two ideas and offer activities to investigate them more fully.

NAMING WHAT YOU KNOW

In a staff meeting, workshop, or class setting, we begin with an experience to explore what people already think about the big ideas we've selected as our focus. Constructivist theory tells us that people construct new knowledge by connecting their current understandings and experiences to new information and ideas. In other words, these existing experiences and ideas are the foundation of any new learning and understanding. Knowing this, we plan our first activity of a training with the goal of uncovering who and where our students are in relation to the topic at hand.

Our opening activities help participants identify and name "the knowing" they already bring to the big ideas under consideration. (Incidentally, participants become aware of the responsibility and power they have for their own learning.) Responses to these initial activities also provide an indication as to what to emphasize as the training progresses. Knowing the range of knowledge and experiences in the group helps to individualize our interactions and connect the larger body of big ideas to participants' interests, needs, and emerging questions.

The activities we offer involve concrete experiences and playful, active participation appropriate for adults. We view these activities as critical to adult learning, just as we know play and concrete experiences are critical for children's learning. Inventing these activities is one of the most enjoyable and creative aspects of our work as trainers.

Examples of activities we've used to begin a training on learning environments might involve recalling a childhood experience or going through a guided imagery. For instance, we might ask the group to consider one of the following.

- Think about a place where you find it really easy to accomplish things, where you feel comfortable and at ease with yourself, where you feel like you belong and fit in.

• Remember an environment where you always felt intrigued and found things you wanted to know more about.

Usually we ask teachers to think or write quietly to themselves as they remember their experiences and uncover their ideas and feelings. Then we suggest they work together in small groups or pairs to describe what they recalled. Our task during this time is to move around to the groups, encouraging involvement, supporting their ideas, and posing questions. When each teacher has recalled an experience to someone else, we move to the next stage in the landscaping process—debriefing the activity.

PROPAGATE, GERMINATE, CULTIVATE

In most of our trainings, teachers spend much more time talking than we do. Our strategies are primarily cooperative learning activities, designed to discuss questions, problems, observations, or discoveries. A question that helps teachers name what they know about a topic almost always generates the very discussion we would have wanted from a lecture. Through the discussion we gain more insight into what information or understanding teachers additionally need. With their context to work with, we can more meaningfully relate the body of ideas and activities we've brought to a training.

The discussions at the end of active learning experiences are critical to the construction and consolidation of knowledge. In fact, the teaching and learning process is not complete without this debriefing. This is where the trainer facilitates the describing and naming of the participants' experiences, helping connect them to the big ideas under consideration. Points we might otherwise have included in a presentation almost always get made by one of the participants. If not, we include these points in our dialogue with them. Different than a summation, the goal of the debriefing process is to help students reframe and connect new information to the ideas and experiences they uncovered during the activity time.

Having begun with an activity structured to explore their own experience, we invite teachers to dialogue not only with us, but also with each other. This process means that we are co-constructing our knowledge, collaborating in analyzing and making meaning out of the relationship between experience and ideas. We are not the experts passing on knowledge, but rather the facilitators of a process that leads to further knowledge on the part of students and ourselves.

During the debriefing discussion, we watch and listen and build on participants' ideas and stories. We help interpret and connect people, their experiences, and ideas to each other. Raising questions may uncover contradictions and expose further complexity to be explored.

This approach is significantly different than testing their comprehension or putting them through hoops to grasp the expertise of the trainer. Because students are so used to the more traditional methods of teaching, from the beginning we acknowledge that our ways may seem unconventional. We explain the theory and rationale behind what we are asking them to do. And there are assurances that we plan no surprises, manipulation, or putting people on the spot. Rather, our role will be to provide opportunities for teachers to become more aware of their own learning process.

We've discovered that explaining the what and why of our training heightens the recognition that participants are in charge of their own learning and are involved in the learning process of others. We emphasize metacognition—an awareness of how this little piece fits into the bigger picture of teaching and learning. Asking teachers to think about their own learning contributes to consolidating understandings and helps them identify what they want to know next.

Learning to facilitate debriefing discussions has been an intuitive process that we've been inventing as we go. The discussion follows the participants' ideas, stories, and interactions with other students and the trainer. We watch, listen, and continually restate and summarize the discussion, inserting thoughts about its relationship to the bigger ideas. Observing each other and our colleagues has helped us to name, define, and refine the facilitating behaviors and language that seem the most effective.

The basic elements we've found effective in a debriefing process include the following.

• establish encouraging ground rules
• ask participants to describe their experience to each other
• restate responses and reframe within the conceptual framework and language of the big ideas
• offer more stories or examples
• apply the five examinations framework
• probe with more questions
• allow silence
• encourage collaborative thinking

The following section is an example of these elements at work in a debriefing of one of the opening activities on learning environments described above. Consider this a chance to walk in the garden and smell the flowers before we take you to the toolshed.

A WALK IN THE GARDEN
Opening activity: Think about a place where you find it really easy to accomplish something, where you feel comfortable and at ease with yourself, where you feel like you belong and fit in.

Establish encouraging ground rules
During the debriefing discussion, we want to ensure that teachers feel comfortable and safe to express their views and share their stories. Our goal is not just interaction between the student and trainers, but a peer exchange where all ideas and experiences are valued. To create a climate for this we set ground rules at the beginning of a class. We tell students they will not be put on the spot. They can listen or participate in ways that are most comfortable for them. When they do speak up, we make sure we listen closely and offer encouraging verbal and nonverbal responses so they know they've been heard. We paraphrase to clarify if we've understood what they said.

Describe experiences to each other
After time to recall and talk to a partner or small group about their memories, we ask participants to tell the whole group some of the elements of their stories. We listen closely to the discussion, recording on chart paper their elements, perhaps

followed by a phrase that reframes what is said in the language of the core knowledge and our big ideas about learning environments for children. The *hope to see* list we may have generated in our planning or the content of any presentation we might have delivered now becomes the information we weave into the dialogue. Instead of starting with these ideas as objectives to be presented, we list them as reflections of the experiences and current understandings of the participants in the group. We add any of our own which we feel to be pertinent to the big picture.

Our chart might look like this:

A place for me
- Room to spread out (adequate space)
- Needed materials and tools nearby (available and accessible)
- Comfortable setting and furniture to work in (size appropriate)
- A place to concentrate and not be interrupted (alone space)
- Enough time to really get into the task and complete it (adequate time)
- Soothing colors; cozy furniture for stretching out or curling up (aesthetic and soft elements)
- A bathtub/hot tub with water (availability of water)
- Not too cluttered, but also not too stark (inviting elements)
- Natural lighting and materials; plants, trees, rocks, water, sunshine, woods, garden (aspects of nature)
- My personal favorite things around me (personal space and security items)
- People who look and act like me (culturally relevant)

Restate and reframe

When a teacher shares an idea, we'll restate what she said in a different form, extending on it with references to the big ideas. This process helps teachers immediately see the connections between their own experiences and the larger body of knowledge. When RayAnn says, "I get really annoyed when supplies for my projects aren't right where I need them and I have to go searching for something." We may respond, "Yes, that's really frustrating and you probably lose your train of thought and momentum to keep working. This is what happens with children as well, and often they don't know where to go for what they need."

When Agda shares, "My office has pictures of my family and other things that are special to me. It's my favorite place to be. I can work and then look up at all of the things that make me feel good." We offer, "That's such an important concept. Children too need to have things that feel familiar and special around them in their child care programs. It helps them feel safe, valued, and know they belong there. Having a cubbyhole with their name on it, a picture of them and their family, something that belongs to them that they can be in charge of, really contributes to a child's positive feelings of who they are in the program."

As we model these connections, we encourage teachers to do the same by asking: "How might what you just shared about yourself be true in an environment for children?" or "How could we create that positive feeling you have in the environment for children?"

Teachers enjoy and need to talk about their own lives and experiences. We want to offer time for this, as well as keep the discussion on track and related to children. Reframing their experiences with the big ideas under consideration provides opportunities for both to occur.

Offer more stories or examples

Another element in the debriefing process is to offer an additional story or example from our observations of children related to the idea or experience a teacher just described. This becomes a further illustration of the points under consideration. For example, when Jane dreamily recalls, "I just feel so comfortable and relaxed in my bedroom. There are soft pillows and a down comforter, I go there when I want to get away from it all," we offer, "Places like that are so important. I've visited a classroom where teachers have created a space like that for the children. They've emptied a deep closet, taken the doors off and lined the walls with pale blue fabric, like the calming presence of the ocean. Pillows, blankets, and stuffed toys create an inviting spot for children to curl up all by themselves. Often children who are having a difficult day choose to spend time there."

Our observations and stories generate more anecdotes from the teachers and their programs, so that the ideas and information under consideration come to life with numerous concrete examples.

Apply the five examinations framework

The five examination considerations we use as a framework for exploring the big ideas are also woven into our debriefing discussion. We offer these as a methodology for teachers to examine aspects of the core knowledge and its application to their work.

After using this method for some time, we discovered that in Selma Wasserman's book *Serious Players in the Primary Classroom* (Teachers College Press, 1992), Wasserman describes a process like this as a "thinking lens." We remind teachers that as they wrestle with the ongoing issues of their work, this five examinations framework will help them explore and clarify what needs to happen. It will also develop a disposition toward reflection. Here's how we might use this framework in a discussion about learning environments.

- *Examining our own filters*
  Are you aware of the kinds of environments in which you feel most comfortable? Who feels comfortable in the environment you've created in the classroom? You? The children? The parents?

- *Examining the environment*
  What are all of the aspects of an environment that should be considered? How does the current environment you've created influence various situations (such as, choices available to children, traffic patterns, conflicts that erupt, cleanup routines)?

- *Examining child development*
  Have you noticed how children of different ages respond to various aspects

During debriefing, the teacher is likely also to raise questions that call for comparisons to be made, for hypotheses to be generated, for assumptions to be examined. These operations create a "thinking lens" through which knowledge is filtered, so that students are cognitively processing information, instead of merely receiving it.

Selma Wasserman, *Serious Players in the Primary Classroom* [4] of the environment? Who frequently plays with or avoids what? What changes in the environment could better support different developmental needs in the group?

- *Examining issues of cultural sensitivity and inclusiveness*
Are all the children of your group and their families reflected in the classroom environment? Does one kind of identity dominate the images, while others are tokenized or obviously different? How might you reflect more of the diversity of how people in the wider community live today?

- *Examining teacher roles and strategies*
What role do I play in the environment while children are at play? Is there something else I might do to encourage their interests and learning goals?

We make these questions explicit by referring to them as a methodology for examining all of our work with children. In this way teachers can draw on this five examination framework in a variety of circumstances to explore their concerns.

Probe with more questions

As teachers offer their thoughts and experiences, we probe for more information, asking questions like the following.

- Can you say more about that?
- What does that look like?
- Tell us why you think that.
- What was it like in your childhood?
- Can you remember where that feeling comes from?

We assure participants that we're not trying to put them on the spot, nor are we looking for a "right" answer. The purpose of our questions is to help them clarify and name their thoughts, creating a stronger foundation for connecting with any new information. Also, their further explanations spark deeper thinking and analysis for the rest of us, contributing to the co-construction of new ideas and learning. We remind them that we often learn just as much as the participants during these sessions. They introduce concepts and information we may never have included in a pre-planned presentation.

Allow silence

A waiting period after a question has been asked is another important strategy for encouraging participation. Often times any silence that follows a question can be uncomfortable for a trainer. We've come to realize that it takes time for teachers to think and respond during discussions. Thus we intentionally wait before we offer our own answers or move on.

If we've probed with a question such as, "Can you remember where that feeling of wanting to avoid cleaning up comes from?" and no one immediately responds, we mentally count to twenty before saying anything else. This usually allows enough time for an experience to occur to someone, such as, "Oh, I think every time my parents told me to clean up my room I just felt totally overwhelmed and thought I could never figure out where to put all that stuff." This gives us a chance to connect this experience with one of our big ideas about learning environments, for example, how the organization of materials influences children's ability to engage in self-directed learning.

Encourage collaborative thinking

We use a number of approaches to encourage collaborative thinking. When someone asks a question, we sometimes offer it to the group for suggestions. When it is pertinent to the continuing discussion, we may refer to an example or comment someone brought up earlier. If a participant has shared something especially relevant with us in writing or in a conversation during a break, we often ask if they would bring it up with the class. We are continually alert to the ways in which each person can contribute to all of our learning and we provide opportunities and a comfortable climate for them to do so.

We were amazed to discover that in her book, Wasserman describes a "play-debrief-replay" process for engaging children's thinking, similar to what we do with adults. Her description of interactions that promote reflection are particularly applicable. In the following paragraph, try substituting the word "teacher" for "children" each time Wasserman uses it.

> How you choose to respond to each child's idea is influenced by your goal of examining the big ideas. Your responses are also guided by the need to allow children adequate time for reflection of the surface or observable data, before challenging their thinking at higher levels. In every response above, respect for children and for their ideas is clearly manifest. Time for thinking, for reflection on ideas, and a climate of safety for children to express their thoughts without fear of being wrong are all incorporated into the interactions. These skills combine to form the masterful art of debriefing interactions.[5]

If it is to aid in the construction of ideas, the art of debriefing takes practice.

ONCE IS NOT ENOUGH

To help teachers continue to consolidate their understandings, we provide time and encouragement to practice applying the ideas that were initially uncovered during the first activity and discussion. For example, as a follow-up to the charting of ideas about learning environments, we invite participants to use the list we generated to evaluate the environment in which we are meeting for the training. We may use the list to watch for examples in a videotape of an environment for children; or we might provide open-ended materials (such as wood, fabric, yarn, paper, and markers), asking teachers to represent an environment using the list as a guide. These activities provide opportunities to try out the ideas introduced, and they help uncover further complexity and new questions.

The discussions following these practice activities include elements similar to the initial debriefing discussion described above. In addition, we encourage participants to decide on next steps for themselves in using these ideas or pursuing new questions. We send teachers home with follow-up possibilities, such as articles, questions for reflective writing, or observation forms, to continue their exploration and practice around the big ideas.

Because we've seen how teachers blossom with this process, we find it far more inviting than a prepared presentation. This method has further enabled us to trust ourselves and, most of all, to put trust in the teachers with whom we work. The truth is that teachers are always in charge of their own learning, despite how often we think we know best and try to control or direct their education. It's fitting that our approach now reflects and utilizes this fact, rather than interrupts it.

We've walked you through our garden to get a taste of what's there, and now we've arrived at the toolshed. You will find that there are four basic types of tools we use, each with numerous variations. We are hesitant to share these strategies without a word of caution. Used as a quick fix without a thoughtful plan for your garden, these tools may be dull or ineffective. We have not provided an instruction book because we honestly believe that the information will be more useful to you if you develop it for yourself.

As you go about planning teacher training, we hope you will return to this toolshed often, asking, for instance, "How might I use a childhood memory activity on this topic?" or, "Are there metaphors or props that would help teachers explore the ideas here?"

Keep in mind that partner and small group activities are a foundation for most of these strategies. Whatever the group size, we find that peer exchanges create safe and valuable opportunities to explore new ideas and hear others' views. Like children, most adults are social beings and learn best when interacting with others. We want to reinforce the notion that the trainer is but one resource in the room.

Welcome to our toolshed. The door is always open and we think you'll see how each strategy relates to the elements of our training methodology outlined above. When used often, some of these tools may need sharpening. We're sure you'll find your favorites and leave the others to gather dust and cobwebs. From time to time you may do spring cleaning and reorganize how you store these tools, transferring them to topical notebooks or card files, or setting up folders with related forms and handouts from appendices. Do what works for you. Pick up that shovel and dig right in.

Chapter 4
Awareness Tools

Because one of our primary goals is to help teachers become observant and self-reflective, we are constantly designing training strategies that promote these dispositions and cultivate the necessary skills. Awareness tools are exercises we use to provoke memories of past experiences and acquired knowledge, as well as alertness in everyday environments and events. Bringing up memories of everyday happenings often turns ordinary encounters into extraordinary insights for effective teaching.

CHILDHOOD MEMORIES

We use childhood memories strategies for a couple of reasons. The more we as adults can remember childhood feelings, the more able we are to plan for them. As we've discussed earlier, teachers further benefit from examining the source of their own values and behaviors so that their responses to children become intentional, rather than unconscious or based on immediate feelings.

Knowing that there can be unpleasant memories, we design these strategies with care. In introducing them, we acknowledge that some of us have had unhappy childhoods. We ask participants to tap into memories that will be helpful, but that will not block their learning. A number of teachers have thanked us for this guideline and said that it made the activity useful for them.

Whether in a class, workshop, or staff meeting, devoting time to childhood memory activities can provide teachers with insights into themselves and their coworkers.

Strategy: Introduce Yourself as a Childhood Message

To begin a discussion or training on any early childhood topic, suggest participants think back to a related childhood experience. For instance, if the topic is "building self-esteem in children" ask, "As a child what was the consistent message you got, verbally or non-verbally, about yourself?" If the subject is child guidance, you might ask them to remember the consistent message in their childhood about how to handle conflict. Remind participants they can be as light or as serious as they'd like.

Ask people to get up and walk around the room introducing themselves by repeating to each person their name and a phrase which captures this childhood message. We then clearly hear the different things we were taught: "Hello, I'm Deb and I need to stop being so moody." "My name is Margie and I know it's important to keep quiet when disagreements arise."

During the debriefing of this activity, we ask people how they feel about themselves after repeating this phrase over and over again. We explore their responses to how others have introduced themselves. If there are any messages that reflect conflicting values, it's useful to consider how these could lead to staff tensions.

Charlotte's comments during a debriefing discussion demonstrate the effectiveness of this training strategy. "Now I see that my constant emphasis on clean up is what was done to me as a child. I really didn't like it, but here I am repeating the same thing to the kids in my room. I don't want our classroom to become a mess, but now I see how the children must feel when I bug them so much about this." As Charlotte's disposition to be self-reflective grew during the months we worked with her, so did the ease with which she conducted cleanup in her classroom.

Strategy: Share Your Memories of Mealtime

Through this strategy, you can enhance a number of training topics in early childhood education—such as, health and nutrition, social-emotional development, building verbal expression, and routines that foster self-help and self-esteem. Examining childhood experiences around food and mealtimes can also help staff team members consider the conflict of values and customs they shape into lunch and snack time rules, routines, and interactions.

Ask participants to discuss the following questions in small groups to explore positive and negative memories of their childhood mealtimes. The debriefing discussion helps them uncover the influences in their own mealtime and nutrition habits and determine which of these they want to continue with children. We consider things such as the preparation, setting, and conversation of mealtimes, as well as availability and selection of food. As the example suggests, issues of manners, choices, and regulations are also part of the discussion.

> - eat your peas
> - think of the starving children in the world
> - no dessert until you finish
> - no real mealtime, lots of peanut butter and crackers
> - Dad never ate with us
> - telling stories of how our day went
> - sneaking food during long prayers

Mealtime questions:
- What do you remember about mealtimes you had as a child?
- Where did you eat?
- Who did you eat with?
- What was the atmosphere?
- What kinds of foods do you remember eating?
- What were your favorite foods? least favorite?
- What messages did you receive about food and eating habits from your family?
- What influences do you think these experiences have had on your habits today?

• Do you consider yourself a healthy eater today?
• Do you enjoy mealtime?

We end this activity where many might have thought to begin it—by exploring appropriate principles for mealtimes in programs for young children. Rather than a lecture or list developed by the trainer, these principles are collectively developed with participants working out agreements across the diverse experiences and conflict of values that may be present.

Strategy: Remember Your Favorite Times

To explore our intuitive and sensory knowledge of developmentally appropriate practice, we ask teachers to brainstorm a list of the activities they fondly remember from their childhoods. Participants can first develop their own lists, work in pairs to do this, or call out memories as they come to them. At the point we choose to create a collective list, we try to record responses in columns of similar examples, making a mental note of the heading for each and only filling in the column headings after the lists are developed. Below is an example of a list.

Time with special people
• Visiting my grandmother and making cookies
• Helping my neighbor fix things with all of her tools
• Sitting on my father's lap, reading a book together
• Going camping with my whole family
• Learning how to fish with my uncle
• Taking care of my baby brother before he could walk or talk
• Exploring the empty lot next door with my dog

Outdoor/Sensory activities
• Playing in the mud, sand, water
• Looking for and catching bugs
• Collecting shells, rocks, leaves
• Lying on the ground and looking up through the trees
• Using sidewalk chalk to draw, play games, write graffiti

Large muscle activities
• Swinging really high and feeling the wind on my face
• Roller-skating very fast
• Running up and down hills
• Playing in the waves at the beach
• Climbing as high as I could on climbers, trees, buildings, and looking out over the world

Independent projects
- Building a fort with scrap materials
- Operating a lemonade stand in my front yard
- Putting on a neighborhood carnival

Sneaking around, being mischievous
- Climbing over the fences in the neighborhood
- Trying on my mom's special dresses when she was out at the store
- Sneaking into the movie theater without paying
- Putting a toy spider in my sister's milk glass
- Calling strangers on the phone with knock-knock jokes

The lists participants develop and the headings we give them become an introductory overview of children's needs, interests, and developmentally appropriate curriculum practices. We ask people to reflect on these lists and discuss the implications they have for the programs they provide for young children. This activity is particularly useful for child care for school-aged children where programs typically reflect boredom, chaos, or another version of school.

NAME IT

Learning theory informs us that people acquire new knowledge and skills by building on their previous understandings and experience. It seems to us that this implies a specific practice for those who do adult education: Devise ways for students to uncover what they've already learned about a topic and identify the experiences that led to this understanding; offer encouragement and opportunities to explain this to others; assist them in analyzing their views in light of a larger context or body of ideas. This process of naming what you know while considering new information clarifies one's thinking, uncovers real questions, and motivates one towards finding answers and new behaviors.

The activities that follow are responsive to the diverse levels of knowledge and experience that participants bring to a training. When we start with *their* knowledge, rather than ours, participants can immediately enter into the process.

Strategy: Making Friends with a Baby

While most child care work is viewed by those outside the field as baby-sitting, this is especially true for infant and toddler caregivers. Those who have experience with this age group benefit from naming their expertise, while the inexperienced learn some basic child development principles through the same process.

We ask participants to work in small groups to brainstorm answers to the following questions:

- What do you do to make friends with a baby?
- Why does this work?
- What does a baby offer you as a friend?

In the whole group, we first discuss ideas on making friends with a baby, noticing and combining similar ideas on chart paper, offering additional ideas that may have been overlooked. These teacher behaviors form an overview of developmentally appropriate practice for infants. It becomes easy to contrast this with inappropriate, or non-friendly practices.

Discussing why these things work with babies and what they offer in return provides a snapshot of the principles of child development, the characteristics and needs of children of this age. Participants not only get a picture of this age and stage, but an affirmation of their own intuition and knowledge. This is an important foundation for understanding what curriculum for infants is really about—building on the things on this list.

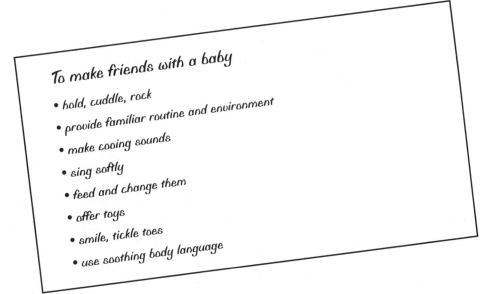

To make friends with a baby

- hold, cuddle, rock
- provide familiar routine and environment
- make cooing sounds
- sing softly
- feed and change them
- offer toys
- smile, tickle toes
- use soothing body language

Strategy: Principles for Working with Parents

To help teachers develop responses to parent concerns about a given issue (for example, biting, academics, or sex play), we first pose this general discussion question for small groups: "How have you handled parent requests that you disagree with? Discuss some specific examples." As they share their experiences, teachers offer each other valuable ideas and new considerations on the complexities involved. Analyze these specific examples with the whole group and develop a chart titled "Principles for Working with Parents."

Developed in this fashion, teachers are more likely to put these principles to use than if you had delivered a lecture or circulated a memo.

Strategy: The Job Game

To use teachers' own experiences to get to the heart of the child care staffing crisis, we worked with colleague Wendy Harris to create the job game. This activity usually generates initial laughter, but quickly involves people in a lively discussion. As teachers share their experiences with each other, they find a commonality that enables them to speak with confidence about what they know. Their courage, advocacy skills, and activism are often enhanced.

We create index cards with a job title written on each one. In making the cards, we choose occupations that have an aspect of child care work: public relations specialist, health care provider, counselor, gym teacher, mediator, musician, statistician, building inspector, journalist, plumber, data analyst, chemist, scatologist, interior decorator, furniture repair person, fund-raiser, purchasing agent, photographer, and so forth. The group circulates, trading cards until they have several that they want to keep. Asking everyone to be seated, we explore the following questions.

- How many of you have a card that has nothing to do with child care work?
- How many have a card that includes some aspect of your work in child care?
- How many of your occupation cards earn less than what a child care worker earns?
- More than what we earn?
- There are scores of occupations here, nearly all of which include aspects of our work but are rewarded with substantially higher paychecks. What's the name of this problem?

Strategy: Kinds of Learning

We have several strategies that give teachers the opportunity to directly examine their own learning process, relate this to the learning process of children, and the kinds of learning Piaget defined.

Ask participants to identify something they have learned as an adult and discuss the following questions with a partner.

- How did you go about learning this?
- What was most helpful in your learning process?
- When you encountered stumbling blocks, what got you through them?
- How did you feel about yourself in this process?

Social Learning	Physical Learning	Logico-Mathematical Learning	Dispositional Learning
• read instructions	• tried doing it	• pictured in my mind	• was curious
• Andrena told me	• ran fingers over bumps	• drew conclusions from picture	• felt stupid

During the debriefing, we ask one or two participants to share their answers. Using the kinds of learning formulated by Piaget, we note and classify the teacher's experiences under column headings of "social learning," "physical learning," and "logico-mathematical learning."[6] We add a fourth column with the heading "dispositional learning" to keep this concept in the forefront as well.

REFLECTIVE WRITING

In conducting staff meetings as a director or in leading workshops or classes, we've often used reflective writing as a training tool. This fosters self-examination and teacher dispositions towards being a researcher.

Many people are not initially comfortable expressing themselves in writing.

We introduce the idea as a way to gather one's thoughts, **and** stress **that we** are not looking for right answers or writing skills. In most cas**es we don't collect or** read what's written, and on the occasions we do, like in an ongoing class, we never correct any aspect of students' writing. Rather, we become pen pals, interacting with the concerns teachers are raising, offering a way to consider them in a larger framework.

Usually we use reflective writing as an opening, transitional, or concluding strategy. We may ask if there is anyone who wants to read aloud what they have written and a useful discussion often follows.

As a director, a nice touch is to provide notebooks or personalized journals for teachers to regularly write in at the beginning or end of a staff meeting. Even if no one reads aloud and there is no discussion, the time spent reflecting is valuable, and when done repeatedly, it has a cumulative effect in making teachers more thoughtful and intentional in their behaviors.

Sometimes we call for open-ended writing, while at other times we pose questions for reflection to help focus the adults' thinking. Here are some examples of each.

Strategy: Open-Ended Writing

- Write about something that made you laugh today.
- Is there anything that happened with a child this week that left you with questions running around in your head?
- If you were given $500 for your classroom today, what would you spend it on?

Strategy: Focused Writing

- Describe a time in your childhood when a big change occurred. What were your fears? What brought you comfort?
- Write about your own thresholds for safety and risk taking. Give some examples in your life. Consider how you think this influences your interactions with children.
- What do you think are the primary influences in your current self-concept? What insights does this give you about working with children?
- Describe the kind of child you are most interested in. Describe the kind of child you are least drawn to. What do you think accounts for that?
- List ten values you want to pass on to children. Choose the five that are most important to you. Prioritize the top two and describe some strategies you are using to get those across.

Strategy: Questions to Guide Writing

For those who are not at ease with writing, we have a set of questions that we use to spark their thinking. We may offer one or more of these to start off those participants, either individually or as a group. Sometimes we use these questions when we are engaging in a written dialogue with the reflective writing of students in our classes. In any case, we've found them useful in giving more confidence to inexperienced writers.

- What are the main ideas you want to write about?
- What influenced you in your thinking about this? Can you describe an experience, something you observed, something you read?
- How do you see your ideas as the same or different as other people's views on this?
- What change do you think would happen if everybody acted on this idea?

OBSERVATION CHECKLISTS

A meaningful way for adults to learn about children is through reflecting on their direct experiences with them. Reflection on what happened is at the core of constructing new knowledge. During one session or ongoing training settings, we nearly always suggest a follow-up activity that involves looking for the concepts we have been exploring. A straightforward strategy toward that end is to offer an observation checklist. These are useful when teachers visit other classrooms as well as when they reflect on their own.

There are any number of checklists available in our field. Those related to the Child Development Associate (CDA) Credential, NAEYC Accreditation, or the Harms Environmental Rating Scale are commonly used. Drawing on these, we are continually experimenting, in both content and form, with checklists that serve as training tools. To be useful, checklists need to be simple, focused, and inclusive of the important aspects of the big ideas under consideration. Whatever the format, we want specific examples of items on the checklist to be noted.

Numerous examples of observation forms we've used are found in appendix A. Some have been created on the spot and handwritten with a teacher, while others have been labored over on our computer. In either case, the goal is to provide a tool that will sharpen observation skills and focus attention on some important aspect of the core knowledge of early childhood education.

Chapter 5
Active Tools

Adults, like children, are usually active learners. Whatever their way of knowing or kind of intelligence (see Chapter 1), most adults enjoy and benefit from moving around during a training, especially at the end of a long work day.

Training strategies we call active tools don't require that one be physically fit, or even especially competent. Most strategies are quite suitable for participants who are differently abled. What we are after with these tools is an interactive experience that includes the body as well as the mind. Our intuition is that these tools foster the sensory integration process, enhancing the learning of all participants.

SIMULATING EXPERIENCES

Because we understand the critical role direct experience plays in learning, we like participatory activities that simulate an experience of the idea we want to explore. These activities take various forms but are designed to create a common experience for us to discuss together.

Strategy: Dance the WHIRR WHIRR WHIRR

To create an immediate experience of learning theory in action, we've created a dance for people to learn in four ways. Photocopy and hand out the "Dance the WHIRR WHIRR WHIRR" description below, asking participants to read silently for a few minutes and then turn their papers over. Take them through the four ways of learning, providing guidance only as indicated.

Dance the WHIRR WHIRR WHIRR

- Clap your hands together in front of your body eight times
- Stomp both your feet four times
- Clap your hands over your head eight times
- Clap in front of your body five times, stop for two beats and then clap ten times
- Shake your head back and forth eight times
- Twirl around three times, saying WHIRR WHIRR WHIRR as you twirl
- Repeat sequence two more times

Learning the dance

- Ask participants to stand and dance the WHIRR WHIRR WHIRR without reminders from you or the paper.
- Have participants listen while the full set of instructions are read and then ask them to dance the WHIRR WHIRR WHIRR.
- As participants watch, demonstrate the instructions as you read them. Then have everyone do the dance.

• Have participants work with a partner to discuss the directions, share strategies and teach each other the dance. Then ask the whole group to do the dance together.

This activity is great fun and provides a simulation of the effectiveness of certain teaching strategies. In the debriefing we refer to the "How People Learn"[7] illustration below, inviting discussion about how each of the strategies they experienced relates to the learning theory. We explore how this relates to the role of play and active learning for children.

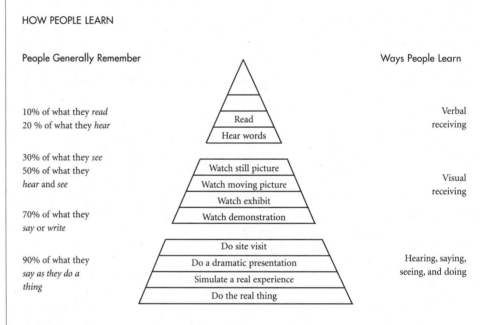

HOW PEOPLE LEARN

People Generally Remember		Ways People Learn
10% of what they *read*	Read	Verbal receiving
20 % of what they *hear*	Hear words	
30% of what they *see*	Watch still picture	Visual receiving
50% of what they *hear* and *see*	Watch moving picture	
	Watch exhibit	
70% of what they *say* or *write*	Watch demonstration	
	Do site visit	Hearing, saying, seeing, and doing
90% of what they *say as they do a thing*	Do a dramatic presentation	
	Simulate a real experience	
	Do the real thing	

Strategy: Contrasting Teaching Styles

With participants in small groups, we provide each with the same basic materials, but a different set of instructions. Asking each group to choose someone to be the teacher, we give them written instructions that either call for a structured, teacher-directed activity, or an open-ended approach to using the materials. Participants are not told what the teacher's instructions are, or that they are different.

Structured Teacher

• Keep all supplies to yourself until needed.

• Make or draw a model for group to copy.

• Give step-by-step instructions, moving on only when all are ready.

• Correct those who don't get it right; praise those that look like yours.

• Keep everyone working individually and quietly.

• Take over for those who have trouble.

Open-Ended Teacher

• Place basic supplies on table within everyone's reach.

• Suggest everyone explore and create as they'd like.

- Watch, listen, offer additional materials as needed (such as scissors or wire).

- Describe what you see happening, offer positive remarks.

- Encourage cooperation, refer children to each other for problem solving.

For example, we give all groups straws or a stack of newspaper and masking tape. Instructions for the teacher-directed groups are to provide a model for all to copy, to carefully ration materials, and to take participants through a step-by-step set of directions, requiring them to work individually without looking or talking to each other. Instructions for the open-ended groups suggest that the teacher put the materials on the table and invite participants to explore and see how they might want to use them. As they do so, the teacher is to listen, watch, and provide additional materials to support their endeavors. The open-ended teacher uses descriptive language and encouraging words as he sits with the group.

After five or ten minutes, we ask the groups to finish up and begin our debriefing discussion. Participants are always eager to share their excitement or displeasure. Usually the open-ended groups have made ingenious creations and report having much fun, conversation, creative thinking, and cooperative problem-solving. The teacher-directed groups often misbehave during the activity and complain that they felt bored, angry, unsure of themselves, anxious to please, unrecognized for their interests and needs, competitive, and often like a failure.

From this discussion we are able to generate several lists related to developmentally appropriate practice:

- How Children Learn Best
- What Makes a Toy or Learning Material Good?
- Teacher Behaviors that Promote Learning

Strategy: A Playful Experience

To experience the value of play for children as well as adults, we create activities in which participants play with materials for long periods of time. The play experience and questions for reflection are structured around the topic of the training. Modeling roles teachers might assume with children, we provide an ample supply of open-ended materials—large blocks, fabric, rope, buttons, toilet paper rolls, masking tape, and an extended period of time to play. We remind them to play as adults rather than pretend they are children. If there are those who would prefer to be observers, rather than players, this adds a further dimension to the debriefing.

For example, in a three-hour workshop on topics such as learning through play, developmentally appropriate curriculum, or academics in preschool, we provided sets of large, hollow blocks in a large open space. We suggested that the players explore the blocks, do what intrigued or engaged them, play with whomever they like, and let us know if there are additional supplies they need. Observers can be asked to record what they see:

- How are the blocks specifically being used?
- In what ways are the block builders working together?
- What do they understand about blocks and construction?

• What are they trying to figure out as they play? What themes are emerging?
• Can you translate any of this play into academic goals?

Initially, some adults are reluctant to play or may think the activity is trite, foolish, or too unclear. Others may have forgotten how to play, seemingly not curious, unable to do much sensory exploration, take risks, and be spontaneous. There are always those who jump right in and eventually everyone finds something of interest to engage with. In fact, we are continually delighted and amazed at how engaged people become in these play opportunities and at the quality of play they create. Observers refine their skills and make valuable contributions to the debriefing discussion.

Sometimes directors or trainers are reluctant to devote such a large amount of precious in-service time to "just playing." But debriefing discussions consistently reveal the value of this experience for teachers, both in terms of its renewal for them personally and the insights and new articulation about the value of play this activity affords.

Strategy: How Do You Learn?

A variation of the kinds of learning strategy found in Chapter 4 involves giving small groups of participants materials and a task that requires them to learn something new or use complex thinking to solve a problem. We typically have five or six tasks, one for each of the groups to use.

Small group tasks:
• a selection of scarves with an instruction booklet on fashionable ways of tying them
• the combined pieces of ten different puzzles to unscramble and put together
• a set of Legos with instructions to create a structure to match a given picture
• the pieces of a marble maze set with instructions to create a working structure that uses all the pieces
• handbooks outlining the benefits of several insurance policies with a description of a family's health needs and instructions to choose the best policy
• a working but dismantled appliance to reassemble for proper functioning

We use the same four-column debriefing approach described in the kinds of learning strategies under "Name It" in Chapter 4, asking participants to describe how they approached their task, what worked, what didn't, and what dispositions aided or hindered them.

SCAVENGER HUNTS
What better way to reinforce the role of the teacher as researcher and archaeologist than to have participants explore the environment for the concepts we are addressing in a staff meeting or class? Scavenger hunts get people up and moving. They provoke a fresh look at familiar surroundings, spark creativity, and enhance spontaneity and playfulness. Here are some favorites of teachers in programs where we've worked.

Strategy: Search and Find

From colleague Marilyn Jacobson we learned a scavenger hunt strategy to convey ideas about ECE environments. Meeting in a children's classroom when children are not present, ask teachers to gather in pairs. Give each an index card containing a list of three to five items to find.

Items listed should be those we'd hope to find in a quality classroom:

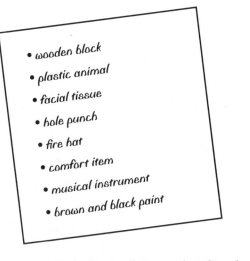

- wooden block
- plastic animal
- facial tissue
- hole punch
- fire hat
- comfort item
- musical instrument
- brown and black paint

As pairs find everything on their list, they return to a designated place in the room to be checked in and receive further instructions. Then ask pairs to exchange their items and return each to where it belongs.

This activity helps teachers look at the supply, organization, and display of materials in a classroom. The debriefing discussion can consider the impact of these on children's self-esteem, their ability to independently pursue their interests and problem solve, and develop their classification skills to easily put things away.

Strategy: Outdoor Play Possibilities

It's possible that teachers have never explored the program's outdoor play area from a child's point of view, or considered its potential for sharing their own interests with children. With the assignment to bring back an example, representation, or story of each item from an outdoor play area, possible scavenger hunt lists could include the following:

Find contrasting elements; something. . .
- heavy and light
- smooth and rough
- dark and bright
- natural and man-made
- huge and tiny
- scary and comforting

Find four kinds of. . .
- holes
- sounds
- things that move
- smells
- places that challenge your body

- symbols or writing
- dangers

Find places of pretending where you are. . .
- powerful
- small as an insect
- at home
- on TV
- a detective
- an artist
- a scientist

Find the natural world
- a new texture to explore
- an intriguing shadow
- something the wind does
- animal tracks
- something alive
- something dead

Strategy: A Place Where I Belong

To consider how an environment fosters or defeats a sense of belonging, we send people on a scavenger hunt around the building to find something that represents each of the following:

- Something that sparks a favorite childhood memory
- Something you don't understand
- Something that makes you feel respected
- Something that insults your intelligence
- Something you would take to a deserted island
- Something that has at least three other uses other than the obvious

The objects that get brought to the group discussion help us get to know each other better as well as provide a new look at our work and learning environments. We sometimes end this activity by brainstorming a list of changes we'd like to bring about in our work environment.

GAMES

To help teachers learn what Piaget would call "the social knowledge"[8] of early childhood education—useful vocabulary and terms related to specific practices, requirements, or regulations to be followed—we design fun ways to acquire what may otherwise be seen as boring information. Making games out of material to be memorized is more effective and enjoyable than delivering it in the form of a memo, lecture, or test.

Strategy: Hazard Pictionary Guessing Game

A fun way to alert teachers to common risk-filled situations is to have them play a version of the commercial game Pictionary. Taking information from a study on high-risk factors in child care centers, we created 3x5 cards with phrases describing these factors. Some examples of the high-risk factors are below. The game is simple: Rotating team members choose cards and draw pictures to convey the idea for their teammates to guess. With images and a fun time to

```
Hazard Pictionary cards

• Staff are not feeling well

• Substitutes unfamiliar with the children

• Staff preoccupied with an uncooperative child

• Tension between teachers

• Room is understaffed

• Extremely cold weather

• Conditions are rushed

• New children in the group

• Rules not carefully explained
```

associate with important information, teachers are more likely to keep the factors in mind.

Strategy: DAP Sorting

To encourage teachers to see the *Developmentally Appropriate Practice (DAP)* book as a valuable reference material, we have turned the lists on its pages into a game.[8] The object is to sort and classify the statements according to appropriate and inappropriate and to identify any gray or uncertain areas. Here's how we made the game.

- First we use a photocopier to enlarge the appropriate and inappropriate columns of the integrated components pages of the book.
- We cut each component into its own small section and place both the appropriate and inappropriate statements in one envelope for each age group.
- With each age group envelope, we attach two sheets of paper, one labeled Appropriate Practice (AP) and the other Inappropriate Practice (IP).
- During our workshop, we divide participants into children's age groups and give each their envelopes and AP and IP sheets.
- We ask them to first sort the enlarged statements onto the AP and IP sheets. Next, we have them arrange the AP and IP statements so that those referring to the same component were directly opposite each other.
- In addition to the statements in the book, we added less obvious or more controversial ones that we refer to as the gray areas. Teachers are asked to discuss and classify these as well, and to add any of their own gray areas.

In using this game we find that most participants are fairly confident in sorting the appropriate and inappropriate components. More experienced teachers offer explanations to newer teachers with questions or uncertainty. We suggest teachers use the DAP book to cross-check their answers.

The gray areas usually generate the liveliest discussions. Is calendar time appropriate for four year olds? *Should* infants be given a bottle whenever they seem cranky and unable to be otherwise comforted? *Are* table manners important to stress with three year olds? Teachers search through the DAP book to see if they can find any reference to these statements. Though the specific statements aren't listed, there are related components that participants can use to argue their position.

This game is a great way to uncover different cultural values and child-rearing practices among staff members. It illuminates the way these differences might become conflicts between staff and parents. We now include an additional reference book for this game, *Multicultural Issues in Child Care* by J. Gonzalez-Mena (Mayfield Publishing, 1993), which has many examples of different cultural attitudes and approaches to raising children.

We recommend that teachers stay alert to possible gray areas of practice in their program and bring these up for discussion in their staff meetings. Some of these may require cultural sensitivity and a renewed commitment to mutual respect.

KINESTHETIC ACTIVITIES

Many people are kinesthetic learners; they can function and gather their knowledge better if they move around during training sessions. Understandably, some teachers have trouble staying alert in a training held during naptime, in the evening after a stressful day of work, or when required to sit in children's chairs or on the rug. Whenever possible we include activities that invite participants to use their bodies to represent their experience and ideas. These are usually lively, as well as helpful to the adult learning process. They provide a model and reinforce the active, playful disposition we hope teachers will bring to children.

Strategy: Put Yourself on the Continuum

In training on children's learning and developmental theory, we've adapted a chart Jane Meade-Roberts developed (see appendix B) that outlines adult tasks along a Piagetian continuum of sensory motor to formal operations.[9] Mapping out this continuum on the floor, we ask people to move to the spot that reflects their level of ability in each of several daily tasks. As participants explain why they are standing in a particular spot and listen to the reasoning of others, we put these comments in the context of the stages of child development according to Piaget. The kinesthetic aspect to activities like this often enables people to consolidate new understandings.

Cooking (I am able to . . .)

Boil water and heat frozen food	make things from mixes	prepare simple meals i.e. broil meat, bake potato	follow recipes	create gourmet meals & invent delicious dishes

Bowling (I am able to . . .)

Pick up the ball	Roll the ball and avoid the gutter	Pick up most spares	Regularly pick up 7-10 splits	Consistently bowl games of 290-300

Strategy: Obstacles to Worthy Wages

To help child care teachers critically analyze the complexity of issues behind their inadequate compensation, we give them statements to consider with instructions to move to one side of the room or another, depending on whether they think the statement is true or false. We intentionally word the statements so that they can be interpreted in different ways in order to heighten teachers' eagerness to speak up.

Physically taking a stand seems to help people clarify their thinking and risk debating with others. We begin by asking the whole group to stand and listen to the statement that we are about to read. We point to one side of the room saying, "If you think this statement is true, stand there" and point to the other side of the room saying, "If you think it is false, stand here." Then we read the statements one at a time, allowing time for people on each side of the room to talk to each other, and then debriefing with the whole group before moving on to the next statement.

We make a rule that participants must choose one side of the room or another—true or false (no fence straddlers), but they are welcome to change their minds and move if they hear a persuasive argument. Here are the statements we typically use.

Obstacles to worthy wages—true or false

- We don't have enough data to prove that there is a relationship between salaries and the quality of care children receive.
- There are not enough men working in child care.
- Conditions of employment are a private matter between the employee and the boss.
- With the current economic climate we don't have a leg to stand on.
- You can't command a high salary for unskilled work.
- Child care employees are isolated and lack the opportunity to discuss compensation issues and explore action and solutions.
- Most child care workers aren't the head of the household and therefore don't need a higher salary.
- We just have to wait for the government to put money into child care.
- The child care work force is disinterested in, if not opposed to, the idea of organizing for change.
- This work can be done by anyone.
- Child care workers care so much about parents that they are willing to work for low wages in order to keep parents' fees down.
- The problem is overwhelming and there is no real solution.

Throughout this book there are other examples of ways we provide kinesthetic learning activities. We generally plan activities in various parts of the room so participants move around, explore objects, and talk to each other.

Chapter 6
Story Tools

Many trainers, no doubt, use stories in the course of their training. We find them to be especially useful in combination with the use of simple props. Nearly every story we use is based on a real-life situation. Unless there is a particular reason not to, we change the names to keep people and programs anonymous.

Stories used as training strategies can be presented in many forms. Whether told by the trainer, written as a scenario to start discussion, read in a body of literature, or seen on a videotape, stories provide a visual image and personal face to many of the ideas we want teachers to consider.

STORYTELLING

While children explore concepts in dramatic play, adults engage in similar exploration through literature. Knowing that storytelling is a primary mode of teaching in many cultures around the world, we've begun creating stories to examine some of the concepts and ethical dilemmas of our profession. This allows us to present information and pose questions in an engaging manner. In contrast to role plays, stories invite participants to enter into the world of the characters without having to do any acting themselves.

We use storytelling in one of two ways. Sometimes we create a story to tell and at other times we ask participants to create stories that convey information we all need to know. In both cases, we usually employ some form of simple prop to heighten the presentation.

Most of our stories come from real incidents we've encountered, heard, or read about. We sometimes turn descriptions from books into stories. Each of the following examples has an introductory explanation and the full text of a story we use.

Strategy: Sensitivity Theater

We all have good intentions, but we sometimes say or do things that are insensitive to others. The following short stories are based on real situations and are useful in teacher meetings to provoke discussion on working with parents or staff members. The stories remind us not to assume that our own lifestyle and culture are the norm for everyone.

Telling each story with a different face mask or large photo creates a sense of theater and eases the ability to wrestle with sensitive or emotionally charged content.

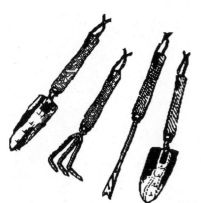

Willie's Mama
When my son's teacher, Patty, called to schedule a conference about his work in Head Start, I agreed to come on Wednesday. On Monday Patty called to remind me of the date and I told her my two-year-old Willie was really excited about coming to his big brother's school. There was a silence on the other end of the phone you could cut with a knife. Then Patty suggested I get a sitter for

Willie or exchange child care with another mom who also needs care for her baby when she comes in for a conference. I can't afford a baby-sitter and why does she think I would leave Willie with someone I don't even know?

Clara's Mama

During our home visit I told Clara's teacher that I want to get a job and get off welfare. This morning she told me about a part-time job at her church. She said that the people were really nice and I could start getting some job skills. I'm embarrassed to turn it down because she'll think I really don't want to work. She doesn't know that if I work part-time my welfare benefits will be reduced. I'd also have to find child care for the baby and I don't know what would happen with my medical coupons.

Josie's Mama

The other day Josie's teacher told me how much Josie likes playing at the water table at school. She suggested I let her play in the sink at home or help me wash the dishes. When I told her I knew she'd make a mess, she told me to use towels on the floor to make the clean up easy. She doesn't understand how expensive it is for me to do a load of laundry.

Marissa's Mama

I wanted Marissa to have nice clothes for her first school experience so I saved up money over the summer and bought her some really nice outfits. Now her teachers are telling me she shouldn't wear new clothes to school because they'll just get dirty. I want my daughter to look nice when she goes to school. Why can't they keep her from getting so dirty? Don't they know I can't afford new clothes very often?

Wen Fong's Mama

I hate to lie, but I told Wen Fong's teacher I already had plans and couldn't come to the parent meeting. The truth is it's the end of the month and I've run out of money. I can't afford to take anything to the potluck.

Strategy: ABZ Child Care Center Story

We put this story in an illustrated big book format to convey the meaning of the child care staffing crisis to teachers, directors, parents, employers, and policy makers.[10] After we read the story, we have small groups take on each of the characters and record on "thought bubbles" how this person might be feeling about this situation. The debriefing never fails to expose the seriousness and impact of the high teacher turnover in early childhood programs. It has spurred many into becoming worthy wage activists or advocates.

ABZ Child Care Center Story

Page 1.

Once upon a time, it could have been yesterday or today, the ABZ Child Care Center served families with children ages six weeks to five years old. ABZ Child Care is a happy, loving place where people have worked hard to create a family environment. Three years ago the program became accredited by NAEYC.

Page 2.

This is Cathy. She used to work at ABZ Child Care, but left three months ago to work as a parking lot attendant for $12.00/hr. Cathy is still friends with people at ABZ. She didn't want to leave. She loved working with kids and even took some child development classes to get better at it.

Page 3.

Here is Cathy on the phone to Sonja, a teacher who still works at ABZ. "Sonja, I really miss the kids."

"They really miss you, too. Casaundra asks about you every day."

"Oh, don't tell me that. I feel so bad. My new job is really boring. It doesn't challenge me at all. Here if I make a mistake, the only harm that's done is money lost on a parking stall.

"But I make so much more money that I'm getting all my bills paid off. You know what? They're going to be hiring again. I told my boss I knew someone who might want the job. What do you think?"

Page 4.

Sonja is torn, but knows she can't resist this offer. She's already had to train two people since Cathy left. She's exhausted and frustrated. She's having a harder and harder time stretching her paycheck to make ends meet. She goes to Joyce, the director, to tell her she's leaving for a better paying job.

Page 5.

Ted is Sonja's co-teacher. He is an enthusiastic, bright young man who thought it would be fun to work with kids. Ted has no background in child development or experience juggling the multitude of tasks involved in running a classroom. He's alone in the room right now while Sonja is off talking to the director. It's hard for him when his co-teacher leaves, even for a few minutes. Both he and the kids depend on her a great deal.

Page 6.

See Joyce, the director of ABZ Child Care, with her head in her hands. See the tears in her eyes. See the scream forming inside her. See all the names crossed off of her substitute teacher list? In the last six months Joyce has had to find four new teachers. How will she ever be able to reassure the parents in Sonja's room now that she is leaving?

Page 7.

Here's Maria who has two children, Malcolm who's 8 months old and Casaundra, age 4. Maria was glad to find ABZ. It seemed just right for her family needs. But one month after she enrolled her kids, one of Malcolm's caregivers left. Then Casaundra's favorite teacher, Cathy, left. Maria has a lot of stress on her job and her kids have started waking her up several times during the night.

Page 8.

Casaundra has learned to write her name. Every day she works at the art table making pictures with hearts. She always asks Ted or Sonja to help her write "TO CATHY" on her hearts. Today she's making a picture for Sonja too.

Page 9.

Malcolm is in the infant room. He cries a lot more than he used to. He's driving his new caregiver crazy.

Page 10.

There is no end to this story. It is repeating itself over and over again in child care centers all across our country. This is a story that needs to be told in all kinds of settings to all kinds of people. It is not a naptime story. This storytelling must wake people up before it's too late.

Another way this story has been used is in a serialized form with each page becoming a chapter of the story told between speakers, giving other presentations to an audience. When used this way the first chapter is introduced with accompanying remarks about a troupe of storytellers who are here to tell a story that should never be forgotten. Each storyteller then begins with a one sentence summary of what was heard in the last chapter of the ABZ story and ends with a "what will happen next?" type of question. For instance, "Will Sonja leave her job to go take care of parking stalls? Stay tuned for the next chapter of the ABZ Child Care Center story."

This story inspired our colleagues Jim Morin and Marcy Whitebook to write another titled *If the Shoe Fits: A Worthy Wage Fairy Tale*, included in Appendix B.

Strategy: A Day at Sunnyday Co-Op Preschool

We created this story as a way for teachers, parent educators, and directors to examine classroom events from different people's perspectives. This enables them to appreciate why the adults are behaving as they are and better assist them with some new insights and skills.

The Sunnyday Story

Sunnyday Co-op Preschool has recently hired an experienced teacher, Susan, to work each day with parent volunteers. The parents who interviewed Susan felt her years of experience and classes made her just the right person to prepare their four-year-old children for kindergarten.

Today Susan has planned an activity to teach the children about temperature. She instructs the parent volunteers to have the children color two predrawn thermometers, using blue for cold temperatures and red for hot. Marking pens are put in the middle of each table.

Sunny, one parent volunteer, moves around to the tables to help the children. "See the number on the thermometer? This one says 20 degrees. That means it is very cold, so color it blue. See the number on this one? It says 90 degrees. That means it's very hot, so color this one red." Ben is drawing other pictures all over his paper and ignoring the thermometers. Seeing Masayo coloring her thermometers neatly with the red and the blue markers, Sunny says, "What a good job you're doing Masayo."

Marilyn, another parent, is trying to keep children at her table focused on the activity. Josh and Charles have decided that their thermometers look like race tracks. They turn markers into cars and move them across the thermometers, making car sounds and racing each other. Marilyn nervously says, "We are not playing cars right now, boys. You need to color in your thermometers." Aiesha, Marilyn's daughter, says, "I want to make mine purple," and begins scribbling with a purple marker. Handing her a red marker, Marilyn speaks in a firm voice, "You need to use red now! You can use purple another time."

Donna, the third parent, is coloring thermometers right along with the children. She says, "Look outside, is it cold or hot?" Remember this summer when you wore bathing suits and went swimming? That's when it's hot. Use the red to show the hot one. Red is the color of fire and fire is hot." Lana says, "We have a fire at our house." Donna begins testing who knows their colors. "What color is this?" The children say "blue." "What color is this?" "Red." She continues holding up all the markers for the children to name. "Wow, you all know your colors. You are really smart. You'll be ready to go to kindergarten next year."

Susan comes over and says, "Yes, we've been working really hard at learning our colors."

Layla, the parent educator (or director), has been observing all this time. Her background is in parent education, with no training in early childhood education, but she senses Susan may not know how to plan appropriate activities for this age group. She is equally concerned about some of the parent responses. She really likes these women and doesn't want to jeopardize her relationship with them. She's at a loss as to what to do.

After reading the story, we give small groups the task of exploring each character's point of view. During the debriefing, we consider how the director or parent educator, Layla, might work with each of the other characters.

Strategy: Persona Doll Stories

The *Anti-Bias Curriculum* describes Kay Taus' development of persona doll stories to explore diversity with children.[11] Unlike other dolls that may be found in a classroom, persona dolls are given a life story by the teacher as a way to capture the children's imagination about some particular issue the teacher may want explored. The teacher introduces the doll as a friend who has come to visit the classroom and then tells a story about some aspect of the doll's life.

This idea can be adapted for use with teachers, asking them to work in small clusters to create a family story about particular children. We've used several different approaches with this activity, sometimes asking them to create a story reflecting a particular identity group, while at other times leaving the assignments open-ended to discover if the clusters develop stories reflecting any diversity.

In any case, the discussion following the storytelling usually provides ample opportunity to explore assumptions and stereotypes, invisibility as a form of bias, and diversity within a specific identity group. Racial and gender diversity issues can be further prompted by giving each cluster a simple face mask to represent their persona story, easily made by bending wire hangers into face shapes and covering them with nylon stockings of different skin colors, with felt scraps and yarn for features.

SCENARIOS

To help teachers practice analyzing and responding to situations they typically face, we create short scenarios around training topics for small groups to discuss. Specific scenarios make early childhood concepts real. Sometimes we follow a scenario with possible teacher responses to choose from, and other times we leave it to the participants to initiate their own ideas.

Strategy: Child Guidance Scenarios

In staff meetings, workshops, or classes, our training on child guidance is always built around the big idea of observing and reflecting on the child's point of view, rather than immediately jumping to reinforce rules or solve conflicts. Teachers typically want to immediately problem solve, so we've found it helpful to provide them with questions to guide their discussion of a scenario toward our big idea (and to remind them not to discuss solutions to the problems).

Discussion questions:
• What is this child trying to achieve and why?
• How would you describe the problem from the child's perspective?
• How might this child describe her or his feelings or point of view here?

Stuck-Up Lee

Lee is working at the art table. For the past few minutes he has tried to paste a piece of cotton onto his paper, but the cotton keeps sticking to his finger. He picks up the container of cotton balls and throws it on the floor saying, "You stupid old cotton balls."

Jamal's boss

The children are playing outside and when you tell them it's time to come in, Jamal yells at you and says, "No way! I'm staying outside. You're not the boss of me."

Jennifer has the blues

You are handing out name tags and letting children choose the one they want. Jennifer picks a blue name tag, then changes her mind and trades it for a pink one. She goes to play, but soon returns saying, "I changed my mind. I want the blue one back." You tell her the blue ones are all gone. She begins to cry loudly, "I wanted the blue one. You said I could have a blue one."

Carmella's conundrum

You see Carmella wandering around outside the classroom. You go over and tell her that she needs to go back to her room. She says, "I don't want to. I hate that teacher in there. She's really mean."

Casey strikes out

Randy and Casey are playing together in the sandbox. Casey is very controlling with the toys and won't let Randy play with certain ones. Randy leaves saying, "I'm not playing with you anymore." Casey comes to you sobbing, "Randy's mean. He won't play with me."

Strategy: Deciding on Strategies to Support Play

We use the scenarios of this activity to reinforce teacher dispositions and encourage teachers to observe and reflect before involving themselves in children's play. We stress that there are many possible responses and no one right answer.

In using these scenarios, we have small groups discuss the scene and each of the possible responses listed. We ask them to consider these questions:

- How might the child feel or interpret this response?
- Does this response help the teacher learn more about the child's play and thinking?
- How might this response impact the play?
- Is there another response you would prefer?

SCENE 1: Samantha at work

Samantha was working in the carpentry area. She put a long piece of wood in the vise, tightened it, and then measured off a space with her fingers. She sawed off a piece about 6 inches long. She moved the wood in the vise and laid the cut piece on top of it to saw the next piece the same size. She placed the two cut pieces on top of each other and, using two hands, began hammering a nail through the top piece. She hit the nail head every third or fourth try and periodically stopped to reposition the wood which slid around the table. When she realized the nail wasn't attaching the two pieces together she left the area. The next time the teacher noticed her, Samantha was back in the carpentry area with a bottle of glue. Having attached the two pieces of wood together, she began gluing some Styrofoam circles on the side. The teacher said:
a) "Oh, what a nice car you are making."

b) "I noticed how you used the vise to hold the wood while you measured and sawed."

c) "There's some paint in the art area, would you like to paint your car?"

d) "How many wheels does a car need?"

e) nothing; she stood back and watched to see what Samantha would do next.

SCENE 2: Mario and the sand

Mario seemed to be enjoying himself in the sand area. He started filling a baby bottle using his hand as a scoop; then a cup as a scoop; then he turned the baby bottle over and used it as a scoop. Then he used a funnel as a scoop and noticed that the sand ran out both ends of the funnel into the bottle. The teacher:

a) picks up a bigger funnel and asks, "Which of these funnels is bigger, yours or mine?"

b) picks up a funnel and tries using it just like Mario and thinks to herself, "Maybe if I get a container and funnel and use them the same way he does, Mario will say something to me about his play."

c) says to Mario, "You figured out how to get sand into that bottle two different ways!"

d) says, "Mario, are you making a birthday cake?"

e) says, "Mario, why don't you pour your sand over this truck and bury it?"

SCENE 3: LaToya and the beauty shop

LaToya hung around the edges of the beauty parlor play in the dress-up corner, looking as if she would like to join in. She held a purse and some rollers and watched the "beauty girl" and the girl in the chair getting her hair done. The teacher:

a) says to the other children, "LaToya wants to play. Why don't you be nice and invite her to play with you?"

b) thinks to herself, "Maybe if I get a purse and some rollers I could say, 'Hi, I'd sure like to get my hair fixed too.' I'll wait to see if LaToya wants to keep watching or if she wants to join in the play."

c) asks, "I see you have a purse and some rollers with you. Are you going to fix the doll's hair?"

d) says, "Only four people are allowed in the dress-up area, LaToya, so you'll have to find somewhere else to play until someone leaves this area."

e) says, "Hey beauty parlor lady, you have another customer waiting for her appointment."

SCENE 4: Jessica and Ryan's game

Jessica and Ryan are playing in the block area. They are balancing long blocks vertically in one corner and from the other side rolling cylinder shaped blocks towards the long blocks, trying to knock them over. As blocks get knocked down, they remind each other of the score and whose turn is next. The teacher

a) says, "Tell me about what you two are doing."

b) says, "That's not a safe way to use the blocks. Blocks are for building."

c) watches the children, smiles, and walks away. She jots down this quick note for her observation file. "Jessica and Ryan invented a bowling type game. They took turns and kept track of the score, counting how many each of them knocked down and who had more."

d) brings a pad of paper and marker to the block area and puts it on the shelf. She says, "Here's a score pad if you want to keep track of how many you knock down and whose turn it is."

e) takes a Polaroid photograph of what Jessica and Ryan are doing. At circle time she shows that picture and others she has taken to the group and asks them to tell a story about Jessica and Ryan's play time.

ROLE PLAYS

Role plays are another form of storytelling or using scenarios as training strategies. We approach role plays with caution because we've found many people hesitant to be a part of them. Sometimes we do the role play ourselves, asking for one or two volunteers to take on a small part. When we do have participants play all the parts, we provide specific instructions about the role so that each is clear about what is expected. Those who don't assume roles become observers to analyze and offer reflections during the debriefing.

Most of our role plays are written about specific situations we have encountered. As we write the parts, we try to build in real complexities people encounter and avoid making anyone a fool or bad guy in the scene. Role plays are useful ways to look at the practical application of early childhood concepts, as well as explore attitudes and skills that lead to staff conflicts and communication problems. Following are two examples that we've found especially useful for the latter.

Strategy: Conflict at Little Darlings Child Care Center

This role play has participants working in pairs, with each assuming one of the two roles outlined below. Everyone receives a description of the scene, but only their role to see. We give the pairs ten minutes to play out their roles and then come together for discussion. In the debriefing we ask whether each felt the conference was a success or not and what made it so. Together we construct a list of effective communication strategies.

The scene

After seven years with Frances, a director adored by all the teachers, Little Darlings Child Care Center has just hired a new director, Carla. Right away Carla began changing the way supervision was carried out at Little Darlings. One of her changes was to hold thirty-minute staff meetings at the end of the day after the center closed. Carla also has individual conferences with each staff member to discuss how things are going. This scene is set in Carla's office where she is beginning a conference with Juanita, a well-respected teacher who has been at the center for three years.

ROLE: Teacher Juanita

You became good friends with Frances, the old director, and really miss her leadership at the center. Her style left you with definite ideas about what kind of supervision works and doesn't work.

You are bothered by some of the changes Carla is making and you've also heard other teachers griping. As a respected teacher you feel a responsibility to speak for the group and not let gossip and staff morale get out of hand. You're glad for this conference with Carla but you don't know whether to trust her. You come with a specific list of concerns that you want to bring up.

1. When Carla explains what she wants, she uses examples from the corporate world which seem elitist, if not irrelevant.
2. The new office arrangements seem to stifle interaction and group participation in problem solving. You liked it the old way.
3. The staff meetings held at the end of the day are inconvenient for many and it's hard to sit and listen to a bunch of details at that time of day.
4. You have many demands on your time and you resent the amount of training she is instituting as a requirement.
5. You have heard that Carla is tough on staff evaluations and you feel uncomfortable with that. Your reputation as a competent professional is very important to you.

ROLE: Director Carla

As far as you are concerned, the changes you are making, and particularly the end-of-the-day staff meetings, are going well. When you ask for it, staff feedback is positive. You know that Frances was a well-loved director and you feel you need to make your mark here as quickly as possible to get staff loyalties transferred to you.

Recently, you've noticed staff getting together to talk in twos or threes during their break time and the room always falls silent when you enter. Perhaps this has to do with you or maybe they are just becoming lax in their work habits and some new reminders are in order.

The staff member, Juanita, who is coming to see you today has been quite standoffish. She participates little during the staff meetings and because she is well-liked by the other teachers, you would like her to take a more active role in implementing some of the changes you have in mind for the center. You may need to convince her that these changes are for the better and remind her that you expect all staff to have a positive attitude.

Strategy: Tension in Head Start

Here is another example of a role play that helps uncover multiple issues for discussion—staff relations, communication skills and systems, pre-packaged curriculum, and developmentally appropriate practice.

The scene

Louise is in her third year as a lead teacher of Good Beginnings Head Start and Martha has been her education coordinator for the last three months. Good Beginnings is a well-established program of twelve years, serving children four and five years old who are income eligible. The finances, enrollment, and overall administration of the program are in good order and stable, even though some systems are outdated and not the most efficient to work with.

As a new teacher, it has taken Louise the first two years to learn all her job entails. Now she feels like the classroom is "hers" and she can begin to make some changes. Of particular concern to her is some tension she feels with her two aides. She is not sure what is going on and hopes she can get them to work together on some of her new ideas.

Martha, after the three months of getting to know her new job, now wants to know individual staff members better. She is holding conferences with each of them.

Role: Teacher Louise

You actually are a bit unsure about this new education coordinator, Martha. The tension you have been feeling on the staff wasn't there until she came. Are Martha and the staff talking behind your back? Often Martha is already in your room when you arrive and you are not quite sure how she is spending her time or what she is up to. She seems friendly but you haven't had much time to get to know her. You have a sense that there are things she doesn't like about how you run your classroom.

There is a wonderful curriculum model you have just discovered called Readiness 1-2-3 and you want to begin using it. The materials are somewhat pricey, but it includes a year's worth of weekly lesson plans, stencils, dittos, books, and bulletin board displays. A curriculum like this will help take the burden off you having to plan activities since your aides haven't been helping with that. You feel this will really appeal to parents and can increase their confidence that Head Start is getting their children ready for school. You want Martha to purchase this curriculum for your classroom and perhaps adopt Readiness-1-2-3 as the official curriculum of the program.

Role: Education Coordinator Martha

You are pleased that Louise has asked you to come look over some curriculum plans with her. Up until now she has been so busy that you have had trouble getting any time with her to develop a working relationship. During these first few months you have gotten to know Louise's aides better than you know her. As they have gotten more comfortable with you, they have begun to confide that they have some problems with Louise. They feel she never really plans much for the kids to do and she wants them to do things outside their job description.

Louise does strike you as somewhat cold, perhaps over-compensating for some insecurities on the job. Nonetheless, you have encouraged her aides to speak directly to Louise about their concerns.

It seems to you that the staff at Good Beginnings lacks understanding of developmentally appropriate curriculum and especially the role of play in children's learning. Louise, in particular, plans group activities for the children to do all morning: circle time, music, an art project, and even group games on the playground. You get the idea that this is a long tradition in the program and you are groping for ways to bring it into question.

One of Louise's aides, Casandra, specifically complained to you that she didn't want to be spending so much time cutting out stuff for art projects. She said that she didn't think this really promoted creativity in children. You sense Casandra may have a disposition for learning new approaches and putting some effort into changing how things are done. But she lacks formal training, and, being only an aide, it could cause some tension if you use her ideas as a model. As you hear what Louise's plans are, you hope to raise the possibility of her involving Casandra more in the thinking process of curriculum planning.

LITERATURE, BIOGRAPHIES, AND VIDEOS

In teaching an ongoing class, we sometimes use novels, biographies, and videos as assignments related to the ideas we are exploring. For staff meetings or workshops a couple of paragraphs or pages can often be extracted for the same purpose.

We've found that stories about people's lives are especially powerful in conveying ideas about cultural diversity. Books by those who share observations of nature can heighten the art of observing children. Literature speaks to people on a level different than the typical teaching handout. Using it as part of our training has the additional benefit of fostering a disposition toward reading for pleasure.

Bringing teachers together for an informal evening of discussing a video can be a form of team building for a staff, as well as learning about the lives of others. We are careful in our selection of videos because, as with books, some can reinforce the very stereotypes or images that we are trying to undo.

Discussion questions for literature or videos

• How would you summarize the message of this story?
• From what cultural, social, or economic perspective was it told?
• Were individual characters or groups of people portrayed in terms of any positive or negative images?
• How did this story reinforce or challenge any of your previously held stereotypes?
• If you were a member of a group portrayed in this story, how would you feel in viewing this?
• How is this similar or different from your own perspective?

Books on diversity
- *Growing up Black*, Jay David
- *The Education of Little Tree,* Forrest Carter
- *Joy Luck Club*, Amy Tan
- *Autobiography of Malcolm X*, Alex Haley
- *Floating World*, Cynthia Kahdota
- *Oranges Are Not the Only Fruit*, Jeannette Winterson
- *Grapes of Wrath*, John Steinbeck
- *Annie on My Mind*, Nancy Garden
- *The Bean Trees*, Barbara Kingsolver
- *Worlds of Pain*, Lillian Rubin
- *The Woman Warrior*, Maxine Hong Kingston
- *Cat's Eye*, Margaret Atwood
- *Ceremony*, Leslie Silko
- *Bastard Out of Carolina*, Dorothy Allison

Books on observing nature
- *The Moon by Whalelight*, Diane Ackerman
- *Seasons at the Point,* Jack Conner
- *Pilgrim at Tinker Creek*, Annie Dillard
- *Desert Notes, River Notes*, Barry Lopez
- *The Ghostwalker*, R. D. Lawrence
- *Celebrating the Land: Women's Nature Writings 1850–1991*, Karen Knowles

Videos reflecting diversity
- *Brother's Keeper*
- *Spirit Island*
- *Long Walk Home*
- *Driving Miss Daisy*
- *Pow Wow Highway*
- *The Wash*
- *Milagro Bean Field War*
- *Torch Song Trilogy*
- *Norma Rae*
- *Boys in the Hood*
- *Map of the Human Heart*
- *Children of a Lesser God*
- *Straight Out of Brooklyn*
- *Come See the Paradise*
- *My Left Foot*
- *Streetwise*
- *Wedding Banquet*
- *Ballad of Little Jo*
- *Desert Hearts*
- *Fried Green Tomatoes*
- *Philadelphia*

CLASSROOM VIDEO CLIPS

Though we have produced them ourselves, we are cautious in our use of commercial videotapes for training, especially the "talking head" type. Precious time allotted for in-service training should be involving of participants, allowing for interaction and practice. If they illuminate the big ideas we're considering, we occasionally use pieces of produced videos, but most videos are too long to use in their entirety.

On the other hand, directors, education coordinators, or trainers working consistently in one program can use an inexpensive camcorder to capture valuable video clips for training. When we film we seldom focus on the teacher unless specifically asked to do so. Videotapes of camera-anxious teachers are hardly useful. Most importantly, to be consistent with the philosophy we teach, the focus in an early childhood classroom should be on the children more than the teachers.

Simple video clips of children at play are powerful tools to sensitize adults to children's interests and development. They spark curiosity and delight. We use video clips for group discussion on applying particular theories or skills in a given situation. Sometimes we'll show some footage without the sound and ask teachers to supply a narration from a child's point of view, or from inside the teacher's head. Video clips are great for practicing observation skills. For this purpose we often show the same clip several times with a progressive set of questions for each viewing.

As teachers become familiar with the feedback video clips offer them, they are often eager to have a camera in their room. Sometimes we've done filming in response to a question or problem a teacher has brought to us. Time permitting, we watch the tape together, or if not, we send the tape home with a teacher accompanied by a few informally written questions to guide viewing.

On some occasions we suggest teachers mount the camera on a tripod, pointing toward the block or dress-up area to capture the activity there. Recently, we've experimented with showing the tape we've just made to the children along with the teachers. This is a fun way to immediately represent and reflect their experience and to share their immediate reactions.

Sometimes we've spontaneously captured some children in action that we feel would be valuable viewing for any teacher. In this case we leave a release form for parents to sign, giving us permission to use the tape in training settings.

SAMPLE RELEASE FORM

I hereby authorize _____ to use footage of my child's activities in child care in the production of training videotapes for early childhood educators and parents. I agree that I am to receive no compensation for my child's appearance and that this appearance or participation confers on me no ownership rights whatsoever.

Child's Name _____

Parent or Guardian _____

Address _____ Phone _____

Date _____

By plugging our camcorder into our VCR, we make a rough but adequately edited tape for easy use. To give you an idea of the possibilities, following are descriptions of two video clips we use along with questions to guide discussion.

Strategy: Action in the Art Area

While filming in a class of three year olds, we spotted some great action in the art area. One of the children was meticulously painting her hands, forearms, and all her fingers. Another was grinning from ear to ear as he exchanged paint brushes between containers of paint and watched the new color emerge in the strokes of his brushes across the paper. A third child at the easel was carefully painting dots of the same size and color around the edges of her entire paper.

Sample discussion questions
- What did you specifically see in the art area?
- What do you think each child is discovering?
- What does each child seem to understand about paint and painting?
- Does this give you any ideas about some other materials each child might enjoy investigating?

Strategy: Snowmen and Buttons

A homemade video clip of a child exploring buttons has been a favorite every time we've used it. Depending on how we shape the questions, it can help teachers discover what children learn from open-ended materials, appropriate responses to children's and coworkers' behaviors, and how to develop individual plans from close observations of children.

The short clip shows a set of teacher-made snowmen designed to teach math skills. Each snowman has a numeral on the bottom snowball, a face and hat on the top snowball, and blank space in the middle. It becomes clear that the teacher's goal is for children to place a corresponding number of buttons on the snowman's body to match the numeral.

We filmed a child who worked alone for fifteen minutes carefully choosing and comparing buttons and placing them in three straight lines down the snowman in one to one correspondence. Upon closer look we see he is using a pattern of light to dark and large to small in his meticulous arrangement of buttons. Not noticing this, the teacher joins him at the table, sweeps the buttons off of his snowman and proceeds to teach him the "right" way to use the game.

Sample discussion questions
- What did you specifically see this child doing?
- What do you think this child is exploring with these buttons?
- How would you describe what this child knows and can do?
- If you were his teacher, how might you have responded to this child?
- If this were your coworker, what might you say to this teacher in discussing how the activity went?
- Based on this observation, what individual plans might you develop for this child?

Chapter 7
Symbolic Tools

Early childhood educators provide numerous materials to children so they can represent their ideas and experience. Teachers think of this as planning for creative expression, not always aware that these acts of representation support a key aspect of cognitive growth in young children—the development of symbolic thinking.

Symbolic thinking allows the mind to move in other realms beyond the concrete here and now. Whether those realms involve the complexities of chemistry and physics or the simple aspects of reading, writing, and arithmetic, we must learn to function with some mastery in the world of symbols. All the more so if we want to pursue mythology, music, or the arts.

For these reasons, and for the just plain fun of it, symbolic tools are some of our favorite training strategies. Asking teachers to represent their thinking through objects or to use objects to provoke their thinking nearly always means a good time will be had by all. Symbolic tools stretch the mind and creative spirit and nudge along a playful disposition.

PROPS TO REPRESENT IDEAS

Constructivist learning principles call for direct encounters with phenomena.[12] To help teachers engage with phenomena that are abstract concepts, we use activities that require a concrete representation of an idea in the form of props or transformed materials. These activities are useful for diverse learning styles because they require participants to step outside the use of spoken or written language. They provide experiences for adults to think and learn as children do, through direct manipulation of concrete materials. With the opportunity to be playful in their expressions, adults also have their disposition toward valuing play reinforced.

Strategy: Picture this Environment

We have a collection of photos of a variety of different environments cut from magazines. These represent a wide array of environmental aspects, including elements of nature, soft and hard textures, nature or man-made from diverse cultures, contrasting colors, organization of space, and lighting. Though they aren't pictures of specific early childhood settings, they symbolize elements that we hope will be found in those classroom environments.

We have participants work in small groups to examine the pictures and answer the following questions. Their discussion generates a list of environmental considerations for planning spaces for children.

- How do these environments make you feel?
- How might you behave if you were in these environments?
- What about the environment do you think contributes to your responses?

Strategy: Represent Self-Esteem

In staff meetings or workshops focused on the development of children's self-concept, we provide such things as scissors, glue, magazines, old calendars, clay, corks, bottle caps, string, paper and markers. We ask small groups to think of a specific child with positive self-esteem and represent or symbolize his or her characteristics with the materials.

With materials to choose from and manipulate, most teachers become creative and playful. Their representations show remarkable understandings of the concepts underpinning the formation of a positive self-identity. We find we can readily identify teacher misunderstandings or omissions and address these in the discussion. For example, when exploring the development of children's identity, aspects of culture or family structure may have been omitted and we can refer to a symbol that might have been included to represent that.

This activity is another example of using what participants already know as the basis for exploring a topic. To this we add new information and a framework for thinking about identity formation, citing how their examples fit in.

Strategy: Represent Environmental Dimensions

softness / hardness

open / closed

simple / complex

intrusion / seclusion

high mobility / low mobility

To review the important elements of classroom environments, we've created an activity drawing on a valuable set of formulations by Elizabeth Prescott.[13] We give five small groups a written description of one of the dimensions Prescott describes (see below), along with materials such as blocks, spools, fabric, yarn, paper tubes, small boxes, and empty containers. Their task is to transform these materials into a representation of a classroom that reflects the elements described on their card.

As they work on this task, participants engage with ideas we might otherwise have delivered in a lecture or handout. As the representations are presented to the whole group, participants discover that together they have constructed a well-organized, aesthetically pleasing and inviting classroom environment. Many are eager to then duplicate this in their own rooms. During the debriefing, we can also discuss the arrangements of the representations as a whole, looking at how space is divided, possible traffic patterns, and cultural considerations. We find that teachers leave eager to read Prescott's article that puts the concrete experience they have just had into a larger theoretical framework.

Softness/Hardness:
Objects that are responsive to touch and include a variety of tactile sensory stimuli—sand, water, used coffee grounds, grass, swings, rugs, pillows, couches, finger paints, playdough, clay, and laps to sit on. Having only hard surroundings (tiled floors, wooden furniture, asphalt playgrounds) gives the message "you better shape up and do what the environment requires" and ultimately leads to tension and fatigue.

Open/Closed:
Play equipment that is open and has no one right way to be used—sand, collage materials, dress-up clothes. Closed equipment can only be manipulated one way to come out right, like a puzzle or lotto game. Legos and tinker toys are examples of equipment that is in between.

Simple/Complex:
Simple equipment has one manipulatable aspect while a complex one has two or more kinds of materials combined, usually sustaining attention for a longer period. For example, a sand pile with no equipment is simple, but when digging equipment and water are added it becomes complex; playdough is simple by itself, but with toothpicks, cookie cutters, and rolling pins, more complex play is created.

Intrusion/Seclusion:
Space arranged to accommodate group activities and social interactions versus opportunities for privacy and control over one's own territory. For example the block or dress-up areas in contrast to a cozy corner with a pillow, puppets, books, or Walkman tape player, and a small table with nature collections, prisms, a magnifying glass, water colors, clipboard, and pencil.

High Mobility/Low Mobility:
Activities that permit the use of the whole body—running, climbing, jumping, trike-riding—or ones that require children to sit still, such as puzzles and books. Playing with musical instruments, dress-ups, or blocks are in-between activities.

Strategy: Props for Teacher Roles

In our efforts to help teachers become conscious about the roles they play with children, we gather props that suggest a particular role a teacher might assume with children—firefighter and police helmets, a squirt bottle, megaphone, plume pen, magnifying glass, blueprints, director's chair, umpire's shirt, coach's hat, magic wand, camera, clown nose, and stopwatch.

We ask someone to relate an incident that occurred with the children, describing only the children's—not the adult's—behavior. After hearing the description, participants consider possible teacher responses by choosing a prop to represent what they might say or do. For instance, if the incident described is about two children fighting, someone might choose the police helmet and say, "I saw that. You know the rules. I'm putting you on time out." Or they might choose the stopwatch saying, "We have to take turns. Taiko can have the toy for five minutes and then it's Becca's turn."

We encourage discussion about the roles that empower and foster self-esteem and initiative in children. Which roles are disempowering and keep the children dependent on the teacher's judgment or power? Using props in this way results in a playful, concrete way to stimulate thinking and discussion.

Strategy: Representing the Project Approach to Curriculum

As the project approach to curriculum planning has gained wider recognition in our profession, we have used a variation of this as a training strategy with teachers in our classes and in child care programs where we train.[14] Giving them an observation oriented "research project" is a wonderful way to engage teachers in active investigation of child development, how children learn, and where certain curriculum materials or ideas might lead.

Teachers might, for example, research all the ways children in their group are exploring spatial relations and document that. They could provide an initial experience, or in the language of Reggio Emilia "a provocation," with something like a set of bones, and study what the children do with it over time—what they find interesting, invent, reveal about their thoughts and questions.

Whatever the content topic, the key component to training with a project approach is to have small groups doing practical research together over time. They formulate questions to pursue, design methods of investigation, and make representations of their discoveries. We offer guidelines to help the groups focus their efforts, but the emphasis is on their own process of inquiry and discovery, rather than a formal presentation of their findings.

We've found that in working on a "research project," most teachers can't refrain from sharing their ongoing discoveries. The actual representations they develop become a documentation of their learning process. These include collections of photos, samples of materials used, children's transformations of the materials, drawings, quotations, videotapes, audiotapes, stories, and observation notes of children, all representing what they did and what they learned.

In *our* ideal world, the project approach would be the primary pedagogy used for teacher education. However, most training programs are compartmentalized and tightly scheduled, making engaged study over time difficult to achieve. Our effort to counter this is three pronged. We use the project approach in designing classes wherever we can. In all training we foster a disposition in teachers to see themselves as continuous researchers and representers of children's experiences, so that their daily work takes on the nature of a project approach.

As teachers acknowledge how much they have learned from training designed with a project approach, we seize this opportunity to encourage them to advocate for this approach in other arenas. We encourage them to meet with or write to department chairpersons, conference organizers, and/or their program director to explain the benefits of this type of training. Sometimes we even take time for participants to role play or write such letters at the end of a training. We pass along to chairpeople and training organizers the written evaluations students complete at the end of our sessions.

Trainers can advocate for institutional changes in training approaches in other ways as well. When we are contacted to provide a training, we can inquire as to how the training they want from us fits into the larger training plan and goals of the agency. Many, in fact, aren't developing focused training plans, but using a smorgasbord model with little theoretical consistency or systematic thinking in mind. Our inquiry often leads to an important dialogue and increasingly leads to more formal consultations on how to design an overall staff development plan for an agency. You can find further discussion of this in Chapter 19.

Finally, trainers as well as directors and teachers can write articles for our AEYC affiliate newsletters and other ECE publications promoting this approach to training.

METAPHORS TO EXPLORE CONCEPTS

A playful way to help teachers explore new ways to think about their work is through the use of metaphors. Closely related to our strategies of having teachers think of new names for the roles they play with children, or finding props to represent these roles, are metaphor activities we've created for self-reflection and new insights into early childhood concepts. Often involving a kinesthetic element, these strategies are especially useful for tapping into diverse learning and communication styles.

Strategy: True Confessions in Four Corners

To get people moving and talking about their experiences and points of view, we playfully tell them it's time for true confessions. We pose a series of questions and designate four possible answers for them to choose from. Though it may not be immediately obvious, the questions are related to the topic at hand.

We frame the possible answers metaphorically to stretch the participant's thinking and draw on their own experiences to define the meaning. As we state the question, we assign a possible answer for people to choose in each of the four corners. After each participant has moved to a corner, we ask them to discuss with others why they are there.

Depending on the time available, the debriefing process for this activity can be brief or extensive. Either way the elements of an effective debriefing process discussed earlier in Chapter 3 are important here. The reframing process described in that chapter can be seen as a cycle as we help participants connect an abstract metaphor to a common experience and then to an aspect of a big idea we are exploring. After a brief or extended discussion on why people are in particular corners, we pose another question on the topic, again assigning a corner for them to move to. Here are some sample questions and their answer choices used in various staff meetings and workshops.

Topic: Curriculum Planning

If I were to describe myself as a planner I'd say I am a
• ship
• hot air balloon
• bicycle
• wagon train

When it comes to curriculum decisions, you might think I am a
• city crow
• German shepherd
• coyote
• giraffe

The tool I most need to help me plan is a
• hammer
• plumber's friend
• wrench
• chain saw

Topic: Staff Team Building

When it comes to handling conflict, I'm a/an
- fish out of water
- beaver
- moth
- ostrich

The worst days in my classroom are like
- half-time at a football game
- the national budget deficit
- boot camp
- the environmental crisis

Growing up, you could say my family's motto was
- time flies when you're having fun
- haste makes waste
- time is on my side
- never put off to tomorrow what you can do today

Topic: Director Burnout

As I set off for work each day, this song is on my mind:
- This Land is Your Land, This Land is My Land
- What's Love Got to do With It?
- Nobody Knows the Trouble I've Seen
- We Shall Overcome

For me, being at work is like being
- at the zoo
- in a mystery novel
- at a family reunion
- in the Rose Bowl locker room

When I tell people that I work in early childhood, their response makes me feel like a/an
- fish out of water
- pit bull
- ostrich
- mother duckling

In these activities, participants may choose a corner for the same or different reasons. In addition to discussing points specific to the training topic, the debriefing can highlight how we have different frames of reference for the same words. Our experiences, culture, and learning styles influence our relationship to language and images. Metaphor activities provoke laughter, self-reflection, and new understandings about our coworkers.

PLANTING THE SEED

Having provided you with multiple opportunities to become acquainted with the tools we use in harvesting effective teacher training strategies, we think you will now benefit from a deeper look at their theoretical underpinnings. Put in terms of Wasserman's formulation, play-debrief-replay, you've had a chance to play in our garden and the next sections of the book will offer further debriefing and a chance to play again with more training activities.

The progression of this book provides an opportunity to consolidate and deepen understandings, illuminate confusions and uncertainties, and draft new plans for the coming growing season. In Sections 3 and 4, we more fully explore the primary emphasis in all of our training—teacher dispositions and roles and culturally sensitive and anti-bias practices. Subsequent sections offer a fuller picture of training considerations in different settings and an overview of a college class on child centered curriculum practices. These chapters allow you to pursue the cycle of reflection and practical application as you move through your seasons of developing as a teacher trainer.

Section 3
Dispositions and Roles for Effective Teaching

CHAPTER 8: TEACHER EXPECTATIONS
CHAPTER 9: CLARIFYING CORE DISPOSITIONS
CHAPTER 10: NEW ROLES FOR TEACHERS

*O*ver several decades ECE has evolved as a recognized profession with a body of core knowledge to be mastered and applied by its practitioners. Defining this core knowledge, which includes topics such as child development, guidance, learning environments, and curriculum planning, has been a tremendous advance for our profession. It has impacted pre-service and in-service teacher training, our professional self-image and awareness, and our advocacy efforts to be viewed as more than baby-sitters.

Further refinement of our professional consensus is underway with efforts to clarify appropriate levels of education, career paths, and compensation for those who work with young children. Though there is reference to the idea of teacher dispositions, little emphasis is placed on this in professional discourse.[2] We see this as a serious omission.

For over twenty years Lilian Katz, one of the most recognized voices in early childhood teacher education, has been writing about the importance of strengthening *worthwhile dispositions* in teachers. However, most teacher training programs continue to emphasize knowledge and competency-based education with minimal attention to this critical factor in teacher success. In fact, this was an omission in our own practice for a number of years. Finally, when we analyzed what teachers consistently said and did, alongside our efforts to apply constructivist theory to adult learning, we redefined our goals for teacher training. Fostering core dispositions is now as essential to our practice as is the core knowledge base. Here's why.

Widespread enthusiasm for performance-based teacher education, and for competency-based education in general, seems to be associated with the risk of under-emphasizing the development of desirable dispositions in what [the teacher] learns. We suggest that when deciding what responses to make to teachers, it is reasonable to choose those which are likely to strengthen enduring dispositions thought to be related to effective teaching. Similarly, responses to teachers should focus on weakening those dispositions which might undermine effective teaching.

Lilian Katz, Helping Others Learn to Teach: Some Principles and Techniques for Inservice Educators [1]

Chapter 8
Teacher Expectations

Because their training is usually focused on the acquisition of knowledge and skills, teachers replicate this with children—with the expectation all will be well. When things with the children don't go according to plans, teachers often turn to tighter controls and group structures and wrestle with a sense of inadequacy. Many teachers leave the field frustrated and stressed out. They feel they are "not cut out for this work." Along with adequate compensation and working conditions, what has actually been "cut out" of our profession is an emphasis on preparing teachers for the spontaneous events of a classroom. One new teacher described her experience this way.

> My memory of the first classroom of three year olds I taught is crystal clear. I had just graduated with an ECE degree and was armed with an array of discipline methods and curriculum themes. My practicum in the lab school had reassured me that I had mastered the skills of good teaching. I was so excited to be in charge of my very own classroom.
>
> It was a discouraging year, full of disasters, as I've since heard many new teachers report. I'll never forget the day I planned a fingerpainting project with the royal blue paint. Applying what I learned in my curriculum class, I put dabs of paint directly on the table top in front of each child and then set about trying to make prints with paper from their design on the table. Most of my time was spent regulating turn taking, getting the right name on the right paper, and keeping paint off of the kids and their clothes. The children seemed more interested in pushing and rearranging the chairs for turn taking than making paint prints.
>
> By the end of the morning the room and the children were coated with blue paint and I was a frazzled, short-tempered teacher. I cleaned things up as best I could and finally got everyone fed and down for a nap. Just as I was catching my breath, my director came in and, horrified by the mess, began taking clothes off of sleeping children so they could be washed and dried by the time parents arrived. As often happened that year, I spent hours cleaning up the room after the children went home. In the end, the fingerpaint prints really didn't look good enough for a bulletin board display and I felt deflated and nervous that parents wouldn't think I was teaching their children enough. I knew I loved children, but that day, and often during that year, I began to think I didn't have what it takes to be a preschool teacher.

Teaching is a complex task requiring continual on-the-spot decision making. Without a disposition to expect this and a method to analyze classroom events, teachers often feel like failures. Some place the blame on the children or on their parents, not understanding the ongoing reflection that teaching requires.

With years of observing in early childhood classrooms, we now have a working definition of effective or *master teachers*. They have certain qualities that distinguish them from teachers who depend on curriculum activity books, follow the same theme plans year after year, or struggle daily to get the children involved in anything productive. Their knowledge and skills are not necessarily different from other teachers. Rather, it is a set of attitudes and habits of mind

It seems obvious that we cannot teach all the knowledge, skills, methods, techniques, etc., which are of potential use to teachers. This being the case, it seems advisable to teach teachers and caregivers in such a way as to strengthen their dispositions to go on learning, to be resourceful and to be inventive long after the inservice educator's work with them is over. . .while we indeed want to help teachers with specific skills and methods, it is important to do so without undermining their "self-helpful" disposition. In short, we should guard against helping a teacher acquire competencies in a way that might strengthen or engender a disposition to be dependent, uninventive and/or helpless.

Lilian Katz, Helping Others Learn to Teach: Some Principles and Techniques for Inservice Educators[3]

that enable them to respond to the classroom dynamics and multiple needs of children with the readiness of an improvisational artist. Here are our notes of one master teacher at work.

Anna reported that on her way to the center this morning she saw a fall harvest display she thought would enhance the children's understanding of the curriculum theme she had planned for this month. She made a note to take a little field trip with her class to see it.

Entering her room she surveyed both the order and aesthetics and described things as looking a bit tattered and scattered, not particularly inviting. As she set about straightening up she considered several ways to rearrange and organize things so that the children might "discover" some of the interesting materials she had for her curriculum theme.

Suddenly a group of children arrived, talking excitedly about a small bag of bones. Anna laid an African batik cloth on a table and suggested the bag of bones be spread out there for everyone to see. She went in search of a magnifying class but got drawn into exploring a handful of leaves another child arrived with.

Before the day ended, many children had been drawn to the table to explore the bones, some using the magnifying glass. There was a chart over the table listing all the guesses the children had about where the bones came from. At some point the leaves were put on the table, hiding the bones as a game for children to share with arriving parents.

By the end of the week the bone collection had expanded, as had books about both animal and human bones. Anna told the children that she learned about things she wanted to know by reading books and talking to others. She enlisted the children's help in writing a letter to a neighborhood veterinarian and the local museum, asking for their assistance in identifying the bones. The children also helped her rearrange the room so that there was more space to accommodate the growing interest in activities related to bones. She readily saw she had harvested a new curriculum theme.

As the month moved along, the children had classroom visits from a veterinarian and a parent who was a dentist. They took pictures of the bones and displayed them next to X-rays the parent had donated. One child invented white paint on black paper to represent X-rays, and soon the room was filled with child-created X-rays of all sorts of bones. They took a field trip to the museum to look at dinosaur bones and soon found themselves with a bunch of questions about how and why things die. This led to a trip to the library and a cemetery, followed by a display and ongoing discussion and activities related to Dia de los Muertos, and the celebrations of the Days of the Dead and All Souls Day in many cultures around the world.

It was not her teacher education program, but rather the book *Zen and the Art of Motorcycle Maintenance* that influenced Anna to approach her classroom in this manner. Rather than approaching her day as a predetermined plan for the children and herself, Anna's disposition toward teaching was to anticipate ways to stay in the moment with the group. Through evaluating the organization and aesthetics of the environment, she attended to the children's discovery rather than a disposition to control. Her delight in their interests allowed her to follow the children's lead.

Anna's behavior also embodies an expectation and responsiveness to the ongoing changes that work with children involves and an alertness for opportunities to introduce diversity in meaningful ways. As this description reveals, these dispositions toward the life of a classroom result in valuable, engaging activities for the children and teacher.

Chapter 9
Clarifying Core Dispositions

Watching Anna gave us some new thoughts about teacher training. Rather than conclude that some people are "born teachers," why not try to identify the habits of mind that characterize master teachers and then consistently foster those in our teacher training efforts? Isn't this the approach we hope teachers themselves will take with young children, supporting their efforts to learn through curiosity, observation, experimentation, and reflection?

Re-reading Katz's writing on teacher dispositions and reflecting on our observations of teachers like Anna, we identified seven dispositions as central to the development of effective teaching and thus to our goals in teacher training.

DISPOSITION: Delight in and be curious about children's development

Most teachers enjoy children and their learning process. This enjoyment is a primary motivation for taking on the work of teaching young children. Once on the job, however, with the pressures of trying to conduct activities, manage behaviors, and maintain order in the classroom, it's not uncommon to lose that sense of delight. Teachers soon become more focused on the goals of their curriculum plans rather than on the learning process children are engaged in. Typically, teachers jump to control misbehavior, rather than ponder the reason for a child's actions.

When considering in-service training needs, teachers often assume that more curriculum ideas or behavior management techniques will improve their practice. In our experience, training that enhances a disposition towards curiosity about children's learning and behavior has a greater impact on teacher effectiveness than a workshop on "make and takes" or guidance techniques. Curiosity also leads to more job satisfaction. Here's a teacher who is acquiring this disposition.

> Jerry created a counting game by cutting out images of snowmen. He put a numeral on each and placed the snowmen on the table with a large bowl of buttons. He watched Tianna as she discovered the game. She spent a long time fingering and looking at different buttons, and began carefully arranging them on the snowman. She made a line of buttons from the neck of the snowman to the bottom. She worked to place the buttons in each consecutive row in one-to-one correspondence with the one beside it. Tianna used various patterns in the rows. Some were matched by color and others by the size of the buttons. She covered all the white space on the snowman with buttons, but took care not to cover the face or the numeral.
>
> Initially, Jerry thought to himself, "She's not counting the buttons to match the numerals. I should show her how." But then he observed Tianna more closely. "She definitely has a plan. She seems to be making patterns, classifying, and putting buttons in a series. I wonder why she didn't put any buttons on the face or the numeral? Is she working on something about spatial relations? Wow, what she's doing is much more complex than what I had in mind."

Rather than pursue his teaching agenda, Jerry stopped to watch, question, and marvel at what Tianna was doing. Imagine the outcome if he had interrupted Tianna's investigation and learning with his goal of teaching her the "right way" to do the counting game.

Many well-intentioned teachers would do just that. Teachers are primarily trained in a deficit model—to pay attention to what children don't know, so they can practice and correct this. Jerry's disposition supports a developmental education model that allows him to see Tianna more clearly.

This disposition also influences Jerry's ability to plan for a wider range of abilities. His approach to materials shifts from, "What can I have the children make with this?" to "What might the children do with this?" He provides learning materials for the children to show him what they already know, what questions they are pursuing, and what interests they have.

A disposition of curiosity is equally as useful in response to behavior issues with children. Rather than immediately intervening when one child strikes out to keep other children out of the block area, Jerry searches for that child's perspective. "What is that child wanting here? How is he using the block area? Is there something he's trying to figure out that I can support?"

Delight and curiosity come easily when one truly watches children. From Eleanor Duckworth we learned the benefits of teachers seeing themselves as researchers. Toward that end, most of our training is now infused with strategies that get teachers involved in observing children.

There is both an art and a skill to being an observer. While we want to promote a disposition towards seeing through the interpretive eyes of an artist, we know that helping teachers acquire the skills of objective observation is the cornerstone of this process. Unless they've taken course work specifically focused on observing children, most teachers need a methodology and coaching in this area.

We train teachers to first specifically describe what they are seeing, holding at bay their desire to interpret and draw quick conclusions as to any meaning this might have. Next, we encourage them to understand this experience from the child's point of view. How might the child describe what is happening?

Strategy: Pose Questions for Observing Children

Whether in a workshop with video clips or doing on-site coaching, the following questions usually enhance observation skills and provoke teacher delight and curiosity about children's development.

• What did you specifically see?
• How would you name the essence of this experience for this child?[5]
• What does this child know how to do?
• What does this child find frustrating?
• How does this child feel about herself or himself?
• What would support this child's continued involvement in this activity?

Strategy: Children as the Focus of our Research

During on-site consultations and coaching sessions, we model the role of researcher for the teachers we work with. We narrate what we see children doing as we move about the classroom, speaking out loud the questions that are on our mind. To show our delight in children's activities, we write up anecdotal stories of our observations and post or leave them with teachers. Discussing with teachers what we are seeing, we caution them to wait and watch before intervening in children's play, their conflicts, or their efforts to master a skill. Observing children continues to be the source of much delight and rejuvenation for our own work as trainers. Inspiring teachers to share this with us enhances our jobs even more.

DISPOSITION: Value children's play

Closely related to the disposition of delight in and curiosity about children's development is one of valuing children's play. When children are independently involved in play, it often goes unnoticed by teachers who use this time for other pressing needs in their job—record-keeping, housekeeping, resource gathering and filing, or consulting with a coworker, parent, or supervisor. Yet observation of children at play is sure to bring teachers delight as well as insight.

Play is of value in and of itself, but adults easily lose track of this. As a focus for preschool programming, play has moved in and out of favor. Still, developmental theory tells us that children who are given ample time to play are usually "ready" for school. For in this play they are constructing their understandings of the world and themselves. The closer attention adults pay to children's play, the better they understand this. And with this sharper understanding, teachers are better able to articulate and advocate for appropriate programs for children.

There are a number of valuable, practical resources to enhance teacher delight and understandings about children at play. But because some teachers don't learn best through reading and many can't find the time to do so, we develop training strategies around the insights found in these books, rather than assume teachers will read them firsthand. We draw stories from them to read to teachers or develop into handouts to explore possible teacher responses. After hearing excerpts, teachers sometimes enjoy writing about a child in their care in the style of one of the books, for instance, Daniel Stern's *Diary of a Baby*. A list of books we regularly draw from is found in the Recommended Resources section.

Finally, teachers who value play recognize that the best curriculum emerges out of the themes children are investigating and expressing, rather than from a commercial activity book or file of last year's plans. When teachers can identify the kinds of play occurring in their classrooms, they deepen their understandings of child development and get better at planning for individual children.

Strategy: Recognizing the Kinds of Play

In classes and workshop settings, we structure what Jones calls a "closed means—open ends" training activity to promote a sharper interest in children's play.[8] The one that consistently gets rave reviews goes like this:

Put teachers into small groups and ask them to choose the role of either player or observer. Each group is given a set of open-ended materials and, while the observers take notes, the players are given a sequence of instructions (unknown to the observers) to be done for about five minutes each. The instructions for the players are as follows:

"Ready" children come to school with a repertoire of play skills based in scripts which represent their understanding of the world as they have so far encountered it. A developmentally appropriate school acknowledges and expands that repertoire while extending children's skills in creating representations of their experience.

Elizabeth Jones, "Playing Is My Job"[6]

Piaget's constructivism, as we have come to understand it, is a powerful rationale for the essential role of play in both cognitive and moral development. It supplements our long-standing awareness of the role of play in socioemotional development and enables us to be more articulate in our advocacy of play.

Elizabeth Jones and Gretchen Reynolds, *The Play's the Thing: Teachers' Roles in Children's Play*[7]

Round #1: Non-verbally explore the materials as if you have never seen them before. Explore with your senses and discover the attributes of the materials. Arrange, manipulate, or transform the materials in any way that helps you get to know them, but don't make anything with them.

Round #2: Explore what you can make with the materials, verbally or non-verbally.

Round #3: Use the materials as props in dramatic play you create together, assuming roles and talking with each other.

Round #4: Use the materials and play a made-up game with rules that get created as you go along.

This activity generates understandings about the different kinds of children's play and a productive discussion about adult interactions that disrupt or keep the play going.

Kinds of Play

I. Exploration
- How does this feel, sound, taste, smell, move?
- What parts and properties does this have?
- What can I make this thing do?

II. Construction
- How can I combine these different things?
- What can I build with these?
- Can I make this look like something I know?

III. Dramatic Play
- What can I make this thing be?
- How can it become a prop for my role play?
- What can these other things and people become in my play?

IV. Games
- Can I turn these things into a game to play?
- What rules are needed for this game?
- How can I change the rules to make this game more fun?

Strategy: Caution—No Adults at Play

Ultimately, it's hard to genuinely value play for children if we as adults don't have it in our own lives. Thus, at the heart of our planning for any training are the following questions:

- How can we set up playful ways for the adults to explore this topic?
- What experiences will not only deepen their understandings, but also renew their spirits and desire to play?

Teachers already valuing a play curriculum also find playful training activities useful as this enhances their ability to articulate the significance of play to parents (who are pressing for more academics in their young child's day). Play opportunities for adults are woven throughout the training activities in this book.

DISPOSITION: Expect continuous change and challenge

Someone once described going into the twenty-first century as akin to living in permanent white water. Child care teachers know this feeling well and, depending on their disposition, put their energies into damming the waters, ferociously paddling to keep up, or actively scanning for the optimal balance between challenge and safety. Helping teachers cultivate a disposition to expect continuous change and challenge enhances their responsiveness to classroom dynamics and sustains their ability to ride out the continual demands and frustrations of their job.

Consider the approach of two preschool teachers regarded as highly competent.

Gladys. In September Gladys prepared an outline of her entire year's curriculum for her classroom of four-year-olds. Her plans were rich with activities around themes that she had developed during the last five years of her teaching career; she had a large collection of resources to enrich these themes. Because she devoted so much of her time planning and provisioning for her curriculum, Gladys rarely veered from her scheduled activities. One day it snowed, a rare occurrence in Gladys' town. The children were extremely excited about the snow and could think of little else. They sneaked to the window to watch the winter wonderland and swap stories of what they had discovered to do in and with the snow. Gladys politely listened and then redirected the children back to her curriculum activities, which were around the theme of turkeys. Things didn't go as smoothly as she would have liked because the children's interest in the snowfall prevailed. In the staff room she grumbled about the loss of "valuable learning time" when so much time must be spent contending with wet clothes and concerns about cold fingers and toes.

Gladys was invested in creating an interesting curriculum so children would learn what they needed to know. Her response to the children's preoccupation with the snow came from a cultivated disposition toward "covering the curriculum." She saw the snow as an unfortunate diversion from what the children needed to be learning. After all, her weather unit wasn't scheduled until January.

Sandria. The teacher in the room next door was just as excited about the snowfall as the children were. Sandria struggled to keep her mind on the activities she had planned for the children. When the children flocked to the window, Sandria briefly joined them to enjoy the snow, but soon sighed and sent them back to their "regular" learning stations. She didn't know how to maintain classroom control when excitement got out of hand.

Because unexpected events are viewed as disruptions rather than part of the learning process, they bring stress to teachers such as Gladys and Sandria. As a result, the fertile opportunities for learning are lost to the children. Like many others whose teacher education emphasized curriculum planning with a theme to be covered, group activities, and products to be made, Gladys and Sandria were unprepared to support the spontaneous interests and actions that are part of children's learning process. What a difference if these teachers had received training that encouraged them to expect such occurrences, anticipating them both emotionally and physically in their planning for children.

The nature of early childhood involves intense change and challenge. And, in this day and age, all of our lives are fast-paced and stressful. This is the context for the daily work of teachers, requiring them to make continuous on-the-spot decisions and judgment calls. Teachers are more effective when they expect constant changes and challenges and make them central to their work with children. After all, children's immediate lives and experiences are the most meaningful context for their learning, a concept central to the practice of developmentally appropriate curriculum.

For example, in the spring of 1992 teachers in Los Angeles were faced with a "rebellion curriculum" as a result of events in their city.[9] Later that year, after Hurricane Andrew struck, teachers in Florida found themselves with an unprecedented weather curriculum. During the summer of 1993 when the Mississippi River repeatedly flooded, teachers in the Midwest faced the same curriculum. In the winter of 1994 the whole country watched earth shake in Southern California.

These unplanned curriculum events may be ones of monumental disaster, or something in the daily context of a child's life that has captured their attention and imagination—a new baby in the family, a parent's loss of employment, a brother beat up in a drug deal, the family glued to TV coverage of a sports event, death from AIDS, the latest war, or election results. Teachers can't plan for many of the happenings that impact children's lives, but they can cultivate a disposition to respond to them, shifting the focus of what is considered as curriculum in the life of the classroom. We feel that ignoring this is both irresponsible and ineffective in providing for the real understandings and skills children need to be secure and successful in the world.

Early childhood teachers are familiar with the concept of "a teachable moment" and many are moving towards a practice of following "emergent curriculum." Concurrently, there is now an enthusiastic voice in our profession for the model of Reggio Emilia and the project approach to curriculum planning.[10] These approaches to curriculum require teachers who are observant, responsive, and able to follow the children's lead. We favor teacher training that promotes this flexible approach to programming for young children, and fosters a teacher disposition that abets change and challenge, not deters it.

A cornerstone in this disposition is divergent thinking—there's no one right answer. We've encountered teachers in search of correct formulas and curriculum recipes who often respond as if this disposition were an organ transplant—they involuntarily want to reject it. But with practice, and the steady experience of breathing in and out, the habit of welcoming challenge and change can find a home in most teachers. Creating training strategies that encourage teachers to expect uncertainties and respond creatively is an important contribution we can make toward cultivating this disposition. Some of these can be playful activities aimed at releasing inventive intuition. Others are designed with the goal of enhancing a more serious, yet spontaneous response.

Strategy: Together Make a Sentence

Ask two pairs of teachers to work with you at the front of the room. Have one pair enter from the left side and the other from the right, conducting a conversation with the following guidelines:

Each pair is to speak with one voice on a given topic. When they meet the opposite pair coming toward them, they should greet each other and carry on a conversation, but within a pair each person is limited to saying one word at a time. The pair has to develop sentences one word at a time, alternating back and forth, spontaneously building the conversation with the other pair. When a sentence or thought appears to be complete, the other pair begins to respond in the same fashion.

Note: Assign the topic for discussion only after you have explained the guidelines. The object is to learn to improvise, not plan ahead. Topics might be child care related or not. For example, ask one pair to be a teacher and the other a parent to talk about toilet training, their child's creativity, or the teachers' need for worthy wages.

Strategy: Professional Preschool Teacher

Lilian Katz's chapter "The Professional Preschool Teacher" in *More Talks With Teachers* (Eric, 1984) can become the basis of a training strategy that helps teachers think divergently and analyze the possible outcomes of their responses and approaches with children. First, present a typical scenario such as the one Katz describes:

> Imagine a teacher of a group of twenty four year olds whose outdoor equipment includes only two tricycles. In a group of American four year olds in such a situation, squabbles will inevitably arise concerning whose turn it is to use one of the tricycles.
>
> Specifically imagine that a child named Robin goes to the teacher and protests, saying, "Leslie won't let me have a turn!"[11]

As Katz states, "There are probably scores of 'right' as well as 'wrong' ways to respond in this situation."[12] To help teachers explore all the possible outcomes of their interventions, ask them to first brainstorm a list of the different responses that might be made in this situation, listing these down the left side of chart paper. Then, in a second and third column, have the teachers generate a list of the possible dispositions and the possible behavior outcomes that might result from each response.

Teacher Responses	*Possible Disposition*	*Possible Behavior*
• Okay, Leslie, it's Robin's turn now.	• always a victim needing rescuing	• whining or tattling • always coming to a teacher
• Let's go talk to her.	• I can get help when I need it	

A variation on this is to ask teachers in small groups to brainstorm all the possible learning available for children in this scenario. We then compare their list with the following possible learning outcomes Katz identifies.

Social Skills
• Turn taking
• Negotiating
• Coping

Verbal Skills
• Assertive phrases
• Conversational phases

Social Knowledge
• Social perspective
• Rudiments of justice

Dispositional Learning
• Empathetic and altruistic dispositions
• Experimental disposition
• Understandings about complaining and tattling[13]

In conclusion, ask each group to choose one of these categories of learning to consider in more depth. Which response would most likely foster the learning outcome they desire? This Katz chapter serves as a useful follow-up handout to reinforce the activity and participants' own thinking.

Strategy: Be Honest with Yourself

Another valuable resource from which to build training strategies for teacher dispositions is the out-of-print book by Doreen Croft titled *Be Honest With Yourself: A Self-Evaluation Handbook for Early Childhood Education Teachers* (Wadsworth Publishing, 1976). Each page presents typical early childhood education scenarios with a list of "probable reactions" for teachers to choose from and elaborate upon. They are then asked to consider the feelings each person in the situation might have.

We have used a format of this sort in training on a variety of topics. It not only promotes a disposition towards self-reflection, but also divergent thinking. Scenarios for strategies like these come from real situations we've encountered and are written up in a short and simple format. After each teacher considers their response, we have an open discussion or debriefing along the lines suggested under the Professional Preschool Teacher strategy above. Here's an example.

Scenario: A Father's Concern
When Jacob's dad came to take him home, he saw his son in the dress-up corner wearing girls' clothing, complete with wig and jewelry. He was clearly upset with you, the teacher, for allowing this to happen. He took his son aside and talked to him in a threatening tone.

Check what your first response might be.
____I would confess to the father that I too was feeling uncomfortable with the situation.
____I would leave them alone and pretend I didn't hear anything that went on.
____I would explain to the father that we allowed this kind of play because it didn't hurt anything.
____I would let the father know that we encouraged the children to try out all kinds of roles.
____I would reassure the father that this didn't necessarily mean that his child would grow up to be homosexual.
____I would ask the father to consider that his son might be gay and that it's important not to harm his self-esteem.

Effective teachers have an understanding of the core knowledge of ECE and a repertoire of skills to put this knowledge into practice. In our view, it is equally important for them to be predisposed to welcome challenge and embrace divergent thinking. This leads us to conclude that developing oneself as an improvisational artist is the height of professional development for a teacher. It is what Mary Catherine Bateson calls "life as improvisational art." Her description aptly describes the disposition and skills we think master teachers bring to their work with children and parents.

DISPOSITION: Be willing to take risks and make mistakes

As one comes to expect continual change and challenge, a willingness to take risks and make mistakes naturally follows. We build risk taking into our training by involving teachers in playful activities and engaging them in things they might not ordinarily do. By continually expecting and requesting that teachers look to their own ideas and experiences, we reinforce the value and acceptance we place on them as individuals. Our confidence and trust in them models how we hope they will view themselves, as well as the children in their care. A feeling of confidence and acceptance enables teachers to take risks and make mistakes. Examples of how we encourage this are woven throughout the chapters of this book.

Our goal is to create a climate that fosters metacognition, giving attention to what teachers are discovering about their learning process. Piaget reminds us of the disequilibrium that occurs as a child attempts to integrate new concepts. We've seen this in adults as well. Understanding that risk taking is central to most new learning, we observe carefully to support our adult learners through the discomfort and disequilibrium that usually comes when trying to integrate new ideas and experiences.

Role-play activities usually require people to take risks, which is why people often feel awkward and play the scene in an overly silly or simplistic fashion. We use role plays with caution because we believe they only enhance learning when people are willing to take risks, and we want risk taking to be a positive experience.

The simulated experience of walking in the shoes of someone else requires taking a risk. You must initially suspend your own experience and try to advocate for another. You may undergo disequilibrium as you do this, or when you return to your own shoes and try to incorporate a new experience into your thinking.

As trainers we acknowledge another risk inherent in using role plays. It is dangerous to think that by pretending to be someone else for a short period you can really know this person's experience. We always state this at the beginning of any role-play activity. We also ask teachers to consider where the greatest learning might occur for them—in advocating for an experience very different from their own, or in practicing speaking out about their own experience. Making a conscious choice about this will put the risk-taker fully in charge of their learning.

Strategy: Passion Plays

Role plays centered around topics that engage people's passions are effective when you design them thoughtfully and explain them carefully. You must also remind participants that no acting awards will be given. We prefer to use role plays that don't ask teachers to pretend they are children, but rather to relate to a

For many years I have been interested in the arts of improvisation which involve recombining partly familiar materials in new ways, often in ways especially sensitive to context, interaction and response...improvisation can be either a last resort or an established way of evoking creativity.

Mary Catherine Bateson, *Composing a Life* [14]

In teaching, all we have at a given moment, in a given situation, is our own best judgment. Throughout our lives, we study and reflect in order to refine that judgment; we talk with colleagues, examine our own efforts—all in order to improve our judgment. In the last analysis, our best judgment is all there is. It is important to strive for a balance between having sufficient skepticism to go on learning and sufficient conviction to go on acting— for to teach is to act, and effective teaching requires action with optimum confidence in the rightness of what we are doing.

Lillian Katz, "On Teaching" [15]

role from their own adult experience. In turn, we always develop parts for role plays based on people we've seen in action. That keeps us all grappling with the real issues that require risk taking.

The following is an example of how we develop scenes and parts for role plays of this nature. Ask for volunteers to play the different parts and sit in a circle in the middle of the group, fishbowl style. Read or give a copy of the scenario, along with the different roles to each volunteer and allow a few minutes for them to develop their role before beginning.

Scenario

The staff at Little Peoples' Child Care Center have been meeting to discuss ways to improve their salary and working conditions. Along with the director they have developed plans to create a staff room and ensure adequate break time and paid release time for planning and in-service training.

The budget is currently stretched to its limit and without more revenue, there won't be funds for these plans, let alone significant raises in salaries. Even though parents are already paying high fees, there is a general agreement among the teachers and director that parents will need to pay more or get involved in raising the necessary revenue. They decided to call a parent meeting to explain what the full cost of child care really means.

LaSandra, a teacher, has agreed to lead the meeting. About twenty parents attended, along with the staff and director.

ROLE 1: LaSandra, the leader

At this meeting you expect some hot emotions and flare-ups. You are determined that the parents hear that professional teachers need a staff room, paid training and planning time, as well as adequate salaries and benefits. Your goal is for them to become activists for worthy wages at your center and in the community at large.

You start the meeting by explaining that there is a crisis at the center, as with many programs in the city. You remind them how many staff members have left the center because they are no longer able or willing to subsidize the true cost of care by accepting substandard wages.

Your tone is one of soliciting their help and cooperating in solving this problem. You repeatedly acknowledge that they too have stress and financial limitations in their family, but you emphasize that caregivers are earning even less than they are and if they leave it will have a negative impact on the children.

You are pleased the director has been supportive of efforts to improve salaries, even to the point of raising parent fees. You want to make sure parents know the director is behind the worthy wage campaign.

You call on different people at the meeting, insisting that everyone's voice be heard and that respect and order be maintained. You watch the time so that you can bring the meeting to a close with some clear steps outlined.

ROLE 2: Dorothy, dare-not-speak director

You come to this meeting as both a parent and staff advocate. You are nervous that there will be conflict and especially concerned that staff might quit or parents withdraw their children. Both of these possibilities would make your job even more stressful.

You've decided to let LaSandra take the leadership for the meeting and to just sit quietly in the background. When anyone asks your opinion or makes a reference to you, just smile and defer to LaSandra or the other staff.

ROLE 3: Helpful Hannah, parent

You love your child's teacher and think it's awful that she is paid so little. You want to do whatever you can to help solve this problem. As a single mother with two kids, your time and money are both limited. You acknowledge you would love to work in child care, but could never afford to do so. During the meeting you continually support the staff and keep suggesting that the group do problem solving rather than complaining or fighting.

ROLE 4: Irene, an irate parent

You have come to this meeting really angry because you've heard there is going to be a dramatic fee increase for parents. You are stretched to your limit and you are going to let them know that in no uncertain terms.

During the meeting you support all parent efforts to stop the fee increase while getting increasingly hostile towards the director and staff.

ROLE 5: Squeak-on-by-Sam, parent

As a parent who is a college student, you haven't had much time to get involved in your child's center. Your wife mentioned that she thinks parent fees are about to be raised and you decided to attend the meeting to find out why. You have a tight budget and aren't sure what you'll do if more money is needed for child care.

When you hear the salary figures you are shocked and express your belief that the staff is worth much more than that. You want to support them, but you really don't see how you could pay a higher fee. You just hope that fees will stay the same for one more year until your child goes on to kindergarten.

Your posture in the meeting is to express concern and sympathy, but to try and stall any proposal to increase fees. You want to hear the director's opinions on these matters and repeatedly ask her to express them.

ROLE 6: Sukio, parent and strong staff supporter

You understand how critical staff training and stability is to the quality of care your child will receive. You've come to this meeting with many ideas about how parents can become involved in the worthy wage issue. You are convinced that if parents lobbied their legislators and employers, wrote letters to the editor, along with ones to big corporations and foundations, this problem would be turned around.

In the meeting you look for every opportunity to suggest these ideas. You encourage every little indication you see of parents or staff willing to become an activist in behalf of child care workers.

Strategy: Think of a Time

We encourage teachers to draw on their own memory bank of positive experiences with risk taking and mistakes. You can simply ask: Think about a time you took a risk with a positive result. How would you name that risk? What happened? What did you learn?

DISPOSITION: Provide time for regular reflection and self-examination

The old adage that people learn from experience is only half of the story. People learn from *reflecting* on their experience, analyzing events, dynamics, conclusions; and from comparing the "official word" or theory with their own intuition and experience. Reflection may confirm or contradict previous understandings. Either way, it deepens insights and the disposition towards seeing oneself as a lifelong learner.

Teachers not predisposed to self-reflection and evaluation tend to attribute all classroom difficulties to someone else: it's the children who are too immature,

For those who have been trained to believe in teaching as "direct instruction" only, the idea of teaching as reflection-on-action may be hard to swallow; yet, it is a significant aspect of a teacher's professional functioning. It is the level at which experts operate in all professions.

Selma Wasserman, *Serious Players in the Primary Classroom* [16]

disrespectful, or out of control; the director or parents present unfair demands; the room is too small; there's nothing to do on the playground and on and on. Some of these things may be true, but again, that's only half of the story. We want teachers to continually examine their own behaviors with children, to consider learning objectives for themselves in meeting classroom challenges.

Adults bring a great deal of our own childhood experience to teaching and parenting situations. We (sometimes unknowingly) repeat how our family dealt with an issue such as mealtime or bedtime, illness, orderliness, or conflict. Or, disdainful of how something was handled in our childhoods, adults may consciously try to respond differently. As trainers we continually use strategies that help adults gain perspective on how their own childhood experiences impact their teaching practice.

Adult-child interactions are laced with issues of power. When we feel we have no power or our power is being challenged, it's normal to respond with raw feelings and ingrained patterns. Without self-awareness and a framework for thinking about the power dynamics in interactions and unfolding events, teachers find it difficult to formulate thoughtful responses. Some use their power over others inappropriately, while others fail to claim and act on their own power.

Our adult lives continue to be full of power struggles and experiences of powerlessness. Rather than see themselves as victims of the program's limitations or the behaviors of the children, parents, or supervisor, teachers do well to identify their own source and use of power in situations they face. We find it enormously helpful to involve teachers in activities and discussions that reveal unexamined values, family of origin patterns, and cultural contexts that influence their responses to the daily events and people they encounter. This is obviously pertinent when it comes to approaches towards discipline, but we weave these self-reflective opportunities into all training topics.

Strategy: Reflective Writing

Reflective writing or guided visualizations are easy strategies to use. Write about the degree of orderliness or mess in your childhood environment. How did you know what was acceptable and what was not? How do you think this influences your organization of your classroom and your threshold for mess? What pushes you over the edge?

Strategy: Bedtime Memory

Close your eyes and think about bedtime in your family. Who was there? What was it like? Is there anything about this experience that influences your rules or demeanor around naptime with children in your classroom?

Strategy: Examine Attitudes Toward Mistakes

Remember a time in your childhood when you witnessed an adult grappling with the consequences of making a mistake. What did they do or say? How were people who made mistakes viewed? When you make a mistake now as an adult, is your attitude the same or different? How do you feel when children make mistakes such as spilling their milk, running in the classroom, or grabbing a toy from another child?

Strategy: Define Personal Space

This training strategy is useful to help teachers who are timid about asserting themselves, for instance, when they are being run over by children or other adults. We learned it from our colleague, Wendy Harris, who has studied martial arts.

Ask people to form two lines, each line facing the other, with people in each line standing at least an arm's length from those on either side. The two lines should be about 10 feet apart, with each person facing a partner. All those in one line should close their eyes. Those in the other line should walk slowly toward their partner. When those with their eyes closed sense that their partner has moved too close, tell them to call out, "Stop." Allow time for discussion and then have the partners switch roles.

DISPOSITION: Seek collaboration and peer support

Though working with children can be extremely delightful, it can also be isolating for an adult to spend the bulk of their time in the company of young children. It's common for those who do this to lose a broader perspective on their work. When we conduct trainings that bring teachers together from a variety of settings, we see how hungry they are to talk to others who understand what their daily work is like. They could easily spend the bulk of their time just swapping stories, frustrations, and teaching experiences. We build in time for some of this in our agenda planning and encourage them to talk together beyond the training session.

Regular discussion with peers helps teachers sustain their self-reflection process and learn the value of different approaches. These conversations can involve getting feedback on ideas, sharing teaching strategies, and gaining support. We have found that teachers who consistently engage in such peer discussions are more likely to evaluate their work, try out new ideas, and gain more skills.

Most of the training strategies throughout this book involve small group and partner activities. Beyond workshop and class settings, we are continually alert for opportunities to pair teachers together to brainstorm curriculum ideas, discuss children's play, observe in each other's programs, and even develop meeting agendas and workshops together. Here are three of our most successful strategies toward that end.

Strategy: Mentor Teachers

In several areas of the country early childhood teachers are becoming involved in mentor teacher programs.[17] Where they are formally organized, mentor teacher programs identify and recruit master teachers who receive training in adult education. Upon completion of this training, they are matched with beginning teachers for peer training, feedback, and support.

Although our state has yet to adopt a formal mentor teacher program, we have been informally supporting it through our local early childhood state initiatives, AEYC affiliates, and Worthy Wage Campaign. As we identify master teachers, we recruit them into our training of trainers classes and take other teachers to visit their classrooms. We find this to be a powerful tool for helping new teachers develop desirable dispositions, knowledge, and skills. Master teachers benefit by becoming more reflective and renewed in their own work. This becomes a next step in their career path while still allowing them to stay in the classroom with children. We encourage teachers to lobby for recognition of their mentoring expertise through increased compensation and we actively support them in this effort.

Strategy: Two Heads are Better Than One

To give teachers experiences with the value of collaboration, we use a variety of strategies that involve teachers doing a project together, sharing ideas, or interviewing each other. When we move among programs to coach teachers in their classrooms, we make note of the special strengths, skills, and interests that a teacher might have. This becomes an informal resource bank we use to refer teachers to each other for observation and consultation.

During classes and workshops, we use activities that ask teachers to interview one another on topics related to their jobs. Examples of these collaborative approaches are found throughout this book. Following are some of the interview questions that usually result in valuable teacher exchanges.

- How and why did you become involved in working with children?
- What are your strengths and the areas you feel really good about in your work with children?
- What do you find most difficult or challenging in your work with children?
- How do you go about explaining the value of play for young children to their parents?

We also offer scenarios such as this one, for collaborative problem solving.

Edna had been struggling with her group time lately. She worked with ten two- and three-year-olds and was frustrated because she couldn't get them to listen during group time. Her program supervisor gave her critical feedback about the tone of voice she was using with the children during this time. The feedback was that her way of interacting sounded negative and blaming. Edna came to you for advice about what she could do about this situation.

Strategy: Pay a Visit

It may sound obvious, but having teachers visit other programs where there is a teacher skilled in an area of concern is almost always helpful. Sometimes just getting out of the building to talk with another adult during work hours makes a difference in a teacher's attitude or behavior.

When arranging such visits, we typically talk with both teachers involved and often accompany the visiting teacher. In advance we talk about what the focus of the observation will be, often drafting an informal checklist related to the topic. For instance, if the teacher expresses an interest in learning more about fostering self-esteem, our observation checklist might be as simple as the following.

Make a note whenever you see:
• Images of the children and/or people like them posted at their eye level.
• The children's names frequently used in a positive tone.
• A child being valued, appreciated, or encouraged by the teacher.
• The teacher encouraging independence and/or child self-direction.
• The teacher referring one child to another for assistance or problem solving.

If the teacher is fairly skilled at using checklists or written observations, or if this is a skill they are trying to develop, we may use a more formal form developed for the topic. Appendix A has examples of actual forms we've developed for this purpose, but there are many other professional resources such as the NAEYC Accreditation Classroom Observation Forms and CDA Competency checklists.

When helping to arrange a visit, we alert the teacher being observed of the concern or focus of the visiting teacher. We encourage her to do more self-talk during the observation so that the visiting teacher can hear more of her thinking, even if she can't take time away from the children to meet with her visitor. If we accompany the visiting teacher, we, too, often narrate what we see happening related to the focus. Sometimes we offer to step in for the teacher so that she can take ten or fifteen minutes to talk with the visitor. This is of enormous help to the collaboration process and has the benefit to us of a few more moments of direct contact with the children.

DISPOSITION: Be a watchdog and whistle-blower

Classroom teachers are under tremendous pressure to meet other people's needs. It is not only children who present them with numerous demands, but parents, supervisors, and forthcoming school expectations. Without a solid footing in developmental theory and appropriate practices, teachers slip into accepting a push-down academic curriculum. They get caught in the trap of trying to be all things to all people. Our training nurtures a disposition to stay alert to these tendencies, analyzing what this pressure represents and ways to counter it with redefinitions of school readiness that reflect our understandings and convictions.

Because a singular cultural perspective has shaped our profession's approach to early childhood education, teachers also are prone to confuse culturally biased practices with definitions of developmentally appropriate practices. To be truly multicultural in their efforts, teachers need to be continually watchful for inclusiveness—in attitudes towards different child-rearing practices and parent communications; in setting up environments and curriculum activities that represent diversity and allow for divergent learning styles; and in responding to teachable moments with a disposition towards activism to counter bias and unfair practices.

As we encourage alertness and activism on behalf of appropriate and inclusive practices for children and their families, we also foster a disposition in teachers to become advocates for themselves as well. Current economic priorities and conditions, along with societal attitudes, create difficult circumstances for those who choose early childhood education as a profession. In many cases teachers have internalized attitudes about "women's work" and have become self-sacrificing and passive when expected to work with less than adequate ratios, materials, wages, benefits, and working conditions. We want teachers to encourage children to stand up for themselves and each other, and likewise, we embolden them to become advocates for their own needs and for our profession as a whole.

At the heart of our training strategies are activities that model as well as advocate for inclusiveness. We start with the premise that people can't accept others or advocate for them unless they know how to do this for themselves. Providing teachers with positive experiences of having their own identity affirmed creates a climate where an interest in diversity grows.

Strategy: Examine Group Identities

Choose three categories of people to examine. We usually include a common reference group such as "football players"; a group most workshop participants would identify with, like "child care workers"; and a cultural group about which they may have some harmful bias, such as a particular ethnic group, "gay men or lesbians," or "people with disabilities." Write each category on its own sheet of newsprint. Ask the group to brainstorm a list of both positive and negative associations held for each group. Discuss each list, beginning with the common identity group of the participants, i.e., child care workers, asking, "In what way is this list true or untrue about you?"

Child Care Workers

Positive associations	*Negative associations*
• loving	• unskilled
• dedicated	• sloppy dressers
• get kids ready for school	• baby-sitters

This activity usually exposes the ease with which we all stereotype, and the complex web of individual and cultural identities that must be considered. Beginning with misconceptions of one's own identity group builds bridges of understanding to double-check our assumptions about others. We conclude with the question, "What would be the best way for someone to learn about you and your identity group?"

Some teachers have difficulty with this activity as they struggle with their own biases and assumptions. We are sensitive to the unsettling nature of the activity and respond carefully and supportively. The discussion can help teachers develop a framework to guide them in their efforts to learn about children, families, and coworkers in their program rather then unintentionally react to biases that emerge.

Brazilian educator Paulo Freire reminds us that empowerment happens when people learn to read the world as well as read the word.[18] Reading the world means exploring the complexities and analyzing the culture of power and its structures and dynamics, which usually requires reading between the lines. This is a critical part of school readiness that most teachers themselves missed out on.

Whatever the topic, we want to illuminate any built-in bias, asking whose perspectives are represented and whose interests are served by a particular view. Along with stereotypes, omission and invisibility are primary forms of bias we want teachers alerted to. As they move through the world, we hope their disposition will lead them to ask, "What's wrong with this picture?"

Until teachers ask this question in their own behalf, recognizing the discrepancy between the skills and responsibilities of their work and their level of compensation, their inclination is to remain passive, waiting for things to somehow get better. History, of course, tells us that real change only happens when people act in their own behalf and form alliances to get to the root of the problem. Marcy Whitebook, former executive director of the Child Care Employee Project, boldly asserts that learning to be an advocate is an important part of the core knowledge of early childhood education. Toward that end we employ training strategies to foster needed watchdog and whistle-blowing dispositions and skills.

Strategy: TV Game Show

To practice advocating for appropriate school readiness, as opposed to a push-down academic program, we use a TV game show activity. Dividing teachers into small groups, we ask each to devise a sound to signal they have an answer. After learning to recognize every group's signal, the game begins. We read a question for each group to discuss. When they feel they have found the best response, they sound their signal and share it with the group. Following are some sample parent questions about school readiness.

1. Will my child learn the basic math skills he needs in this class?
2. Danita is really smart and knows all the letters of the alphabet. I bought her one of those spelling workbooks but she doesn't seem to get it. If she brought it to preschool, can you help her with it?
3. Every time Sandra writes her name she gets the 'S' backwards. Will you make her do it right?
4. We want to get Ming Gong a Christmas present that will help him learn more English. Do you think those alphabet cards would be good?
5. Can you test my child to see if she's ready for kindergarten? And give her some homework assignments so we can work on the areas where she's behind.

With the development of other types of questions, this same strategy can be used to practice advocating for worthy wages. Following are some sample questions for this topic.

1. As a teacher, I really don't want to rock the boat with all this talk of worthy wages. Don't you feel your commitment is to the children?
2. As a parent, I just can't afford to pay more for child care. What do you expect me to do?
3. Don't you think it's unprofessional and self-serving to be lobbying for higher wages?
4. Won't closing programs for Worthy Wage Day just inconvenience and antagonize parents?
5. Please tell our television audience, just what is it that you people want?

Strategy: Conduct Interviews

Interview activities are other strategies we use to predispose teachers to see themselves as advocates. Two examples follow, one aimed at advocating for diversity, the other for the work of early childhood professionals.

Interview someone from a different culture. Providing a set of questions, ask each staff member to interview someone representing a cultural group with which they have little direct experience. Staff may need some help locating people to interview, so it's useful to develop a resource list of willing interviewees. Prior to the interview, we have teachers make a list of personal assumptions and positive and negative associations held about that group. Interview questions might include the following.

• How do you define yourself culturally?
• Growing up as a child, were you aware of any cultural differences between your family and others with whom you had contact or saw on TV?
• What attitudes about "difference" did your family convey to you?
• Describe expectations your family/culture has of children, of teachers, their community, the government?
• What do you consider to be oppressive in your own culture? Are there attitudes about your culture you would like to change?

If interviews are done with people with the same cultural identity, these can be discussed by the staff together. Teachers can share what they learned about themselves as well as others from doing this activity. A variation on this strategy is to have staff members interview each other or members of their own families.

Interview someone outside the early childhood field. Ask teachers to informally interview ten people who don't know much about ECE to find out what they think a child care worker does. Common responses teachers have shared include:

• Oh, you get to play with kids all day.
• You make sure they don't run out in the street and have accidents and such.
• You have to feed them and toilet them and make sure they stay out of trouble.
• You keep them busy all day so they don't miss their moms.
• Do you baby-sit at night, too, when their parents go out?

Reactions to these responses can be explored together. In the face of general public lack of awareness and undervaluing of child care work, most providers struggle with a sense of themselves as professionals. When they contrast what they actually do with what people think their job is, teachers move from shrugged shoulders and lowered eyes to pride and indignation. This will often propel them into becoming active advocates for the early childhood profession.

Chapter 10
New Roles for Teachers

Most people enter the teaching field with ideas about the role they can play in children's learning. They want to pass along knowledge, shape little minds, do fun crafts, and get children ready for school and future jobs. Our country's approach to education sets the stage for how teachers conceive their roles and how they are educated to carry them out. The acknowledged logic of the banking method of education is to give students all they need to know to be successful in the world. The unacknowledged goal is to maintain the status quo, keep industry moving in the direction it's headed, and ensure that institutions and power structures are held in place. Whether or not they recognize or agree with it, teachers are assigned the roles of sheepherder and gatekeeper.

Given what we know is best for children and for the world, these roles make no sense, pedagogically or futuristically. Predictions abound that during the next century, half of the information required by the average worker to perform a job will become obsolete about every four or five years. In some industries, the figure is already less than a year.[21] Furthermore, all the learning theory research and our profession's thrust toward developmentally appropriate practice suggest very different roles for teachers of young children. Why, then, do teachers continue in obsolete and erroneous behaviors?

The primary educational experience and teacher role model most of us have encountered is that of the teacher as orator, standard bearer, and judge. This leaves the student cast in the role of passive receiver, compliant believer, and perhaps creative conformer. In one form or another, this is the stage and prototype roles teacher education programs strive to replicate. Here and there one finds alternative approaches and innovative thrusts towards "school reform" but, by and large, these still serve the same ends. Any significant deviation is usually branded as liberal experimentation, irrelevant, or without significant accountability. There is a tremendous fear of student misbehavior and challenge, if not failure from untested practice.

While some early childhood programs are based on the banking model, direct instruction, or behaviorist theory, our profession's definition of developmentally appropriate practice is based on developmental theory and child initiated activities for learning. However, even those defining their practice along these lines feel the need to respond to pressures for academic instruction that will get children ready for school. They subsequently slip into roles that subtly, if not directly, undermine children's discovery process. In the name of teaching, these teacher roles continually interrupt learning.

Piaget and constructivist theory tells us that young children learn most things by playing with objects and people. In play children build their understandings of the world and develop their bodies, minds, imagination, language, and social skills. The teacher's role, then, is to set the stage for play and to observe for interests, skills, and emerging understandings. These observations

The skillful teacher of young children is one who makes play possible and helps children keep getting better at it. Many people working with young children, however, have quite a different view of what teachers do: teachers teach. They sit children in circles, lead finger plays, and talk about the calendar. They tell the children the rules for using the slide and for avoiding collisions with the tricycles. When we watch children playing "school," they play stern teachers who give information, enforce discipline, and issue directives. In the school game as played by both children and teachers, there appears to be a consensus that when teachers talk, children learn.

Elizabeth Jones and Gretchen Reynolds, *The Play's the Thing: Teachers' Roles in Children's Play*[19]

The landscape through which we move is in constant flux. Children cannot even know the names of the jobs and careers that will be open to them; they must build their fantasies around temporary surrogates.

Mary Catherine Bateson, *Composing a Life*[20]

Young children learn the most important things not by being told but by constructing knowledge for themselves in interaction with the physical world and with other children—and the way they do this is by playing.

Elizabeth Jones and Gretchen Reynolds, *The Play's the Thing: Teachers' Roles in Children's Play* [22]

Our schools start off with a reconnaissance flight over all the human, environmental, technical, and cultural resources. Then more reconnaissance missions will be made to get a full overview of the situation. Also teachers do reconnaissance trips through workshops, seminars, and meetings with experts in various fields. What educators acquire by discussing, proposing, and launching new ideas is not only a set of professional tools, but also a work ethic that gives more value to being part of a group and to having interpersonal solidarity, while at the same time strengthening intellectual autonomy.

Loris Malaguzzi, *The Hundred Languages of Children* [24]

guide teacher interactions and future curriculum provisions. Suggesting that teachers abandon their sheepherding and gatekeeping roles is like asking them to give up their identity. Even if they are unconsciously playing the part, teachers can't forsake their roles of banker, scorekeeper, or transfer station guard until we have helped them define new roles for themselves.

We began asking ourselves to specifically define what roles master teachers play when they adopt a constructivist approach to helping children learn and be truly ready for school. Our ideas came from years of watching teachers in action, reading professional literature, and talking with Betty Jones and other close colleagues. With exposure to cultural orientations different from our own, we've also been influenced to think more in terms of relationships and metaphors.

As Jones shared her gathering thoughts while writing *The Play's the Thing*, we began developing training strategies to convey these ideas to teachers. Playing with the descriptions Jones and Reynolds use—the teacher as stage manager, assessor, communicator, and scribe—launched us into a multitude of possible metaphors that could help teachers redefine their roles with children. [23]

When teachers consistently provide opportunities for children to construct their knowledge, they are wearing different hats at different times. We challenged ourselves to think of roles in terms of hats. For instance, if two children are squabbling over a toy and the teacher always wears the hat of a firefighter, swooping in to rescue and put out the flames of conflict, what other hat would foster self-help and self-esteem? If he consciously donned the hat of a mediator or interpreter, wouldn't his behaviors better assist children to become their own problem solvers?

The practice of reformulating teachers roles with children is now a centerpiece in our training. We've found that teachers not only have fun with these, but are motivated to learn the behaviors when we characterize them as belonging to master teachers. We have specific training strategies to convey this idea and weave it into many of our strategies on other topics as well. For example, in conducting a three-part workshop for Head Start teachers on writing individual plans for children, we outlined their roles as follows: an archaeologist, sifting through the evidence of children's interests and developmental stage; a forecaster, predicting what children might do with certain materials and having a supply of additional props that might be needed; and a spotter or coach, maintaining a close, supportive presence as children take risks or try out new skills.

The following are some of our most popular strategies. Hopefully, they will spur you into inventing an even wider selection of activities to help teachers explore their roles. See if you can invent one from the Malaguzzi quote on reconnaissance flights.

Strategy: The Teacher's Role by Any Other Name

To encourage people to examine the traditional roles that teachers play, we pass out cards with fictitious names on them made by scrambling the letters in words that describe these roles (examples are listed below). Working in small groups, we ask participants to decode the name, uncovering a typical role a teacher assumes with children. This activity is initially puzzling to some, but as the first discoveries are called out, it becomes lively and involving for most. Teachers are able to laugh as they face descriptions of common behaviors they have with children. This sets the stage for a cast of new roles to be considered in becoming a master teacher.

Sample Cards
Kim Peetere *(Timekeeper)*
Ju Ged *(Judge)*
Rianadi Sciplin *(Disciplinarian)*
Dhere Preesh *(Sheepherder)*
Ora Rot *(Orator)*
Mel Volsprober *(Problem solver)*
Hope Kueseer *(Housekeeper)*
Kate Preege *(Gatekeeper)*

Strategy: Hats, Props, and Videotapes

This activity uses video clips we have made during our visits to classrooms. The clips are easy to make, nothing fancy, but are useful as visual examples of things we want to discuss during trainings. (More discussion of the use of video clips is found in Section 2.)

We gather and display a collection of props to represent various teacher behaviors, giving participants time to look them over. Props include a firefighter's hat, captain's hat, magnifying glass, wand, chain, gavel, plume pen, megaphone, and stopwatch. Watching short video clips of teachers at work with children, participants are asked to choose a prop that represents the role the teacher played. We discuss the teacher's behavior and how that role enhances or defeats our goals with children. Finally, participants decide on an alternate master teacher role that could be played and a prop to represent it. This strategy usually engages teachers so fully that they beg for more!

Strategy: Researching Roles

We want teachers to discover skills and behaviors for roles they can play with children. With reference materials such as a dictionary, encyclopedia, career and occupations resource guides, and job announcements from newspapers, small groups of participants are asked to research a given job—such as architect, coach, broadcaster, mediator, prop manager, observer, or scribe. Together, group members develop a list of the knowledge, skills, and tasks the role entails. Next they consider how aspects of this role might enhance their work with children.

Each group can make a presentation to the others; or, time permitting, they can create a skit for the other groups to uncover how this role might be beneficial for teachers.

Strategy: Observation Checklists and Notepads

To help teachers become more familiar with specific behaviors involved in mastering a particular teacher role, we have developed checklists of concise descriptions. You can use these checklists in a variety of ways: as a self-assessment tool; an observation form for teachers to learn from others; or, in notepad or wall poster form, as a visible reminder. Examples are listed below, with master forms for duplication found in appendix B.

Teachers—like children and everyone else—feel the need to grow in their competencies; they want to transform experiences into thoughts, thoughts into reflections, and reflections into new actions. They also feel a need to make predictions, to try things out, and then interpret them. The act of interpretation is most important. Teachers must learn to interpret ongoing processes rather than wait to evaluate results. In the same way, their role as educators must include understanding children as producers, not as consumers. They must learn to teach nothing to children except what children can learn by themselves.

Loris Malaguzzi, *The Hundred Languages of Children* [25]

TEACHER ROLES

Teacher as Architect
- Evaluating space based on a child's eye view
- Adapting space to the children's play needs and interests, etc.

Teacher as Observer
- Seeing self as a field researcher in child development
- Appreciating the details of children's complex play, etc.

Teacher as Prop Manager
- Suggesting play possibilities through arrangement of materials
- Anticipating play scripts with a supply of related props, etc.

Teacher as Mediator
- Creating a climate of safety for children to speak their needs and feelings
- Seeing conflicts as opportunities to learn social skills, etc.

Teacher as Coach
- Recognizing strengths and providing opportunities to practice them
- Encouraging risk taking with a supportive presence, etc.

Teacher as Scribe
- Modeling that the spoken word can be written down and read
- Making written and pictorial representations of children's play and language, etc.

Teacher as Broadcaster
- Spreading the news of the play stories you observe in your group
- Collecting and displaying examples of children's activities and creations, etc.

Strategy: Early Childhood Junk Mail

Each month our mailboxes are stuffed with slick advertisements featuring samples of curriculum kits, patterns, worksheets, and dittos marketed to preschool teachers. We've recycled this collection into an activity to help teachers compare traditional teacher roles with the ones we've been describing. Giving small groups collections of these publications to analyze, we pose these kinds of questions:

- What do these materials suggest as the expectations, goals, and intended learning outcomes for children?
- How would you describe the role of a teacher in using these materials with children?
- Is there a way to use this material while playing one of the roles of a master teacher we've been discussing?

Strategy: New Roles for the Playground

The role of playground supervisor can make one weary, either from too much to keep track of or not enough interest to keep one awake. Familiar roles that usually take up the most time include: patrol cop, first aid dispenser, referee, and benchwarmer. Sometimes we present these roles through a word scramble or set of props as described in the strategies above.

We then work with the group to create a new set of roles for teachers on the playground, such as body builder, detective, environmentalist, architect, weather forecaster, visitor from another planet, landscaper, inventor, engineer, and pilot. On chart paper, we create three columns and write this list of new roles in the left-hand column. In the next two columns, we brainstorm the possible behaviors and activities teachers might try in each of these new roles with children.

Teacher Role	Teacher Behavior	Possible Activity
• detective	• takes kids to investigate where caterpillars are coming from	• bring out magnifying glasses and bug catcher with screens

PLANTING THE SEED

We've found it challenging and rewarding to re-conceive of training that leads to effective teaching. It's tempting to believe that people's dispositions are set in cement, and, indeed, some are. But we've also seen tremendous change in teachers who have been coached to see children and themselves differently.

It seems to us that trainers and supervisors get better results when we, too, foster certain dispositions in ourselves. Rather than focusing on what's wrong with a teacher and trying to fix it, we do better to focus on what's right and build from that.

Our profession is at a critical juncture. We are losing our workforce and having difficulty finding qualified new recruits. As we seek to address this in the public policy and compensation arenas, we also have the opportunity to rethink our approach to staff development. It's definitely worth the effort.

Section 4
Training for Culturally Sensitive and Anti-Bias Practices

Recently during group time, I passed out feathers to dance with. Immediately, some of the boys stuck the feathers in their hair and said, "Whoo-whoo, me Indian! me Indian!" Then more kids caught on and put their hands on their mouths yelling "whoo-whoo" like stereotypical war cries. A Native American boy in the group did not participate. I became alarmed for him and redirected the play.

Rebecca, teacher

My kindergarten is the only special education program at my school. None of the kids are visibly handicapped, but several are medically fragile. When our kids are on the playground, other children either look frightened by them or laugh at them. I feel their teachers need to address the issue of diversity.

Lucinda, teacher

𝒲hether close at hand in the daily life of early childhood classrooms or at home watching the evening news, there are countless compelling stories driving our commitment to culturally sensitive, anti-bias practices with children and adults. We read about wars based on ethnic cleansing, religious rivalry, and political assassinations around the world. In our own city we watch race and class tensions mount, along with a dramatic rise in hate crimes and violence against targeted groups such as Jews, Japanese people, Asian-Americans mistaken for Japanese people, Arabs, lesbians, and gay men.

The demographics of those in prison, living in poverty, facing chronic health problems and being dismissed or dropping out of school reveal yet another story of the bias and injustice that pervades our communities. Whether in the form of cross burnings, sexual harassment, name calling, or ethnic jokes, it is increasingly common and acceptable for disrespect, if not hatred, to be expressed towards certain groups of people. Mounting unemployment, difficult economic times, and aroused religious fervor fuel an urge to find someone to blame, a scapegoat. Confusion, fear, and ignorance are furthered by the growth of a mean spirit creeping across this land.

In the early childhood field, however, we pride ourselves on being multicultural and fostering cooperation and a "we can all get along" spirit. Why, then, the push for anti-bias practices? We hear this question and confusion from some who take our classes and workshops. We have even encountered resistance and accusations that the anti-bias curriculum promotes a "p.c." (politically correct) approach to education, fostering only one way of thinking or promoting agendas from special interest groups. Some have gone so far as to misrepresent anti-bias education as anti-Christian and anti-family. That couldn't be further from the truth.

The goal of anti-bias work is inclusion, not exclusion, self-esteem for all, empathy, and activism in the face of injustice. These goals were developed

We do not really see through our eyes or hear through our ears, but through our beliefs. To put our beliefs on hold is to cease to exist as ourselves for a moment.

Lisa Delpit, "The Silenced Dialogue"[2]

because there is ample evidence of the early formation of bias in young children.[1] We think these goals are also needed to address the inequities that still exist in our field. Early childhood educators can't always walk our talk.

In our travels as trainers and consultants, we have seen numerous examples of de facto segregation in early childhood education, with children of color predominating certain programs, and European American others. Where populations are expanding and shifting, we typically find Head Start and other programs for low-income families faced with waves of new refugee and immigrant groups, homeless families, and the fallout of violence in children's lives that poverty and upheaval often bring. Teachers tell us they lack the experience, training, and support services to handle many of the multicultural, multilingual, and family arrangements with which they are faced.

We see efforts to teach children about different cultures often reinforcing superficial understandings or stereotypes. In cross-cultural caregiving settings, we too seldom see providers using children's culture as they care for and teach them and too often see providers not understanding culturally relevant practices.

Still, multicultural and anti-bias education are household words in the early childhood field, resulting in a proliferation of new literature, media, and products. We now find "Diversity" workshop tracks at conferences with a range of offerings to get in-step with the current trends in our profession. There are seminars and workshops on specific cultural groups, gender bias, inclusion of children with differing abilities, honoring diverse family structures, and bilingual and culturally relevant practices. Many of these are complementary, but some suggest contradictory approaches. We alternately hear people excited, confused, and exasperated at being expected to know so much (while being paid so little!).

Trying to navigate in these waters is tricky business. It is tempting to stick with what is viewed as accepted practice, avoid controversy, and gravitate toward what is popular and safe. But we have a commitment to continually examine our own biases, and to listen to the voices that have been traditionally silenced. This has put us on a ship with no reverse gear. The chapters in this section reflect a work, indeed, our lives in process. Training with and about diversity is where our personal and professional growth intersect most acutely—listening, watching, acting, reflecting, reading, risking—trying to better understand our own identity and that of others, simultaneously trying to incorporate our learning into our teaching.

Chapter 11
Our Journey and Developmental Process

Understanding concepts of culture, identity, and power has been a developmental process for us. We have moved through a number of stages in our journey of recognizing bias and learning to be culturally sensitive, and there are surely many more stages to come. This journey has involved letting go of some sacred assumptions, putting ourselves in uncomfortable positions where we are the minority culture, and paying attention to the stories, reactions, anger, hesitancy, and strengths of people different from ourselves. Though we don't consider ourselves new to the topic of multicultural and anti-bias practices, we have experienced a recurring cycle of discovery, pain, anxiety, de-centering, insight, and exhilaration.

CULTURAL BLINDERS REGARDING DAP

Because it reflects our own values and views, for a number of years we used the Developmentally Appropriate Practice (DAP) book published by NAEYC as the sacred standard bearer, the truth about what is right and wrong in programming for young children.[3] When we encountered significant divergence from these DAP standards, we pressed heavily for change, failing to distinguish between programs that were genuinely not meeting children's needs and those that were operating within a different cultural framework. As we began to listen more closely to the voices objecting to the sanctification of the DAP book, we could more thoughtfully analyze the resistance. It became clear that cultural domination and racism were woven into some of our definitions of "appropriate." This realization has been an unsettling process, causing us to re-examine our thinking and practice.

It is often easier to recognize things with hindsight than in the moment. Several experiences now stand out to us as lessons we didn't know we were learning. For instance, as a Head Start education coordinator for five years, Deb found herself supervising a large African American staff, most of whom were women. As she tried to impress upon them that developmentally appropriate practice requires teachers to be non-directive and in the background, they politely told her, "but that is not our way." It is only in recent years that we have come to understand the meaning of what they were saying.

These women knew how to teach in a culturally relevant manner with young African American children. They knew how to establish an environment that was familiar and emotionally nourishing to the children. They were skilled in ways of talking and relating such that the children developed a sense of self and security while learning the rules of European American culture by which they would be judged in school.

Margie had experiences parallel to Deb's in her seven-year job as the director

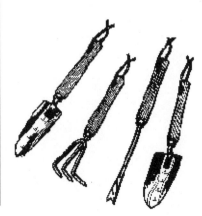

of a multicultural staff in a child care program. For example, she wanted the teachers to unify in their approach to daily routines. She tried to convince them to adopt policies such as having the children address all the adults by their first names and not requiring them to eat all the food on their plates. Some time passed before she understood the discomfort many of these new approaches caused teachers who had different values about showing respect to adults and other well-founded approaches to food issues and mealtime.

On another occasion Deb worked as an education specialist with responsibilities including the oversight of an Indian Head Start program. She was concerned about the lack of materials in the program, while simultaneously amazed at how well the children played together despite this. Thinking she would help the program, Deb arranged for the purchase of several thousand dollars of early childhood supplies for their use. Months after these supplies had been delivered, Deb visited the program and was shocked to find that most of the new purchases were not in use. Putting aside her judgment about this situation, she watched and listened, and, over time, discovered that what was important to the teachers and children in this program was their relationships with each other, not objects to play with.

It's embarrassing to recognize these forms of bias and cultural sensitivity in ourselves. Likewise, we remember practicing a form of multicultural curriculum planning that resembles the one we now try to discourage. As European American women committed to early childhood practices that empower all children, we aren't always aware of the blind spots our power and privilege give us.

Most of our training and, indeed, what is in this book, reflects our allegiance to the NAEYC formulation of developmentally appropriate practices, and we recognize there are other cultural forms of appropriate practice. The point is not to abandon these values and definitions for ourselves, but to be thoughtful and recognize there are other, equally valid perspectives. Cultural sensitivity requires that we be open to change and modification. The general give-and-take we advocate for trainers is especially critical in cross-cultural settings.

FORGETTING WHAT WE KNOW

Embracing the anti-bias curriculum approach came naturally to us,[4] but certainly not without some notable mistakes. We each have a history of activism with issues of peace and social and economic justice in our families, communities, and workplaces. Long before the *Anti-Bias Curriculum* book was published, we were doing this work in classrooms with young children and, in a low-key way, promoting it with other teachers. With the publication of the book we could now name our practice and place it in the larger body of research and literature on the development of identity and cognitive frameworks in young children. As a result, our teacher training became more impassioned and insistent about anti-bias practices.

When we began to examine why our training on this topic wasn't always as enthusiastically received as our other work, we discovered that our devotion to anti-bias practices had begun to overshadow our understandings about adult development. Obviously, we could no more insist that teachers really learn and embrace an anti-bias curriculum than any other topic near and dear to our hearts. Teachers have to put together their own understandings about the need for and approach to take with anti-bias work, just as they must do with setting up learning environments, child guidance, and any other early childhood topic. When asked to look at issues of bias, teachers especially bring a sack-load of childhood experiences that they need support in examining. Relearning this brought us back on track.

GOALS BEYOND EXPOSURE TO DIVERSITY

Through the way we train teachers and our influence on their work with children and families, we hope to steadily chip away at rearranging how power, resources, and respect get distributed in our communities. These goals go beyond exposing children to other cultures in the world through celebrating holidays and making art projects. While we certainly want children to have exposure to and learn to feel comfortable with and even curious about those different from themselves, our goals suggest an approach significantly different.

At times our training presents a conflict for those who have invested themselves in what Louise Derman-Sparks calls a "tourist curriculum." We understand this because our early teaching about diversity included this practice as well. Over time we've gotten more clarity on why this approach is problematic. Being a tourist is for those who are at least somewhat privileged and have the economic means to travel. Tourists typically spend a few days visiting a place. They stay in a hotel and go on excursions catered to them. They return home with superficial information, if not significant misunderstandings, regarding how the people there live, what they value, and so forth.

Teachers often duplicate this tourist pattern when they bring a multicultural "lesson" and artifacts into a classroom. They teach about traditions of "this other group of people" in a way that may make them appear exotic, romantic, strange, or objectified. What's more, children rarely understand what the lesson is about and why they are asked to do this activity. It may be fun, but the characterization of another group's identity is often over-generalized or trivialized. A tourist curriculum usually reinforces stereotypes and simplistic thinking.

> Inappropriate Approaches to Diversity:
> • Teachers believe they're not prejudiced
> • Teachers are proud of being "color blind"
> • Teachers believe that European American children are unaffected by
>   diversity issues
> • Teachers assume that the children they teach are culturally deprived
> • Teachers seek out resources to develop multicultural [tourist] curriculum
>
> Elizabeth Jones and Louise Derman-Sparks
> "Meeting the Challenge of Diversity"[5]

We find other teachers unsettled by our training, as well, for example, those who have worked hard to develop a "color-blind" approach to racial or cultural differences. Our training emphasizes the importance of recognizing and acknowledging differences. Some claim children don't notice these differences until we point them out. Because a primary developmental theme for young children is classification, we believe they do notice differences. The task of early childhood educators is to dispel any fear or negative associations with these differences, and to intervene in the development of bias they will acquire from our society at large.

This week I paid special attention to TV commercials. One night I noted eight all-white, young, "sleek" commercials. The women were all sensual and my reaction was one of offense and disgust. African American men were portrayed as super athletes in a kind of fairyland realm. I did not see any Native Americans or Asians. Then I noticed that in my favorite mail order catalog, all the women and children appear white, beautiful, and well-off.

Stephanie, teacher

Ignoring differences in a classroom often leads to marginalizing those who aren't of the dominant culture, making their lives invisible to themselves and others. While we want to avoid over-generalizing about members of any group, we don't want to deny a person's group identity, for it is part of who each of us is. In fact, many of us have several strong group identities that are important to us—our ethnicity, gender, work, and the like.

The interface and distinction between one's individual and group identity is a complexity we can slowly introduce to children. It involves the same process we use in helping them learn to "hold more than one attribute at a time in their minds." Just as we might point out "these things are all green, but one is also a sock, a plant, a crayon," we can say "Minh, Cam, and Freddy are all Vietnamese Americans, but one of them is tall, one has short hair, and one lives with his grandma." Our training to help teachers develop more comfort and skill in acknowledging differences has improved in direct proportion to our own comfort and skill level in this area. We are convinced this will also become the experience of teachers working with children.

DISPOSITIONS THAT HELP

The activities outlined in this section are consistent with our emphasis on fostering the dispositions discussed in Section 3. In training on cultural sensitivity and anti-bias curriculum practices, we want to encourage enthusiasm and delight regarding diversity, an empathetic heart, and questioning mind rather than reluctance, guilt, or desires to be politically correct.

Self-reflection and a willingness to take risks are obviously key dispositions for working with diversity and general training. Training strategies that encourage these dispositions are as important as strategies specific to multicultural topics. We try to cultivate the habit of internally questioning "What's right and what's wrong with this picture?" as we move through experiences and images in the world. Asking this question helps us better model and foster a disposition of being a watchdog and whistle-blower.

On topics of diversity *and* in working with diverse groups of participants, many trainers may feel less prepared to use the strategies and debriefing approach advocated throughout this book. Indeed, working with diversity is only generally referred to in the body of core knowledge defined as the early childhood profession, and a great deal more homework is required if we are to be effective in this area. Our own growth process has included extensive reading, discussion, and attending of workshops and seminars. We've also joined a support group that meets regularly to share experiences, resources, and social and political analyses. The group challenges us to undo the influence of the "ism brothers" in our lives. To aid you in your journey we've included suggested readings in the Recommended Resources section at the end of this book.

Chapter 12
Guiding Principles and Strategies

As reflected throughout the pages of this book, our training on any topic is guided by concepts of developmental theory and constructivism, goals and principles, all of which influence how we structure our time, activities, and interactions with participants. And because we want to foster student empowerment to act on behalf of broader social change, our effort to be inclusive in our practices is more than a matter of teaching techniques. It's an agenda of values and social theory.

From time to time we try to articulate the foundations of what we believe to be effective training with diversity. We start by naming our assumptions and move on to analyzing what they imply about planning a training program. This evolves into defining some principles to guide our work, and finally the creation of some specific strategies to use. As we continue to read, listen, and evaluate our practice, we come back to this process again, knowing our formulations will continue to change as we internalize new understandings.

NAMING OUR ASSUMPTIONS
The current assumptions we are working with are as follows:

1. Everybody has a culture; culture is learned and includes, but goes beyond, ethnicity.
2. The dominant culture of power in this country has been shaped by European American male perspectives and interests.
3. Bias comes in many forms; invisibility and lack of cultural relevancy are as detrimental as stereotyping.
4. Anti-bias practices require that we recognize European American cultural dominance and learn how its assumptions become a bias when applied universally. We must learn new attitudes, information, and behaviors as we unlearn acquired biases.
5. To be inclusive and genuinely multicultural requires that we make a place for those historically left out, misrepresented, or disenfranchised. Given the stakes, this will likely stir up emotions and conflict that we must learn to work with.
6. Adults come to programs and workshops with a complex web of influences from backgrounds that must be untangled as they learn and unlearn across diversity.
7. As adults come to deeper understandings about themselves and working with diversity, these understandings will influence their work with children, going beyond tokenism to counter biases and be culturally sensitive.

We keep these assumptions in mind as we evaluate our work, especially when tension or conflict arises. Overall we want to remember that all of us are in

As long as the power relationship based on book knowledge or years of work and life experience exists, as long as most college systems require grading, it would be dishonest to pretend that students and teachers share equal power.

Margaret Randall,
Walking to the Edge[6]

a developmental process and at different stages in learning about ourselves, others, and the systems of power and privilege. The *un*learning process can sometimes be more difficult than the learning.

The training practices advocated throughout this book represent the particular theoretical frameworks we embrace and our understandings of the socioeconomic and political context of the United States. We know our perspectives (and privileges) as European American middle-class feminist women may not feel workable for those with other backgrounds and values.

We are familiar with and secure in the "culture of power" and therefore comfortable in school settings (even though we are highly critical of them).[7] Our value system leads us to take a posture of peer relations with our students. This is welcomed by many, but some, whose cultures teach them to revere and defer to the teacher as the authority, have difficulty interacting with us in a peer fashion. We believe students will learn a great deal hearing each other's stories, but this is awkward for those whose culture encourages them not to focus on their individual experiences.

Coming to understand these variations of culture and power, we have begun describing to participants in our training the "why" behind what we do and say. This is our attempt at teaching what Lisa Delpit calls "the rules of power" in our classroom.[8] Explicitly naming what we value and how that might differ from other teachers and school experiences provides our students with a rationale for our activities. They don't have to flounder or guess about how to be successful.

IMPLICATIONS FOR TRAINING

Culture of Power
1. Issues of power are enacted in classrooms.
2. There are codes or rules for participating in power; that is, there is a "culture of power."
3. The rules of the culture of power are a reflection of the rules of the culture of those who have power.
4. If you are not already a participant in the culture of power, being told explicitly the rules of that culture makes acquiring power easier.
5. Those with power are frequently least aware of—or least willing to acknowledge—its existence. Those with less power are often the most aware of its existence.

Lisa Delpit, "The Silenced Dialogue"[9]

Increasingly, we introduce our workshop or class with statements such as the following:

We genuinely value the experiences you bring to this topic and we think your stories will help us learn how to be more effective teachers. And because we believe that you can learn as much from analyzing your experiences with each other as you can from listening to us, small group activities are a big part of how we will spend our time together here. We don't believe we have all the answers or expertise. We see our role as developing activities to help us all learn from our experiences and relate those to the ideas of this class. If this is problematic for you, let us know and we will try to adapt activities so they can enhance your learning.

Another way to describe the teacher training we advocate is providing for "contextual learning." We stress the importance of starting with the participants' experience, planning for different cultural orientations, learning styles, and stages of development. It is also critical to understand how the history of the United States shapes the social and political context of learning and teaching.

In the context of this history, European Americans benefit from particular privileges, some of which are diminished by circumstances of gender, class, education, age, sexual orientation, and physical abilities. Contemporary European Americans did not create this system of privilege, but partake in and benefit from it just the same. This is our legacy. We are not responsible for what happened in the past, but we are responsible for what we do now.

For us, this has particular implications for European American early childhood educators. It is our responsibility to figure out who we are and where we came from, rather than assume the concept of ethnicity applies only to people of color. When we understand that we, too, have lost our ethnicity in the great melting pot schema, we can tackle white racism. We can become allies of people of color, rather than competitors or defenders of the status quo. With reflection and watchdog, whistle-blowing dispositions, we can become activists as we discover injustice.

When the disposition is not one of guilt or defensiveness, European Americans can support efforts by people of color, be they children or adults, to build their identity and power base, even when this means separating ourselves from our sphere of influence. As allies, European Americans can work to prevent people of color from being isolated or singled out. Our challenge is to raise the next generation of European Americans without the mistaken identity that "white is right" and we are the only bona fide citizens deserving access to power. We can share power when it comes to developing policies and procedures, shaping plans, making decisions, determining leadership positions, and distributing resources.

The implications of the historical context of the United States are equally strong for people of color. The legacy of racism has left scars of internalized oppression, often taking the form of self-hatred, a psychology of "I can't," shame, victim-thinking, violence, and self-erasure. In the words of author and professor bell hooks, "people of color need to decolonize our minds." These are understandings that must be integrated into educational settings, with strategies developed to bring forth the voices and experiences to, as Frederick Douglass said, "speak truth to power."

For some, coming to understand our history results in an overnight transformation. In others, it is a step-by-step process of changing attitudes and behaviors. We find the task of integrating new understandings into our training practices a continual challenge, one well worth the effort.

GUIDING PRINCIPLES

We first learned the term "dialogical education" in reading the work of Paulo Freire, but it is a general approach we've seen some instructors use instinctively and informally. For Freire the term implies a pedagogy with the goal, not just of interaction between the student and teacher, but a mutual exchange of influence leading to a basic shift in power relations within the classroom and in the wider

> If you do not know your history, you lose essential memory. And you cannot know yourself. If you remain ignorant of history, you cannot hope to affect change in society or even in your life.
>
> Margaret Randall,
> *Walking to the Edge* [10]

> I am convinced that our future—and the future of our planet—depends upon citizens who possess memory and history, who understand the intersection of race, class, gender, and other cultural issues in their lives, women and men who know their place historically as well as in their society and community. We need people of our full national range: of differing races, ethnicities, sexual preferences, ages, and degrees of ability, who are proud of who they are.
>
> Margaret Randall,
> *Walking to the Edge* [11]

> The handouts I read and mused over this week really served as a tool of enlightenment to me. I realized that I have taken my culture and white privilege for granted without much thought given to it.
>
> Betsy, teacher

world. Because this is our goal as well, we are drawn to a continual study of Freire's pedagogy and social theory.

Dialogue Process

A Freirian classroom has a structured format of a dialogue around problems posed by teacher and students. Our dialogue process is usually begun with an activity structured to have students explore something in their experience that relates to the topic at hand. We invite them to not only dialogue with us, but also with each other. This process means that we are co-constructing our knowledge, collaborating in analyzing and making meaning out of the relationship between experience and ideas. We are not the experts passing on knowledge, but rather the facilitators of a process that, hopefully, leads to further knowledge for students and ourselves.

The stories, problems, and questions students pursue increase our understanding of who they are, and help us assess their current understanding of the topic. This give-and-take enhances our ability to see whose perspectives and interests the body of ideas we're exploring reflect, and how they might need rethinking to meet the goals of empowerment and social change. For us, this is a key aspect of an anti-bias practice.

The dialogue process helps us find our commonalties and our differences and examine how these relate to the larger social and political context. We can integrate discussion of this context into most of our general training on early childhood topics, and give it a particular spotlight when the topic is specifically culturally sensitive or anti-bias training.

Inclusive Practices

Our planning process for inclusive practices in workshops and classes takes into consideration several factors: the format, environment, and setting; language and examples to be used; and activities for dialogue, collaboration, analysis, and practice with different learning styles.

As we begin a training we always give participants an overview of our goals and how we will spend our time. We explain why we think it is important to start with oneself and what one knows best. In doing this we acknowledge the social and political context of human development and learning.

The environment and setting of a training convey an intrinsic message about values and power. If the students are all seated facing the teacher, this arrangement sends out a clear message about where the power and authority is thought to be. When the surfaces are all hard, with sharp edges, uncomfortable seating, and limited vantage points for seeing and hearing clearly, this environment is usually a reflection of the learning process.

In our way of thinking, the language of instruction includes both words and the body. Physical proximity, eye contact, gestures, and facial expressions all convey cultural meaning. The manner as well as language in which people are addressed conveys messages about values and power relations. There may be participants unfamiliar with acronyms typically used in the professional discourse (i.e., DHHS, CPS, DAP, NAEYC). English may be a second language for some and others may have limited literacy, sight, or hearing abilities. All of these must be taken into account, along with the use of the names or labels preferred by people who might be referenced in the discussion.

To evaluate how our plans have taken all these factors into account, we typically use a mental, if not written, checklist.

- What will be done to help everyone feel included, encourage every voice to be heard?
- Are there provisions for different learning styles?
- How do activities support relationships and collaboration among participants?
- Which activities help participants relate their experience to the ideas of the training?
- What groups of people are reflected in the examples or stories used?
- How can we convey diverse cultural perspectives on this topic?
- Does the training provide practice in applying the ideas or skills discussed?
- What follow-up suggestions will support participants in taking their next step in learning about this topic?

Section 5 provides a fuller discussion of how we plan workshops and classes. We end this chapter with examples of how we translate the principles and concepts discussed here into concrete training strategies. Most are simple activities for self-examination and dialogue with others. They are strategies aimed at uncovering all the voices present and designed to promote a fuller understanding of how people's stories relate to the larger context of power and privilege, as well as the specific content of the training.

Many elements of these strategies are parallel to those described in the chapters of Section 2. To remind you how we categorize strategies as types of tools, we again group them with the labels used in Section 2. The debriefing process described there is especially relevant for strategies designed for cultural sensitivity and anti-bias practices.

AWARENESS TOOLS

Strategy: Childhood Message about Yourself as a Learner

In Chapter 4 we describe an activity of introducing yourself as a childhood message. This can be adapted to help participants explore their self-image as a learner and where this came from.

Following the same procedure described in the earlier chapter, ask people to walk around the room and introduce themselves to each other by repeating a phrase that captures a childhood message they received about themselves as a learner. This message could have been received directly or indirectly, from things that were said or not said, or by how they were treated. For instance, "Hi, I'm Margie and I better study hard because girls are not as smart as boys." "My name is Deb and if I don't learn, it's the teacher's fault and not mine."

This activity generates numerous examples of the conditions and messages conducive to a positive "I can do it!" sense of oneself, along with the aspects of entitlement and privilege or discrimination and disenfranchisement we inherit. It alerts both the trainers and participants to the contextual backgrounds brought to the school and learning experience.

Growing up, it seemed that being different was bad and not talked about. If it was talked about, it would be a put down. I had an aunt who was a very heavy woman and my family would say terrible things about her. When I got heavy, they would say things like "Oh, you'd be so pretty if only. . ." Teachers in school thought I was not as smart as the other kids.

Catherine, family home provider

Strategy: Guided Writing

There are a variety of brief writing assignments we use during a training session or in-between classes as a homework assignment. We follow the approach described in Chapter 4 under reflective writing strategies. To focus thinking on issues of identity, family values, culture, and bias, we give writing assignments like the following:

- Sketch out a family tree that defines your family as you were growing up. For each person included, write a phrase or two describing the role they played or what they contributed to the family values or functioning.
- Write about an incident where you saw a child express a strong sense of group identity apart from someone else, for example, along gender, cultural, or socio-economic class lines. What was the reaction from other children and/or adults around? If you had intervened, what might you have said or done?
- Describe a time when you experienced or witnessed some bias. What happened? How did you feel? What would have been helpful at the time? If you were to encounter that situation again, what might you do?

ACTIVE TOOLS

Strategy: Map Out Experiences

For this activity we enlarge a blank map outlining the United States and make several copies of it. We glue each map onto pieces of thick paper or tagboard. We arbitrarily divide the maps into eight sections like a jigsaw puzzle and cut out the pieces. Each shape has one of the eight phrases listed below written on it.

- grew up in a religious family
- has repeated experiences of being an outsider
- grew up in a small town or rural setting
- has close experience with a mental or physical disability
- grew up poor
- has lived with an extended family
- has strong ties with more than one culture
- has broken away from some traditional female roles

Participants are given random shapes with phrases and asked to walk around holding it in front of them. They look for a phrase that they have a personal story about and try to trade their shape for it. The trade happens when both people have a story related to each other's shape. They tell their stories to each other, trade shapes, and move on again, holding the shape in front of them for another trade. After a reasonable amount of time in which everyone has been able to make at least two trades, we ask the group to stop and listen to directions for the next step.

We then ask participants with the same shape to get together in groups and compare their stories related to this phrase. They usually discover that they have both similar and different experiences related to this category. If this activity is part of a larger training, there won't be time for a full debriefing, but rather a summary that captures examples of the idea that, for instance, people in this group all grew up in a religious family, but the religion and its influence on their lives was very different.

For the final step, ask one member of each group to collect all the group's shapes, put them into a stack and come to the center of the room to try and fit the pieces all together in a completed puzzle. Sometimes it takes them awhile to discover that these shapes together represent a map of the country. We end the activity by asking for any final comments related to new insights the activity might have given them about the diversity of the United States.

Strategy: Move to Tell Us about You

This activity is best conducted in three parts, each of which can be done in depth or together as an overview of influences on identity formation. The first part involves physically moving, while the second and third can be done sitting in pairs.

Identify opposite sides of the room for participants to move to, depending on how they respond to specific statements. For instance, say, "When you were growing up, stand here if this was true about you and there if it wasn't." Examples of statements include the following:

• A strong gender identity was stressed for you.
• Religion was a big part of your upbringing.
• You were given a strong ethnic identity.
• Your racial identity was emphasized.
• Your economic circumstances were stressed.
• Your group identity was primary, as opposed to individual identity.
• Most of your life you've felt part of the mainstream culture— "just like everyone else."

After each statement, ask participants to discuss why they are standing there (discuss as a whole group if numbers are small and in partners or small groups if there are many people). Typically participants discover they have both similar and different reasons for being there. For example, they may have been raised with a strong religious identity, but the identity itself could be quite different— Jewish, Catholic, Baptist, Islamic. Having a strong gender identity stressed might have been along traditional sex roles or specifically to counter those—"Just because you're a girl, it doesn't mean you have any limits to what you can do."

During the debriefing of each statement, we ask people to notice whether many of the same people consistently are standing with them, or if they are frequently different. It's useful to look at this particularly in terms of how people responded to having an ethnic group, or individual identity stressed. Unlike most people of color, quite often most European Americans don't think of themselves as having grown up with a racial identity, because being White is taken for granted.

As we move into the second part of this activity, we ask people to sit with a partner to discuss the following questions.

• How did your family help you acquire an identity, directly or indirectly?
• What words, labels, behaviors, and/or activities were used to help you acquire an identity?

My fear of homosexuals is by far the most difficult to deal with. I am so uncomfortable with that whole subject. I remember panicking when I found out that my youngest daughter's drill team instructor was gay. But after being around him and watching him with those girls my eyes were really opened. He wasn't some monster. He was a wonderful caring person with hopes and dreams just like anyone else. While I can't embrace their lifestyle, I don't panic and withdraw like I used to. When the fear was put aside I found human beings —just people with another lifestyle. I can go beyond my stumbling block. I guess that means I've taken another baby step toward progress.

Juanita, teacher

• What words, labels, and/or identity groups do you use today to describe your identity?

We debrief this activity by writing on a flip chart examples of typical phrases they heard while growing up that reinforced their identity.

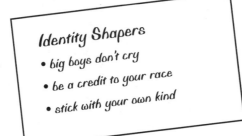

Identity Shapers
• big boys don't cry
• be a credit to your race
• stick with your own kind

For the final portion of this activity, we ask people to talk again in pairs, this time sharing one of the earliest memories they have of noticing someone different than themselves.

• Describe what you remember about noticing this difference.
• What assumptions did you make about this person?
• Did this cause you to have new thoughts about yourself?
• Did you get any messages from your family about this incident or other general messages regarding people different from your family or group identity?

This final debriefing can help clarify the interplay between identity formation, exposure, or the lack thereof to people different from ourselves, and the direct and indirect values we learn from this. Examining these issues leads to self-awareness for teachers and usually a clearer picture of this developmental process for children. This underscores the compelling need for anti-bias practices and open dialogue with children when they notice differences or experience societal messages that suggest some limitations on who they can be.

Strategy: Developmental Milestones on the Road I've Traveled

To counter the discouragement of "I can never learn it all" and to heighten self-awareness of the influences that have been pivotal in participants' growing understandings of culture, identity, and power, we created a developmental map. This activity can be done on paper or plotted on the floor with participants moving to the milestones and telling their stories.

Drawing a long, curving line, with hills and switchbacks to represent a road, mark samples of developmental milestones with examples such as the following:

• my first memory of difference
• my first memory of being part of an identity group
• the first time I remember feeling left out
• a big effort I made to "fit in" with some definition about my primary identity group
• I recognize a strong message my family gave me about people who were different

- I discover something different about myself apart from my identity group
- a time I tried to deny there was a difference between me and a person with a background very different from mine
- a time I felt powerless because I felt unnoticed or unheard because of my identity group
- a time that made a strong impact when I was treated unfairly
- a time I discovered I held a bias based on false assumptions
- an experience of being part of a group that was addressing bias
- a strong action I took to counter a bias that was in the process of happening

If the road is plotted out on the floor, participants move to the different milestones, taking turns telling their stories. This can be done in a parallel fashion pointing to the different milestones along a road created on paper. The ongoing debriefing process and the concluding summary can highlight how positive and negative influences have shaped our understandings and ability to act.

STORY TOOLS

Strategy: Tell the Story of Your Name

From Elise Bryant, labor activist and performer, we learned another simple strategy that simultaneously promotes awareness of one's own background and that of others in the group. Ask people to introduce themselves by telling a short story about how they got their name.

We begin the process ourselves, providing an example of the kind of things that might be said. For instance, "My name is Deborah Curtis. Last names in my family have been a real issue. My mother is a first generation Italian American. Her parents immigrated to the United States before she was born, having given her the name Ida Maria Santoro. As a teenager mom quickly learned that Italians were looked down on, so when she started school she told the teacher to change her name on the roster and call her 'Diane Sutton.' My dad was raised in Salt Lake City with a Morman mother and, unbeknownst to any of us, a Jewish father. Only after a heart attack did my dad call his adult children together and tell us that his real name was Bobby Cohen. He and my grandfather had changed their names to Curtis to avoid the anti-Semitic persecution they were receiving in Utah. My middle name is Claire after my maternal grandmother. All the first born girls on that side of the family have Claire for their middle name. When I was born my parents had a dispute about what to call me. My mom wanted to call me Gabrielle, which my dad thought was too sophisticated, and he wanted to call me Betty after the movie star Betty Grable. It was a compromise to settle on Deborah. It wasn't too fancy and it wasn't too mundane."

"My given name was Margaret Jane Allison. My mother came from a large Irish-Catholic family and named me after her favorite sister whom she called Margie. She always told me that Aunt Margie was the sweetest, dearest person in the world and she hoped I would be just like her. She gave me my middle name, Jane, after my father's sister, whom she said was just a bit wild and outrageous, something she wanted me to have a touch of as well. When my mother remarried, I took my stepfather's name, Bitner, and dropped the Allison. In my early twenties, I married and took my husband's name, Carter, dropping the Bitner to just the initial 'B.' Getting a divorce in my thirties, I considered returning to the

I have really grown a lot in this class. It has helped me be able to look at myself and see what it is I am thinking and why I am teaching what I am. It has taught me to be aware of other people's cultural differences more and to feel comfortable asking them questions.

Colleen, teacher

name Bitner, but decided enough was enough with this name changing business. I wanted my son and I to have the same last name, making this family-name identification business easier for him than it had been for me."

The stories this activity calls forth almost always create interest in getting to know each other better. People get a flavor of the history of this country and how their family related to the "melting pot." Sometimes people have no awareness of how they got their name, reveal they were given a name popular at the time, or recall that they were named after a famous person. European Americans often discover that their backgrounds include more than the shopping mall culture. Repeatedly, we've had people tell us that this activity sent them back doing more investigation about their family history and the larger social context of the times in which relatives lived. We think this self-awareness is critical and will lead to more sound anti-bias practices.

Strategy: Persona Stories about Learners

There are any number of variations of the persona story strategies as coined by Kay Taus and described in Chapter 6. This one alerts participants to different learning styles and the circumstances that may be influencing them.

Give small groups of participants a prop such as a doll, face mask, or photograph to use to create a story. Ask them to give the person a name, family, culture, and set of circumstances that shape how they come to school and their learning situations. After each group has worked together to create their persona, have them share their stories with the group.

Using a chart pad, keep track of information from the stories that might fall into categories of learners, such as kinesthetic, musical, or relational. This helps guide the debriefing process as you explore with the group how this relates to their own experience and the implications for working with young children.

SYMBOLIC TOOLS
Strategy: Choose a Picture to Describe Yourself

To help participants introduce themselves to each other, we arrange an aesthetically pleasing set of pictures on a table for each participant to choose from. The pictures feature a variety of people, cultures, and environments and we ask people to choose one that feels familiar and comfortable to them. Depending on the size of the group and the time available, we ask participants to describe what this picture says about them, initially talking in pairs or to the whole group.

Using a visual representation of some aspect of one's identity is a simple way to connect people to each other as they explore the similarities and differences among those in the group. In addition, most of the stories people associate with these pictures illuminate some aspect of the social and political context of human development, for example, if they grew up in a poorer neighborhood, in a family prominent in the community, or with strong religious teachings. This can be highlighted during the debriefing discussion.

Use each of the above strategies when training on topics not specifically designated as having a focus on cultural sensitivity or anti-bias practices. Several can be used for opening any training where you want people to get to know something about each other. As you move on to the topic at hand, remind participants to keep in mind the diversity present in the room and to draw on these shared and different experiences for a wider look at the ideas that will be discussed.

Integrate many of these strategies into training on topics such as child or human development, building self-esteem, child guidance, and creating learning environments. As we have demonstrated in this book, there are numerous ways to include aspects of diversity in any training offered. It is also important to offer training specifically focused on cultural sensitivity and anti-bias practices. The chapters that follow outline strategies of this nature.

Chapter 13
Training to Heighten Cultural Sensitivity

When most early childhood educators plan for things "cultural," they think in terms of holidays, crafts, and artifacts. These are certainly expressions of peoples' cultures, but the term encompasses far more. Culture refers to how people live. It includes everything from food and language to values, belief systems, and patterns of relating, caretaking, and communicating. Culture may reflect ethnicity, education, class standings, and physical abilities, but it is not limited to these things.

Deep Structure of Culture
- Culture is a set of rules for behavior, influencing, not causing, behaviors themselves.
- Culture is shared behavioral characteristics of groups passed from one generation to the next.
- Culture is learned, not something we are born with.
- Individual members of a culture are embedded to different degrees within their culture, resulting in variations of behaviors and attitudes.
- Cultures borrow and share rules through contact with each other.
- Members of a cultural group may be proficient at cultural behavior but unable to describe the rules.

Carol Brunson Phillips, Culture as a Process[12]

When we think of multiculturalism in child care settings, we are likely to consider images, objects, and people in the environment. To be sure, these things are important. In programs with children from more than one culture, it is also critical to consider diverse child-rearing practices. The way people raise children reflects variations in values, religious beliefs and practices, family structures, and economic circumstances. From time to time these may present conflicts between a family and staff of a child care program, but for the most part, these differences go unacknowledged if not unrecognized.

POSSIBLE CULTURAL CONFLICTS
Alerting ourselves to the need to investigate possible differences is an important step we can take in cultural sensitivity. Even if families in a program look alike and speak the same language, we should not assume they share the same cultural identity, values, and beliefs. Many of the activities described on earlier pages can help teachers in the uncovering process required.

In recent years a handful of valuable resources have been developed to guide early childhood and parent educators in our cross-cultural work. Two of the earliest and most insistent spokespeople in this arena have been Carol Brunson Phillips and Janet Gonzalez-Mena. Their individual articles in *Young Children*, along with Phillips' *Essentials for Child Development Associates Working With Young Children* (Council for Early Childhood Professional Recognition, 1991)

and Gonzalez-Mena's *Multicultural Issues in Child Care* (Mayfield Publishing, 1993) detail cultural differences around such basic caregiving practices as holding, feeding, napping, toilet training, and providing for learning. They each emphasize the awareness and conflict negotiation that must take place if programs are to be culturally sensitive and respectful.

PROVIDING CULTURAL CONTINUITY

The research of Lily Wong Fillmore has also brought us compelling evidence of the relationship between maintaining development in one's home language and providing cultural continuity and bonds for families.[13] This is a critical component in culturally sensitive programming and challenges the current practice of most who serve multilingual populations. In the rush to help children learn English as a second language, we are often sacrificing family bonds and cultural pride to the goal of school readiness.

Many of these issues are effectively covered in the video and accompanying manual *Essential Connections: Ten Keys to Culturally Sensitive Child Care*,[14] which we regularly use to reinforce some of our training strategies. We have found it helpful to do one of the activities suggested in this chapter, show the first part of the video, stop for discussion, view the last half of the video followed by further discussion and "practice" with an activity such as "consider this scene" discussed in the strategies below.

> Essential Connections: Ten Keys to Culturally Sensitive Child Care
> 1. Provide cultural consistency.
> 2. Work toward representative staffing.
> 3. Create small groups.
> 4. Use the home language.
> 5. Make environments relevant.
> 6. Uncover your cultural beliefs.
> 7. Be open to the perspectives of others.
> 8. Seek out cultural and family information.
> 9. Clarify values.
> 10. Negotiate cultural conflicts.[15]

Earlier we spoke of our growing awareness of the cultural bias reflected in our definition of developmentally appropriate practices. Perhaps the best collection of writing on this subject is found in *Diversity and Developmentally Appropriate Practices*, edited by Bruce Mallory and Rebecca New (Teachers College Press, 1994). From studying this book we gained clarity on the interface between culture and an individual child's development, especially regarding developmental accomplishments that transcend culture. Our own training practice was tremendously affirmed by the authors' mandate for reflective practitioners and observation as the primary role of teachers if we are to achieve culturally respectful child care.

To convey the complexity of these concerns with teachers, we design activities to explore their own cultural values and patterns of living, along with those different from themselves. You can adapt various activities from the chapters in Section 2 for this purpose, and what follows are a few we specifically designed to enhance cultural sensitivity. Some are oriented toward ethnic culture, while others focus on the broader issues of culture—how people live—such as those with differing abilities.

I was touched and sobered considering the matter of culture and what it means to different groups, that it involves their very identity and empowerment within the larger society. Yes, children of different groups need skills to make it in America, but they also need their cultural integrity preserved.

Georgia, teacher

The articles impacted me more with the startling realization that when a child's culture is invisible and omitted in society, then his/her very identity is at stake.

Cheryl, family home provider

AWARENESS TOOLS

Strategy: Share Memories of "How We Did It"

Most of us carry on practices in our adult life that we learned as children. Often these are taken for granted and we haven't given much thought to the "why" of it. In the book by Leslie Williams and Yvonne De Gaetano, *Alerta: A Multicultural, Bilingual Approach to Teaching Young Children* (Addison-Wesley, 1985), the *what*, *how*, and *why* of culture are explored as three different levels of culture.

We incorporate this thinking into an activity in which we ask teachers to share examples of how things were done in their family with regard to such practices as health care, meal preparation, and discipline. You can do this in the form of introducing oneself as a childhood message on the subject as described in Chapter 4. Or you can go around the room asking people to describe how their family approached certain situations such as caring for a sick family member, getting food on the table, or correcting a child who disobeyed or transgressed.

Information in the form of words or short phrases from these stories can be plotted on a three-column chart paper under the headings *Alerta* suggests: *What, How, Why.*

WHAT	HOW	WHY
Health care practices (e.g., treating a cough)	• rubbing ointment on chest • coining • using a vaporizer • drinking herb tea • taking cough medicine before going to sleep	• concepts about physiology • belief systems • tradition passed down from mother to daughter • instructions from doctor, tribal healer, etc.

Most of what people will say falls into either the *what* or *how* column. For instance, treating a cough would be put under the *what* column, while rubbing ointment on the chest or coining the back would be listed under the *how* column. Raising questions about the *why* of these practices is where less obvious information and insight are uncovered. This usually results in new understanding and respect, if not agreement on how things are done in different cultures.

Strategy: Red Flags in Magazines and Professional Literature

Because we want people to begin recognizing the particular cultural frameworks implied in popular advice or professional recommendations regarding child rearing, we gather samples to analyze in our workshops. There are any number of parenting magazines on magazine racks, and our professional literature has a growing body of articles on how to handle certain age groups, behaviors, and caregiving practices. We also like to use sections of the NAEYC *Developmental Appropriate Practice* (DAP) book for this activity.

This activity is a good one to follow the viewing of the video *Essential Connections: Ten Keys to Culturally Sensitive Child Care* or the activity just described above where the *what, how,* and *why* of cultural practices are explored. First we brainstorm a list of the areas of child rearing where there might be cultural differences, putting responses into the three-column list of the *What, How,* and *Why* of culture. In our discussion we emphasize that the differing values and belief systems of the *why* column impact how children are treated.

We then highlight some of the contrasting values (such as emphases on individual identity versus collective identity, self-help versus doing for others, and the push towards autonomy versus interdependency) and ask the group to think of these area as red flags representing possible cultural bias. With these in mind we pass out a set of professional and parenting magazines or articles, along with some red Post-it notepads, asking small groups to go through the materials, discussing and noting where any red flags appear.

We end with a full group discussion where examples are shared and a summary of areas of possible cultural conflicts is reviewed.

ACTIVE TOOLS

Strategy: Welcome Those Parents

We came across a handout from one of our community college parent education classes that instructed the teachers to make sure they made eye contact with every parent when they entered the room. Though this is a common practice advocated in most European American circles, it is not a universally accepted positive experience for all.

Some cultures consider it a sign of disrespect if a younger person makes direct eye contact with an older person. Other cultures have gender differences around this practice. There are different customs and expressions of respect with regard to physical proximity in interactions, as well as making physical contact or showing affection. What is acceptable or condoned in casual conversation also varies from culture to culture.

To alert teachers to possible misinterpretations and misunderstandings occurring across cultures, we use descriptions from D. Sawyer and H. Green's book *The Nesa Activities Handbook for Native and Multicultural Classrooms* (Tillacum Library, 1990) and adapt their role play for a parent open house at a Head Start or child care program. We divide into two groups, with two-thirds of the participants assigned to parent roles while the other third assumes the role of teachers welcoming parents at an open house. They are each given one of the descriptions below.

> *Teacher's role* —You are a European American teacher in a program with a large and varied population. Tonight is the first informal parent-teacher meeting. The director has a commitment to good parent-teacher relationships and has asked the teachers to individually welcome the parents and engage each of them in personal conversation. You are eager to meet the parents and "size up" their parenting skills for you feel this will give you more insights into their kids. You look for ways to ask them things about themselves, their family life, cultural background, etc.

> *Parents' roles* —You are invited to a parent-teacher meeting at the school and since you are concerned about your child adapting and doing well in school, you are glad for this opportunity to meet the teachers in the program. You don't know much about them, but you do come with some assumptions. You feel that your background and family life is not the teachers' business and avoid discussing this with them.

Parent #1—Japanese American mother

In your culture it is customary to bow gracefully when you greet someone, rather than shaking hands. It is also your custom to stand about four feet away from a person during conversation. You tend to defer to men, especially your husband, and those who you perceive as having status, for instance, teachers. You often express appreciation, even for small services and polite comments. You avoid direct eye contact.

Parent #2—Arab American father

In your culture people stand so close to one another that they can smell the other's breath, rarely more than a foot away. You engage in direct, long-lasting eye contact that searches the other's eyes for meaning and emotion. You face people fully when speaking to them, eyeball to eyeball. Hand and head gestures are used frequently; shaking your head from side to side means "yes."

Parent #3—Chinese American father

In your culture conversation is more slow and measured and silences are considered positive communication. You feel that expressing one's emotions is rude and immature. You show few emotions through gestures or facial expression. Direct eye contact is considered rude or aggressive and viewed as a violation of private feelings. You like to stand close to equals, but do not like to stand face to face. You cover your mouth when you laugh.

Parent #4—European American mother

In your culture the social distance is about one and a half feet. You should always stand at least this close when conversing with another person. It is also customary to reinforce what you are saying with hand gestures. Conversation is rapid and spontaneous and interruptions are not regarded as highly rude. Emotions are displayed openly and touching is an important part of communicating feelings, especially with those of the same sex.

Parent #5—Native American mother

In your culture it is not important to fill in time with conversation. Unless asked a direct question you tend to remain silent. Also, when in situations you're not familiar with you tend to wait and watch to establish appropriate responses. If you are asked a question you carefully consider your answer before replying in a quiet voice. When shaking hands your hand may remain limp. Direct eye contact is avoided and may be seen as showing disrespect or aggression.

After each group has had time to absorb the instructions for their roles, they are asked to put away their written descriptions. Parents are each given a name tag with their number on it, with multiples of each parent role used in the case of a large group.

In the role play the teachers greet the parents as they arrive, calling them by the name of "Parent 1" or whatever their number is. They refer to the parent's child as "Little Number 1" and so forth, inventing some information to share about each child. Give participants five to ten minutes to simulate the open house, watching and noting how people are treated and responded to as information to bring to the debriefing discussion. Bring the open house to an end with an announcement that it's late and time for everyone to go home. Call the group together for the debriefing.

We begin the debriefing by asking the parents and teachers to describe each other and their experience together. Usually people immediately make judgmental remarks such as "he was really aggressive, rude, or evasive." We ask people to describe what happened to create this impression and the *how* and *why* of their cultural behavior begins to get uncovered. We end the discussion by summarizing the way people get judged on their communication patterns and how this can create misunderstandings, if not antagonisms.

When a larger block of training time is available, we often use a commercially available simulation exercise called BAFA, BAFA.[16] This exercise has some similar elements to the cross-cultural role play of a parent open house. It requires at least two hours, some financial resources, and extended preparation time for the trainer, but it is an activity well worth this investment if one frequently trains on cross-cultural sensitivity.

Strategy: An Integrated Preschool

Using a variety of props to simulate differing abilities, our colleague Wendy Harris taught us a simple role play to use for gaining insights into how an environment without adaptations for special needs children impacts their lives. To aid people in assuming the roles described below, we have them use props such as the following:

- sunglasses smeared with Vaseline (for visual impairment)
- cotton, earplugs, or mufflers (for hearing impairment)
- thera-tubing of different lengths and weights with loops tied at each end (for stretching behind one's back from hand to foot or in various configurations to simulate differing physical conditions). Thera-tubing is available at most medical supply stores that carry materials for physical therapy.

Depending on the size of the group, we ask one or two people to play the part of teachers. We double up some of the children's parts to accommodate the size of the group. It helps to prepare name tags for each role so that people can be addressed as naturally as possible.

The teachers conduct a short circle time activity with a story and song, tell the children to engage in the play of their choice, clean up, and have snack time. As we hand out the parts below, we remind the group that a role play is different from the real experience and we need to caution ourselves if we think we really know what it's like to be this person. We ask participants to use the experience to gain some new insights for themselves, rather than try to win an acting award or get goofy in their participation because role plays can be somewhat awkward.

Kathy, teacher
You have worked with children for many years and are ready for a change of careers. Parents are getting so demanding. Children's needs are more and more complex. Although you have skills and experience, you are feeling frustrated and stressed out by your work.
You call the children to circle time and read a short story. Your co-teacher, Irene, leads them in a song. You then help the children choose an area for the free play time.

Irene, teacher
Although your experience with children is varied, you have never worked with children with special needs. You are fairly open minded and experiment all the time trying new approaches to involve children.
Your co-teacher reads a story, then you lead a song with movement. After the

song, have the children choose play areas. After a short time, you call children to clean up and come to snack.

Paulette, child

You are five and physically very coordinated. Your brain doesn't process things typically. Often you don't understand what other people say, but you are not sure what question to ask to clarify. You enjoy working with things as they are easier to understand than people.

Carol, child

You are three and a very verbal, curious, typically developing child. You recently started having mild seizures. It feels strange in your brain for a few minutes and you can't talk when you are having them. You aren't sure what is going on with you or how to describe it. You haven't started medication yet, as your parents don't understand what is going on either. After eating you tend to have less problems and, as you intuitively realize this, you start wanting a snack frequently.

Micah, child

You are four and a persistent person. You are visually impaired and hard of hearing. You also have balance problems so walking is difficult. You are inquisitive and like to explore everyone and everything with your hands.

Ira, child

You are five and more interested in adults than other children. You are bright and inquisitive. You are able bodied but a late walker and somewhat "tactile defensive." You do not like touching things with your hands or putting pressure on them at any time. You also do not like anyone to touch you. Standing on your feet sometimes feels uncomfortable. You like only bland, untextured foods.

Richard, child

You are four and have a feisty personality. You recently learned to walk and need a great deal of support from furniture, walls, or people. You need something sturdy to help you get from a crawling to a walking position. You are very bright and you are hearing impaired. You do not speak and signing is difficult. Although you understand signs, your coordination is challenged.

Vanessa, child

You are five and a very philosophical but shy person. You are typically developing. You have a younger sister who is hearing impaired and has cerebral palsy. You have learned to sign quite well. Sometimes you worry about your sister or other children. You want everyone to feel included. Other times you just want to play by yourself.

Ken, child

You are four and very observant. You are typically developing in all areas. Your family's home language is Lao and you have lived in this country for six months. You speak this language fluently at home and are feeling shy about speaking English at school. You are beginning to understand what's going on, just by watching closely.

Trisha, child

You are four and have an agreeable, but tentative character. You wear glasses that do not correct your tunnel vision. You sometimes have balance problems but can sit and walk independently. Just recently you figured out running and jumping and you really want people to help you do these activities as much as possible.

Gabrielle, child

You are four and have a very difficult time with focusing your attention. Loud noises and bright lights startle you and make you cry. Also you are afraid of strangers. You like being held and soothed. You also enjoy moving quickly from one activity to the next.

Billie, child

You are four and have recently learned to walk independently. With a mild case of cerebral palsy, you don't have good control over your head, hands, or feet. When you talk, swallow, and eat you don't have very good control over your tongue. You still need a lot of help eating. Still you are a very happy and agreeable child who is eager to make friends and do many things.

Billie's mom

You are pleased that this program is integrating Mickey and you plan to volunteer for a while until you think the teachers and children know how to work with him. You help Mickey get around to different parts of the room and feed him at snack time. You want the other children to accept Mickey and treat him normally. You want them to learn when and how to help him. You help out other kids as needed also.

Trung, child

You recently turned five and have had typical cognitive, physical, and emotional development. Your hearing is normal. However, you are apractic (without speech) and this makes social interactions very difficult. Other people treat you as if you are hearing impaired or do not understand what they are saying. You are a bit shy, but you want to be included and have friends. You take initiative in doing things. You sometimes withdraw when people don't treat you right.

After the role play has gone through the snack time, we step in and bring it to a close, asking everyone to put the props away and return to their seats. To begin the debriefing discussion we ask each person to take a moment for self-reflection. How did you feel during this experience? What messages did you learn about yourself from how people treated you?

After a few minutes of silence to think about these questions we open up the discussion. After participants have all had a chance to speak, we ask them what they noticed about the others in the role play. Who were they drawn to and who did they avoid and why? What did they need to feel and be successful in this classroom?

The experiences people share provide an opportunity to discuss issues of fostering self-esteem, social interactions, and friendships among children. It is also useful in considering adaptations needed for different children, whether this be modifying equipment or activities for them to participate as successfully as possible.

Activities such as this one not only get attitudes out in the open (do we see this child's deficiencies or capabilities first?), but also lead to consideration of specific strategies and adaptations that make a program truly inclusive.

Strategy: Losing Beans

To help counter the bias against low income, unemployed, or welfare recipients, we use an activity adapted by Beverly Sims from the Fair Budget Action Campaign's welfare simulation exercise.

I learned some very valuable ideas in this class and a reminder to try to see things through someone else's eyes. You truly can't "judge a book by its cover."

John, teacher

We create table charts with squares designated for needs in the areas of food, housing, utilities, clothing, furnishings, transportation, child care, insurance, grooming, recreation, gifts, savings, and other choices. Participants are divided into groups of four and told that they represent a family—two parents and two children.

FOOD
a. Included in housing costs (room and board).
b. Cook at home; dinner out once a week. ☐☐
c. Purchase frequent fast food lunches and
    weekly dinner out: cook other meals. ☐☐☐
d. Purchase all meals away from home. ☐☐☐☐

HOUSING
a. Live with relatives or in public housing. ☐
b. Share apartment or house with others. ☐☐
c. Rent a place of your own. ☐☐☐
d. Other (ex. - buying home). ☐☐☐☐

They are given eighty beans, dividing them as they'd like among the squares on their chart. We encourage the small groups to discuss options and allow time to make decisions as to how to use their resources. Once everyone has their beans allotted on the squares, we ring a bell and make an announcement, telling them that due to current economic conditions one parent has lost their job. The result is an immediate loss of thirty beans. We tell them we are coming around to collect these beans and they must decide which squares to take them from.

Participants are told that while the laid-off parent looks for work, the second parent changes jobs moving from part-time to full-time employment so they still have income. A few months later this parent becomes ill and the family immediately loses thirty more beans. We remind them that they must make some immediate decisions as we are coming around to collect these beans. With both parents out of work, the family is now living on disability assistance. After a few more months the disability money runs out and they shift over to welfare assistance, resulting in a loss of another five beans.

By the time we have gotten to this point in the activity, many have thrown in the towel and found it impossible to continue. We begin the debriefing by telling them that the initial allotment of beans was based on our state median income guidelines of $4,000 for a family of four, with each bean equal to $50. How did they feel in the beginning? As the first cutback occurred, how did they choose what to give up? Were there disagreements? As conditions steadily worsened and more beans were lost, how did your families cope?

There is often a variety of responses with some families arguing and nearly breaking up, while others continued to pull together and agree upon sacrifices. When we ask what new insights people now have about welfare recipients, there are often comments about how people now understand why "those people live the way they do."

The culture of poverty is one about which many have misinformation and stereotypes. This activity helps to identify some of the circumstances that lead to ways of living others in more privileged situations criticize.

STORY TOOLS

Strategy: Consider this Scene

Drawing on some of our own experiences, as well as those described by Janet Gonzalez-Mena, Jim Greenman, and Rayko Hashimoto, we have created scenarios for teachers to discuss and represent to each other in a training session. The representation can be in the form of a role play, chart, diagram, or drawing.

One of each of the scenarios below are given to small groups with the following instructions:

As a group, discuss the scenario in light of the following questions. Prepare a brief representation of your group's discussion to present to the whole class.

- How does this situation look to you in terms of NAEYC's definition of developmentally appropriate practice?
- What values do you see at work here on each person's part?
- Could there be a cultural orientation underlying each set of values?
- How might this program work to address the issues here?

Happy Times Child Care Center

Happy Times is a center that believes kids should get dirty and be little explorers. It has a wonderful adventure playground. However, one of the parents has been complaining saying, "I don't want my daughter playing in your sandbox. I spent an hour and a half fixing her hair and two minutes after she's outside, her hair is filled with sand. I can't get that stuff out and we spend our whole evening trying to clean it up. So, please, keep her away from that sandbox and any other place on the playground where she's going to get dirty."

The teachers are frustrated with this and feel they need to educate the parent. Their response is something to the effect of, "Gee, that's too bad. But we wouldn't ever want to limit a child on the playground." Behind this parent's back they mutter, "That's outrageous. That parent only cares about her daughter's appearance and doesn't understand good child development."

Potty Time

A mother and a caregiver are engaged in an intense discussion. "I just can't do what you want," says the caregiver. "I don't have time with all these other children to care for. Besides," she adds hesitantly, "I don't believe in toilet training a one year old."

"But she's already potty trained!" the mother says emphatically. "All you have to do is put her on the potty."

"I really don't think she's trained." The caregiver's voice is still calm but a red flush is beginning to creep up her neck towards her face.

"You just don't understand," says the mother, picking up her daughter and diaper bag and sweeping out the door.

"No. You're the one who doesn't understand," mutters the caregiver, busying herself with a pile of dirty dishes stacked on the counter.

Nap Time

A family enrolled their baby in an infant center. The baby had never slept by himself before, and when he was put into a crib off in a quiet, darkened room, he became very upset. It wasn't the ordinary upset mood of a child who was resisting going to sleep. It was a panic reaction of a child who was fearful of the situation. No matter what the staff tried to do to help this child sleep alone, nothing worked. He would sleep only when near someone, in the midst of the activity of the playroom. Being by himself was an unfamiliar and fearful situation for him.

The director reminded the caregivers that licensing requirements say that infants must sleep alone in a crib in a room separate from the play area, so they will just have to keep working on this until the baby learns to fall asleep there.

Let's Eat

A mother comes to pick up her son from a family child care home. She enters the room to find him seated, waving a spoon in the air with one hand and jamming mushy cereal into his already full mouth with the other. She hurries over to him, frowning. She gruffly says to the caregiver sitting by him, "Where's the washcloth?" She takes the cloth handed to her and, as she briskly cleans up her protesting son, she mumbles under her breath.

Though she hasn't exactly heard the mumbling, the caregiver gets the idea that the mother is upset with the scene. While helping another child clean up, she tries to talk to this woman about self-help skills and sensory experiences for babies, but the angry mother's back is turned to her as she works to clean up her son. She finally gets his hands and face clean, but even with a bib, his clothes show signs of the food he has just enjoyed. The mother hurriedly changes her son's shirt, which now clearly clashes with the pants he is wearing. She looks at the outfit and shakes her head in disgust.

As the mother bustles out the door with her child, she is obviously distressed. She doesn't even say good-bye.

The caregiver, angry herself by now, sits down for a minute to cool off before attending to the other children.

No Baby Talk Here

When the director walks into the baby room with a prospective new parent, the three caregivers are all sitting together at one end of the room on the couch and rocking chair talking to each other about a TV show they have seen. Several hold babies on their laps, but they don't talk directly to them. Other babies are crawling around exploring and one is asleep in the swing.

One of the caregivers stands to acknowledge the director and parent. She relates the details of the great show they have been discussing. As she talks with the director and parent, she picks up a crawling baby and bounces her in her arms. Everyone in the room seems happy and calm. The parent observes that the caregivers seem to notice what is going on around the room, though they are obviously more focused on each other than on the children. As she's leaving she tells the director she thinks she should get a better trained staff for that room. "They obviously don't know how to give the attention that babies need." The director looks puzzled and disappointed. She had hoped this family would enroll in her center. It would make the program a bit more diverse.

Head Start Graduation

Jamie, the new education coordinator, was eager to meet with the committee of parents and teachers to plan the year-end activity for the children and families who would be moving on to kindergarten in the fall.

She opened the discussion with, "Let's all share some ideas of what we might do to celebrate the ending of school in June." (Personally, she was hoping for a family picnic in a park.) Pat, an active parent participant, immediately said, "Oh, every year there's a really neat graduation ceremony and I've been waiting for my son to be one of the ones who gets a diploma."

Another parent chimed in, "Every class does a song or dance and puts on a great program. We can help sew the caps and gowns for the children if the teachers will write something special on each child's diploma."

A teacher adds, "Oh, sure, we always do that. This is one time that all the families, even the aunts, uncles, cousins, and grandparents who live around here, show up. They just love it." Other parents and teachers chime in with equally enthusiastic comments.

Jamie, trying to speak calmly says, "But do you really think a graduation program is appropriate for four and five year olds? I think all the time put into getting kids to do a program could be much better spent, especially with the weather getting warmer." There was an awkward, tense silence.

Each of these scenarios reflects clashes in the views and values of how things should be done with young children. We find that, even with homogeneous groups, the discussion brings out differences. Exploring the *why* behind the conflict is key to building respect. Participants usually need 15 to 20 minutes to discuss differences and another 10 to 15 minutes to decide how they want to represent their understandings of the scenario to the rest of the group. We usually bring a box of props that could be used for those doing role plays.

We debrief the presentation of each group by first exploring the underlying reasons for the clash and noting them on chart paper. We then introduce the basic elements of good communication and problem solving—active listening, paraphrasing, perception checking, and using "I" messages as a way to further analyze how each scenario could be handled with openness and respectful communication.

Strategy: Gina's Story

We've created a persona doll story about a child in a wheelchair to sensitize teachers to the experiences of such children as they begin to integrate into classrooms. This story can also be adapted for use directly with children to either prepare them for including a child in a wheelchair or to expose them to this way of living and address any discomfort or bias they might have.

Our favorite persona dolls come from People of Every Stripe in Portland, Oregon; we've found a realistic and sturdy doll wheelchair through Global Village Books and Toys in Santa Monica, California. See the Recommended Resources section for more information.

Gina's Story

Once upon a time there was a five-year-old girl named Gina who couldn't walk. From the time she was very young, she learned how to move in a wheelchair. She could start, turn, stop, and make her way around people and things. She got very good at using her wheelchair.

For several years Gina's grandmother took care of her while Gina's mother went to work. Recently, Gina and her mother decided that it was time for Gina to go to a child care center where she could play with other children and make new friends.

Gina and her mother went to visit Happy Place Preschool. It was a sunny morning when they arrived and some children were out in the play yard. Gina looked closely but didn't see any other children there who used wheelchairs. She was excited to see the ramp that led up to the door and pointed out to her mother that the ramp would make it easier to come here every day.

Mrs. Butler, the women who talked with Gina and her mother, was nice. She said she thought Gina would like Happy Place because it had been built to help people in wheelchairs move around. As Mrs. Butler took them on a tour, Gina noticed that the hallways and rooms were large enough for her to get

This workshop has served in developing in me an awareness of diversity that wasn't there before. I was ignorant and had tunnel vision as far as seeing others' plight in our society. I must have the lives and cultures of the children I serve represented in the classroom. . .sprinkled all around to validate their person and worth.

Mary Ann, teacher

From this series of classes my eyes have really been opened to how biased our classrooms can so blindly be. I have also realized that I take for granted the privileges that I have as a white woman.

Claire, teacher

None of us can say we are not biased—I think everyone of us is, in some way and to some degree. Anti-bias work will be ongoing, a kind of life-long task, but we are seeing more and better tools to work with towards our goal.

Margo, teacher

through. Mrs. Butler explained that no one who used a wheelchair had come to the center before, so the children would probably be curious about Gina and her wheelchair.

Gina was a little nervous as they entered the first classroom. She knew the children would probably stare at her. Would they come talk to her and be her friend?

When Gina wheeled herself into the room, the children didn't notice her at first. They were busy playing around the big room doing all kinds of fun-looking things. When some of the children saw her, they stopped playing and stared. One ran over to tell the teacher. Then a couple of the children came up to Gina's chair to look at it more closely and touch it. When Gina smiled one child started poking at one of the wheels. Gina's mother asked Gina if she wanted them to give her a push in her chair. "Not now," said Gina. "Let's go see another room." The children said good-bye as she left.

When Gina entered the next room the children noticed her right away. They watched her closely as she moved slowly around the room. Mrs. Butler introduced her to two girls who were playing with blocks. One of the girls asked, "Why are you in that chair?" Another said, "My grandma has a chair like that." More children came over with questions. "Do your legs hurt you?" "Did you get hit by a car?" "When will you get better?" Gina and her mother tried to answer all of the questions.

One little boy stayed as far away from Gina as he could. When Mrs. Butler tried to talk to him and bring him to meet Gina, he started to cry and ran away. Another boy said, "Oh, he's just acting that way 'cause he doesn't want to play with no weird girl."

Gina heard what the boy said and looked like she was going to cry. Mrs. Butler suggested to two girls that they make room for Gina at the playdough table.

After telling the story, we ask teachers what they might be feeling if this were their room. We encourage them to be honest, sharing their own fears and concerns. We sometimes write responses on a three-column chart paper, with column one headed by "Own feelings," column two "Gina's feelings," and column three "Parent's feelings." As we consider these, we then move on to talking about and listing strategies for including Gina into the life of the classroom.

Cultural sensitivity requires wrestling with preconceived notions, stereotypes, judgments, and unresolved conflicts. A curious disposition and one that delights in diversity help us engage in this process. Sharpening listening and observation skills and practicing this role deepens our understanding and keeps judgments at bay. The above training strategies, along with the strategies of "Sensitivity theater" in Chapter 6 and "Examine group identities" in Chapter 9, have repeatedly proven to enhance culturally sensitive child care. Though distinct from what is typically viewed as an anti-bias curriculum, we see cultural sensitivity as a key component of anti-bias practices.

Chapter 14
Specific Training on Anti-Bias Practices

Dear Teacher:
I am a survivor of a concentration camp. My eyes saw what no man should witness:

Gas chambers built by learned engineers. Children poisoned by educated physicians. Infants killed by trained nurses. Women and babies shot and burned by high school and college graduates.

So, I am suspicious of education.

My request is: Help your students become human. Your efforts must never produce learned monsters, skilled psychopaths, educated Eichmanns.

Reading, writing, arithmetic are important only if they serve to make our children more humane.

Haim G. Ginott, *Teacher & Child: A Book for Parents and Teachers*[17]

A brief look at the history and the circumstances of today's world obliges us to consider how to right the wrongs and raise each new generation of children with a commitment to peace and justice. Education is never neutral or value free and the young children our profession is built around are in their critically formative years. Our task is to care for and educate them so that they will not only survive, but thrive.

We have lofty and sometimes seemingly contradictory goals. We want to assist children to like and respect themselves as well as others; to grow to function successfully in the world while simultaneously changing it to a safer and more equitable place. When done thoughtfully, anti-bias practices hold promise for just that.

UNDERSTANDINGS NEEDED
An anti-bias curriculum is more of an approach than it is a set of lessons. Louise Derman-Sparks suggests four goals for this approach and these can guide activities as the teacher plans and responds to emerging events in the classroom.

1. Foster each child's growing personal and group identity and self-esteem.
2. Build comfort and empathy with those who are different.
3. Foster critical thinking about bias.
4. Encourage children to stand up for fairness.[18]

We've found that before teachers can implement an anti-bias approach, they must acquire some basic understanding. First, they need to see how this approach differs from a multicultural one that is more like a tourist visiting various cultures. One of the ways we convey the difference in these approaches is with a discussion of two contrasting diagrams of circles and arrows.

In a tourist approach, we stand in the center of the circle and look out at all the various cultures of the world. We may have a genuine interest in learning

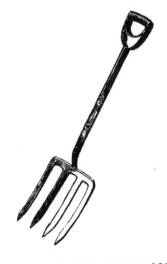

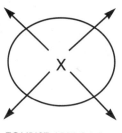

TOURIST APPROACH

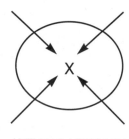

ANTI-BIAS APPROACH

about other cultures, but we still see ourselves as the center of things, or as what is "normal" or "the truth," while the others tend to be different or even exotic.

In an anti-bias approach to multiculturalism, we stand along with all the others around the circle, looking together at different things in the circle, for instance how families look and live and the kinds of transportation, homes, or musical instruments they have. This diagram represents one level of difference between an anti-bias approach and one of multicultural tourism. In terms of the levels of culture formulated in Williams and De Gaetano's book *Alerta,* which we discussed in Chapter 13, these two approaches look at the *what* and *how* of cultures, but in the tourist approach, the *why* is often neglected. A tourist approach and an anti-bias one share the goal of exposing children to differences, but they do so from different perspectives.

The *why* of cultural differences represents different values, belief systems, and positions in the structures of power that govern people's lives. An anti-bias approach has this understanding at its core and seeks to convey this so as to foster critical thinking in children and encourage them to work for justice.

To implement an anti-bias approach, teachers also need to know the developmental tasks of children at different ages. Including this information is an important aspect of Derman-Sparks' *Anti-Bias Curriculum.* Knowing the developmental task helps teachers recognize the questions and themes children are grappling with so as to better understand their interests, comments, and confusions.

Child development knowledge reminds us to keep anti-bias activities focused on the child's developmental stage, which at the preschool level means introducing abstract concepts through concrete experiences. We must avoid the tendency to build curriculum primarily around teacher "talk-abouts." Teachers fired up about anti-bias practices also do well to caution themselves about abstract moralizing and evangelizing. Whereas we want them to be watchdogs and whistle-blowers, we see this as distinct from becoming the "p.c. (politically correct) police" or vigilantes mounted on horseback.

An anti-bias curriculum approach advocates for cultural relevancy and bilingual programs in order to provide cultural continuity for young children not of the dominant culture. This is yet another way to counter bias and the injustice inherent in our society's current arrangements of power and distribution of resources. Thus, anti-bias classrooms may look different from one another as they work towards the four goals of this curriculum approach.

As discussed above, our training to build these understandings in teachers has gone through a number of changes. If we believe the most effective learning starts with who the learner is and what they bring to the learning process, this is absolutely essential when it comes to anti-bias practices. The strategies described reflect our efforts to involve teachers in examining who they are and what they already think while opening themselves up to learning from others.

In some of our in-service training work, we find teachers reluctant, if not resistant, to what they think is yet another formulation on how to approach multicultural education. This posture is especially true when a supervisor calls us in because she has decided that her staff needs anti-bias training, but the teachers themselves had not expressed a need. To be effective, we find we must not only appreciate these circumstances for teachers, but also offer activities that build a sense of pride in who they are as we invite them to look at issues of inequity and a possible role they might play. Here are further strategies towards that end, again arranged with the categories suggested in Section 2.

AWARENESS TOOLS

Strategy: What Is American Culture?

We often begin an anti-bias training by handing out large copies of an outline of a U.S. map to small groups. We ask them to work together to generate individual words or short phrases that represent American culture and to write these on the map.

We allow only a few minutes for this activity and find that the small groups often take different approaches. Some write associations with different regions of the country. Others disregard any regional focus, writing instead impressions from the media. There are those who focus on things they learned in school—mottoes and so-called historical facts. Still others emphasize customs and traditions, which represent positive or negative values for them.

The variations in responses help make our point during the debriefing so we intentionally keep this as an open-ended activity. As we ask each group to show us its list, we suggest they tell us the tenor of their discussion. "What kinds of things did you talk about? Were you all of a like mind?"

Our goal is to get a sense of how participants think of the United States, what understandings they might have of concepts such as oppression, exploitation, and culturally or commercially biased viewpoints. Looking over their lists with them, we categorize responses in terms of those that represent the mainstream or dominant culture values and viewpoints and those that don't. We remind them of how one-sided and biased are the definitions of American culture most of us carry.

Strategy: Walk Down Dominant Culture Way

To convey the idea that there is a dominant culture that marginalizes most who don't fit the narrow definitions of what is "normal" or "typical," we gather samples of things that represent this and put them on display boards. Our collection includes a variety of pictures from newspapers, magazines, and catalogs, greeting cards, wrapping paper, food packaging, travel and career brochures, and typical supermarket toys and coloring books. We also gather together props and posters from educational supply stores and a video with random snatches of TV shows and commercials. We emphasize to the group that we haven't gone out of our way to find these things; they are the typical images in our everyday life.

Looking at the images in the dominant culture from my pretend role as a girl in a wheelchair I saw nothing that I could relate to. Being this character has opened my eyes to how we need to step back and just observe things from different perspectives. Society puts limits on a handicapped person.

Ramona, teacher

Before participants look over our displays, we ask them to sit in small groups and then assign each an identity to assume as they walk down "dominant culture way." Small group members are to first discuss what they believe might be true about this person's life and, from the possibilities, briefly create a persona story about the person to have as their identity when they walk through the displays. The identities we use are listed below.

- European American five-year-old boy, living with his mother and father who are both professionals.
- Cambodian American four-year-old boy whose family recently came to the United States from a refugee camp and speaks no English.
- European American three-year-old girl living with her mother, father, and two brothers in and out of shelters and sometimes out of their car.
- Ukrainian American four-year-old boy whose mother, aunts, uncles, and grandmother moved to this town shortly before he was born. They speak minimal English and work at minimum wage jobs. The boy is in a wheelchair.
- African American four-year-old boy living with his mother and father who work in social services and his two sisters who are in elementary and middle school.
- Latina three-year-old girl living with her middle-class lesbian mothers and has never met her father.
- African American five-year-old girl living with her grandmother and aunt in a housing project.
- European American five-year-old boy living with his grandmother who works at a bowling alley.
- Native American four-year-old boy living in his third foster home with an unemployed European American man and a Native American woman who is a high school teacher.
- Biracial six-year-old girl who is overweight and lives with her Japanese American mother who works as a librarian. She regularly sees her Latino father who is a musician.

Ask the group to look at the displays through the eyes of their personas. We suggest keeping in mind the following questions, their personal child, and the child's parent(s). Suggest they make notes on their walk, returning to further discuss issues with their group.

1. What images of you and your life are reflected here?
2. What do these images tell you about yourself?
3. In what way do you feel part of a group here?
4. In these shoes, with this window on life, how are you feeling?

During the debriefing with the whole group, we ask each small group to briefly describe their persona and their experiences of walking down dominant culture way. During this we notice any stereotypes they may have built into their persona and comment on this.

We also highlight important points that may not have been made, such as who were the travelers and who were the service people on the travel brochures? What about the families of color who try to find an appropriate birthday card for their child? How might the Native American child feel with all the stereotyped caricatures on the birthday cards? The Cambodian American child with the images of Asians on the food packaging? The African American boy whose only role models are sports figures, entertainers, or gang members? The overweight biracial child with all the Barbie doll images of the magazines, media, and toys?

We always end this activity with a reminder that though they can't really understand what it is like to be in someone else's shoes, they can now walk through the world seeing things with a different set of eyes, keeping in mind the question "what's wrong with this picture?"

Strategy: The Label Game

This activity provides a quick reminder of the biases and injustices that pervade our lives. We prepare a stack of index cards, each with a "label" written on it. The labels range from derogatory to accurately descriptive or preferred terms and cover a wide range of categories. The ones we use include the following:

nigger	retard	slut
black	handicapped	women's libber
colored	deaf and dumb	witch
Afro-American	disabled	stacked
wetback	crippled	tomboy
slant eyes	four eyes	single mother
gook	spastic	bitch
Chicano	special needs	feminist
poor	faggot	chick
disadvantaged	gay	fundamentalist
at risk	homosexual	heathen
coolie	queer	pagan
working class	effeminate	Bible thumper
white trash	dyke	Nazi
illegal alien	senile	radical
boat people	old codger	commie pinko
hobo	senior	capitalist pig
homeless	elder	hippie
underprivileged	chrome dome	yuppie
culturally deprived	pip-squeak	freeloader

We arbitrarily pass out cards to each person, asking them to circulate around the room trading cards until they find three they are comfortable with for themselves. We intentionally leave the term "comfortable with" vague because the different interpretations of it prove fruitful in the discussion that follows.

After five minutes we call the group together to discover what we have learned about ourselves. There are several good questions to open up the discussion: "Is everybody happy with the cards that you now have?" "Which cards were the easiest to keep and why?" "Which did you feel the most uncomfortable with?" "Tell us what you understand about that."

The range of experiences and viewpoints that flows from this provides an immediate entree into discussions about diversity, biases, and injustice. Looking at the origins of some of the labels provides further insights. For instance, the term "handicapped" evolved because people with disabilities were on the street with their caps in their hands, outcasts in society, dependent on a few coins from others to survive. "Faggot" actually means a small stick used to start fires and has come to refer to gay men because they were used as kindling when witches were burned at the stake. This term, like the word "black," began as a derogatory one, but has been claimed by those in these groups as a source of pride and determination in maintaining their identity.

After summing up what we've learned about the pervasiveness of bias in our society, we often follow this activity with a few moments of silence, asking everyone to think back to their childhoods to capture their first memory of noticing someone who was different from themselves or feeling different from those around them. From these memories we can recognize how young children feel when they notice others and how easy it is to be afraid of differences or absorb negative connotations.

Strategy: Basis and Forms of Bias

Many people associate the concept of bias with stereotyping or name calling. We want to alert teachers to the many other forms bias can take, so that they can be aware of these in their classroom practices.

This activity is primarily a brainstorming one and it is a good follow-up to the label game previously described. First we ask people to list the kinds of attributes upon which bias is often based. People usually call out such things as race, skin color, sex, and age. With time and a bit of reminding, the list quickly grows much longer to include things listed below.

We then ask people to call out the forms or ways bias gets expressed. We allow time for the list to grow and it often ends up including things we consider to be personal bias or prejudice. This gives us the opportunity to clarify the difference between biases that an individual may hold or act on and those that are woven into the institutions and structures of our society in a systematic fashion. We consider the terms "covert" and "overt" bias, and discuss how bias sometimes operates even when it may be unintentional. Here's a typical list that gets generated from this activity.

Bases of Bias

- race
- skin color
- ethnicity
- national origin
- sex/gender
- sexual orientation
- economic class
- education
- age
- physical ability and physical appearance
- religion
- language or linguistic patterns
- marital status
- family structure
- geography
- life-style
- political preferences
- health practices

Forms of Bias

- stereotyping/over-generalizing
- name calling
- exclusion/discrimination
- laws and legal sanctions
- language/vocabulary/literacy
- lock into historical context

- segregation
- invisibility/lack of representation
- red-lining
- distortion/misinformation/myths
- limit access to resources
- physical violence
- portray out of context
- silencing
- disenfranchising/dislocating
- ghettos/reservations/camps
- misrepresentation
- cultural domination

Strategy: An "Isms" Self-Portrait

From Louise Derman-Sparks we learned an activity that helps participants explore how each individual experiences societal privilege and/or oppression. It is also useful in exploring the way the various "isms" interconnect in each individual's life.

The activity begins by showing the group a chart such as the one below. We explain that each of us is in either a positive or negative relationship to the various "isms" as indicated by the "+" and "—" symbols above and below each word. In other words, a "+" stands for belonging to the dominant group with regard to this issue, members who have societal power and experience privileges; a "—" stands for belonging to the dominated group, members who experience societal bias or oppression with regard to this issue.

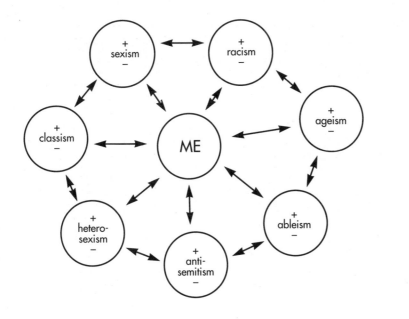

We ask each person to make two columns on their own sheet of paper, one headed with a "+" and the other with a "—." Using the chart we've reviewed, they are to write down which group they belong to, the dominant or dominated, regarding each area. They can add other categories as well. We often demonstrate with our own self-portraits to get them started.

Margie's "Ism" Self-Portrait

+	—
• white	• woman
• middle-class	• lesbian
• educated	• over 50 years old
• able-bodied	

Deb's "Ism" Self-Portrait

+	−
• white	• Jewish
• middle-class	• woman
• heterosexual	
• able-bodied	

Depending on the group, some may or may not want to share their self-portraits. The self-reflection alone will usually lead to a productive discussion on how each of us experiences a combination of privilege and oppression because of our membership in different societally determined groups. It helps people get away from guilt or the "my 'ism' is more awful than yours" syndrome.

A final step Derman-Sparks recommends for this activity is to add the component of individual self-esteem—how each person feels about their membership in the various categories. For this we ask people to indicate their personal feelings next to each item on their self-portrait by using the following symbols:

+ = I like this part of myself
? = I am confused about this part of myself
− = I don't like this part of myself
! = I am most identified with this part of myself

In looking at both societal categories and individual self-esteem, it is important to help people understand the differences and the connections between the two. One is created by society and deals with societal power, while the other is a function of the individual's personal experiences.

Strategy: The Trouble I've Seen

To encourage teachers to recognize bias, offer the following set of examples, posted around the room or as a set of large index cards passed around to choose from. Ask people to think of an incident they've seen that exemplifies this form of bias. Depending on the focus of the training, these incidents can be discussed in terms of how the incident reflects the larger social political context they see or possible ways of responding to such an incident.

• A fellow student, parent, or coworker is one of the only people of color in your group and rarely speaks or participates in activities without repeated coaxing.
• A child care program proudly claims to have a multicultural curriculum, designating a different culture each month as the theme focus.
• You are approached by several parents claiming that a coworker of yours holds biased views.
• You hear frequent remarks between children such as "Your eyes look funny. You can't play with us." "Only boys can play here. You can't come in." "He can't run fast enough. He's a faggot! He's a faggot!"
• A child of color repeatedly refers to herself as white.
• You often hear African American boys referred to as "a problem" and know they are frequently put on "time out."
• A coworker regularly refers to people with cultural stereotypes such as "She's a typical neurotic Jew." "She's Japanese. You can bet she'll be quiet and won't say

anything." "You know she must be a lesbian because she has trouble with men."

- A European American fellow student, coworker, or parent speaks regularly about special privileges "for those kind" and speaks continually of reverse discrimination.
- A person of color on your staff is repeatedly passed over when teachers are encouraged to apply for supervisory positions.

Bias takes many forms in our programs. Examples from this discussion may highlight some that participants may never have considered. Further examples may be discussed, such as a teacher using language, examples, and visual aides reflecting exclusionary practices: referring to all people as "he" and all families as "mommy and daddy," telling stories about people reflecting only European cultures, using visual images that reflect Caucasians accurately but caricature others. We often end this activity with the suggestion that participants keep these kinds of bias in mind as a mental checklist when they return to work in their programs.

Strategy: Face Those Feelings

Before integrating special needs children into a program, it is important to help teachers identify the range of feelings they may have.

We pass out pens and small pieces of paper and ask teachers to write a word on each that describes a feeling a parent or a teacher of a child with special needs might have. They can use as many papers as they'd like. We collect all the papers in a hat and pass the hat around asking each person to take a paper. Going around the group, we give everyone a chance to describe why they think a parent or teacher might have that feeling. The anonymity of this activity allows for honest discussions without fear of criticism and fosters empathy with the difficult feelings that often exist.

Feelings that typically get expressed include pity, compassion, excitement to learn a new aspect of diversity, incompetence, fear, frustration, exhaustion, and anger. Already under stress and underpaid, child care teachers sometimes resent being asked to take on yet another set of specialized responsibilities, often requiring extra hours of unpaid preparation and searches for resources. They need to hear this is a legitimate feeling. It is understandable that they are angry that their colleagues in the public schools get paid twice what they do. The frustration is especially acute knowing these colleagues have aides, therapists, or special education personnel to assist them and to provide lower ratios for individual attention.

More often than not there are staff members who eagerly embrace the opportunity to work with children with differing abilities. This is an asset to a staff, but it can also lead to growing tensions with those who don't share this feeling. Validating all the feelings involved is an important first step in approaching changes in attitudes.

Strategy: Words I've Heard

To help teachers recognize the bias about physical disabilities our language may reflect, we do a simple group brainstorm of a list of terms they have heard used to describe people who are differently abled. Typical terms that are mentioned in this activity include slow, crazy, nuts, deaf and dumb, handicapped, spastic, Mongoloid, four eyes, retard, gimp, and crippled.

We then ask people to share a story of when they first remember hearing one of these terms. This can lead to a good discussion about how quickly fear, judgment, and bias shape our views and language.

We conclude the activity by trying to get accurate descriptions and terms for the different physical conditions that are on our brainstormed list. Developing a set of preferred terms for a program to use enables teachers to speak with knowledge, ease, and respect.

ACTIVE TOOLS

Strategy: Examine Curriculum Collections

To help teachers concretely examine possible biases—particularly in the form of stereotyping or invisibility—in classroom materials they are using, we make use of old catalog pictures of toys and educational supplies. Cutting out examples and gluing them on individual index cards, we give small groups of participants a stack of cards to examine along with small red pieces of paper with the word "warning" printed on each. These are for use in noting concerns they may have about any of the materials. We also provide the following questions to guide their discussions.

1. Are there any forms of bias present (stereotyping, misrepresentation, omissions)? Consider such things as colors represented in the materials, groups of people, and gender role stereotypes.
2. Which of the materials would you eliminate? Why?
3. What else would you add to this collection to reflect an anti-bias classroom?
4. Are there any materials you would keep but use cautiously? If so, use a warning label to describe your concerns and recommendations for use.

As groups finish examining their collection of curriculum materials, we ask them to share with others any warning tags they have made and any additions they suggest to offset potential bias a material conveys. For instance, teachers typically discover that the colors black and brown are not often represented in the classroom and these need to be consciously added to the art area. Often little girls are only represented in frilly dresses, doctors and firefighters are only men, families always have a mommy and daddy and Native Americans are only in traditional costumes.

If these materials are to be kept in a learning environment for children, they must be offset with images that show girls wearing a variety of clothing, females in jobs traditionally limited to men, a variety of families, and Native Americans dressed and living in contemporary ways.

Strategy: Research What Children Notice and Think

In doing anti-bias work it is especially important to enhance teacher dispositions toward being curious about children, especially why they may speak or act in a discriminatory way. Toward that end we have drawn on the suggestions of Patricia Ramsey in *Teaching and Learning in a Diverse World: Multicultural Education for Young Children* (Teachers College Press, 1987) to create an activity for teachers to research what children notice and think about differences.

First participants will need a set of pictures that represent diverse people—a range of cultural, racial, income, and family groups. These can be cut from magazines or purchased from educational supply stores. Participants are to use these pictures, presenting them informally to children over a period of time in their classroom or someone else's classroom.

At first teachers should put the pictures out and invite the children to tell stories about them. We remind teachers that the goal is not to try and teach about differences, but rather to learn what the children already think. We suggest they keep the setting and activity informal, perhaps as a choice during their activity or small group time. They should allow the children to talk together as independently as possible about the pictures, following their conversation and actions with a tape recorder or note taking, and only occasionally asking questions to determine more of the children's thinking.

Any questions should be open-ended and casual, rather than seeming like a test or interrogation. Teachers can ask the children to describe all the things that they notice about a person in the photograph. Whatever the response, the teacher should simply say to the child "Oh," or "I see," making no judgment or response with their opinion.

On another occasion teachers should offer the pictures again, suggesting the children "put the ones together that go together," noting the things they say and criteria they use in grouping people. If they haven't mentioned their reasoning, ask, "Why do you think these people go together?"

A week or so later, put the pictures out again, casually exploring questions like the following: Which one looks like you or your family? Which of these might be friends with each other? Why? Who might not be friends? Why? Who would you like to be if you could be one of these people? Which of these people would you like to have as your friend? Why?

As the teachers document what the children say, we suggest they make note of such things as whether they make fun of or reject any of the people as being "silly" or "yucky" or do they appear curious and interested in knowing more. Were there any particular patterns of response they saw in individual children or in groups of children? How might they account for that? We remind them to

I had an experience a couple of years ago with one of the kids in my family day care. He was half black and half white. His mother, who was white, would not acknowledge that he was black. This little guy was so confused. I know this is going to affect him and his identity for a long time.

Carlos, family home provider

I've learned that there is more than just talking to the children. You must show them. After looking over my day care room, I realized that boys are valued more than girls. I will be making some changes so everyone who comes here feels valued.

Carmella, teacher

refer to the four-page chart "Goals and Developmental Expectations of Anti-Bias, Multicultural Curriculum for Young Children" that Louise Derman-Sparks included in her chapter in *Reaching Potentials: Appropriate Curriculum and Assessment for Young Children* (NAEYC, 1992). They can also refer to the chart we've created in appendix B.

After researching over a period of time, we ask teachers to either discuss or do reflective writing in response to the following questions:

• Did you have any preconceptions confirmed or unsettled?
• What surprised you?
• What insights and ideas does this give you for your future work with children?

Strategy: Adapting Circle Time

Integrating classrooms with special needs children is an honorable anti-bias practice, but one which teachers often balk at; they think they don't have the expertise or appropriate staffing to provide for the needs of these children and those of the rest of the group. Sometimes training on practical strategies for integrating these children will help teachers with their fears and bias. Colleague Randi Solinsky taught us this one.

Pass out the chart below, asking teachers to think of a circle time activity that they have done which would still work for each of these special needs children with little or no adaptation.

Child	Adaptation needed
• a child who is visually impaired	
• a child who is hearing impaired and uses American Sign Language	
• a child with CP who has limited use of her arms	
• a child in a wheelchair	
• a child with ADD who has limited ability to concentrate and sit still	
• a child who is DD and functioning as a two year old	
• a child who is hearing impaired and a child who is visually impaired	
• a child in a wheelchair and a child with CP	
• a child who is ADD and a child who is DD	

STORY TOOLS

Strategy: Explore the Developmental Task

In their eagerness to stop bias in their classrooms, teachers instead sometimes stop the investigating and exploring that children are doing in their efforts to understand similarities and differences. If we are to truly counter the development of bias in young children, we need to pay attention to the context of what is at issue for the child and work with that.

Drawing on the developmental tasks and goals woven throughout the *Anti-Bias Curriculum,* we have made a chart for teachers to use in formulating their responses to children's expressed bias. We distribute this for discussion and then offer scenarios to practice responses based on understandings from the chart. A copy of the chart we use is found in Appendix B. Alternatively, you can use Derman-Sparks' four-page chart referred to on the previous page.

In discussing the scenarios below, we ask participants to use the chart as a reference in considering the following questions:

1. What developmental tasks or themes do you see operating in the scenario?
2. What images and messages are influencing the child or children here?
3. Keeping the developmental task in mind, what would be some anti-bias practices for this scenario?

Weird Food

Nguyen Van Thu's grandmother lives with him and often packs his lunch for school. Today he has rice and vegetables while most of the other children have sandwiches.

Anthony says, "I got a sandwich. You got weird food."

The teacher says, "Thu's food is different than yours, Anthony. But look, Vinh has rice and vegetables just like Thu does. Their food's the same."
Thu says to Vinh, "Did you get that food from my grandma?"

Potty Time

Peggy Sue takes three children to the bathroom and reminds them to pull down their pants and sit on the potty seats.

Casey pulls down his pants and walks over to Maddie and helps her pull down her pants. He bends over to look at her genitals. She moves away a little. Casey follows her, still holding on to her pants and trying to see her more closely.

Peggy Sue says, "Get your hands out of her pants. Don't be dirty."

Dirty Hands

Jamal (an African American child) and Amanda (a Caucasian child) have just come from the bathroom washing their hands for lunch. Amanda says to Jamal, "Your hands are still dirty. You need to wash some more."

Jamal says, "My hands are clean."

Maria, the teacher says, "Amanda, that's not a nice thing to say to Jamal. We need to be nice to our friends."

Teachers usually also want to critique how the teacher handled the situation, but we hold that for the second part of the debriefing discussion. First we have them use the chart to determine what the child is trying to understand in each situation. Discussing this, we then offer suggestions as to how the teacher might have responded to better address the developmental theme the child was working with.

Strategy: Intervening When Bias Occurs

Many teachers are perplexed as to how to respond when children are exclusionary in their play or make biased statements. We offer the following guidelines and then practice using them with small groups discussing the scenarios below.

1. Do a pulse check/heart check/head check.
   • How is this situation making you feel?
   • What is your bias in this situation?
   • What do you want to have happen?

2. Do an environmental check.
   - What societal images and messages are influencing the children in this situation?
   - Is this setting conducive for discussion?
   - How will on-lookers be impacted?
3. Do a developmental check.
   - What developmental task is at work for the children here?
   - What can I say to affirm the identity of each person involved and acknowledge what might be true for each person?
4. Model empathy and empowerment.
   - How can I investigate rather than interrogate?
   - What will acknowledge the feelings of each?
   - What understandings of "fairness" can I build on here?
   - Can I relate this to any model for activism?
   - What will empower the victim of this bias?
5. Make a mental note for follow-up plans.
   - What images, materials, or activities can I insert into our classroom environment to counter this bias?

Classroom Scenarios to practice applying guidelines (adapted from Joan Newcomb and Kathleen McGinnis).

Scene 1: Toddler fear

You are the teacher in a toddler room. You have a two-year-old boy, Jerome, whose father is African American and whose mother is European American. Jerome often plays with Sam, who is European American.

When Jerome's mother picks him up, Sam is interested and friendly to her. When Jerome's father picks him up, Sam runs and hides behind a cabinet and peeks out cautiously.

Scene 2: Dramatic play

Matt, a five-year-old boy in your class, has lesbian parents. One day Matt is playing in the block area when Tanya comes over from the house corner and says, "Hey, Matt, we need a dad in our house. Will you marry me and be the dad?"

Matt says, "I'm busy. Why don't you marry Sarah and then you can both be moms."

Tanya replies, "Girls can't marry girls!"

Matt says, "They can so! My moms married each other. I got to eat cake at their wedding."

Sarah says, "Don't talk crazy, Matt!"

Scene 3: Car talk

Your class includes Karla, a four-year-old girl. Her family recently moved to the area and has been living in their car while the family looks for work and a temporary shelter with space. At snack time the children are describing their bedrooms to each other. Karla says she doesn't have a bedroom now and explains she lives in her car.

Another child says, "I saw a TV show about people who live in their cars. Those people are bad. They are illegal to be here. The police will put them in jail. It's true! I saw it on TV."

Scene 4: Help for mom

Kathy, a young mother, asks for your help in handling a family situation involving her son Tommy and his little sister. "My daughter Theresa is two years old," Kathy tells you, "and we adopted her when she was a baby. At first Tommy didn't seem curious about her background, but now that he is five he is asking a lot of questions. Recently, I was talking to Tommy about Theresa's Native American heritage and that she is a member of the Winnebago Nation. He listened patiently to my explanation and then looked up and asked, 'Mommy, when Theresa grows up, will she kill me?' I was so upset. What should I do?"

In debriefing these scenarios, we ask the groups what responses they felt comfortable with and where they were still unsure. We stress that there are no right answers and that each of us has to work on our own understandings of bias and child development to enhance our skills in handling these difficult situations. Self-awareness is key to this process and making mental notes for follow-up allows us more time to think and find appropriate ways to counter bias.

Strategy: Choices for Responding to Bias

Teachers are often more at ease in responding to bias in children than they are when parents or coworkers express bias. We build on an approach Jean Illsley Clarke takes in her book *Growing Up Again: How to Parent Yourself So You Can Parent Your Children* (Harper, 1989). Teachers have a set of seven choices in how to respond when adults express bias. After reviewing these, we ask people to work in pairs to share stories of bias expressed by parents and to practice identifying responses for each choice. This helps teachers begin to recognize answers that may be assaultive or defensive, as well as practice responses that may foster more awareness and sensitivity in the other person.

We walk them through an example that might go like this.

Story: A father comes to pick up his child and finds him in the housekeeping area, dressed in girls clothing and feeding a baby. He is clearly upset and comes to you saying he wants his son kept away "from that kind of play."

Choice of Responses:

- **Attacking:** We let children play wherever they want, why don't you?
- **Defending:** There's no way I could stop your child from playing dress ups.
- **Empathizing:** It's hard to see your child doing something you disapprove of.
- **Investigating:** Are you worried that he might get teased or picked on?
- **Reframing:** I'd like to understand what harm you think this might do to your child. From what I know, young children who are prevented from exploring their interests and identity in a supervised environment often grow up with confusion, if not shame about who they are.
- **Excusing:** Oh, don't worry, it's just harmless play.
- **Ignoring:** Excuse me, I'm needed out on the playground.

Choice of Responses:
- Attacking
- Defending
- Empathizing
- Investigating
- Reframing
- Excusing
- Ignoring

With each scenario we recommend teachers consider what their goal might be. If it is to put the parent on notice that they won't tolerate that kind of bias, one of the first two responses might get that point across. If they want to avoid much discussion or conflict, the last two responses might be appropriate. Usually our goal is to develop a trusting partnership with parents, sometimes informing or sensitizing them about our understandings and why we do what we do in our programs. This particular scenario calls for some combination of the middle three responses.

A teacher in one of our trainings once commented that the first two choices have to do with oneself, the middle three with the other person, and the last two with no one. Many found that insight a useful understanding in making their choices.

Strategy: How to Decide on Integrating a Child

With the passage of the Americans With Disabilities Act (ADA), many child care programs are faced with tough decision making on whether their program can accommodate children who are differently abled. The task of making a facility wheelchair accessible or ensuring someone on the staff knows American Sign Language (ASL) may seem foreboding enough, but those provisions alone will hardly meet the needs of a child who is wheelchair-bound or hearing impaired in a truly anti-bias manner.

For a child with differing physical abilities, there is a range of adaptive equipment to take under consideration to meet developmental needs and to care for a child with respect and dignity. For example, what aids are needed to give the child the most independence and ability to pursue interests, communications, and friendships? Are tables at a height to accommodate a wheelchair so that a child can eat and work alongside classmates? How will dignified diapering occur for older children who have no ability to use a toilet? Does the playground include discovery, social, and physical opportunities for children with physical disabilities?

Developmentally appropriate quality programs for children meet their social-emotional and cultural needs, as well as their physical and cognitive needs. All children need role models and images of people who look and live as they do as part of their learning environments. Children who are hearing impaired, for example, require communication and social interaction with more than one teacher who knows ASL. To meet their cultural as well as communication needs, a program should have a TDD (telecommunication device for the deaf) and flashing light system to alert these children to the ring of a telephone alarm.

In helping programs weigh all the considerations, we use the following chart and descriptions of children created by colleague Randi Solinsky. In small groups we ask teachers to go through each column, noting what adaptations would be needed to meet the needs of each of these children.

	Physical Adaptations	Curriculum/ Materials	Staffing	Special Training	Resource Identified	Policies and practices modified
Lupita						
Jamal						
David						
Kyle						
Tanika						

Lupita

Five-year-old Lupita needs child care half days only. The other part of the day she attends a program for children with special needs in the public school. Transportation is provided by the school district. Lupita has Down's Syndrome.

Lupita has language abilities but more often gestures to get her needs met. She enjoys dramatic play and joins in at group time in songs and games. Her thinking skills are delayed at about thirty months. This means she can easily follow one part instructions but becomes confused with more complex tasks.

Lupita has a mild heart defect that does not interfere with her activities but requires regular medical follow-up. No medications are indicated.

She drinks from a cup and finger feeds herself well and is learning to use utensils. She is fairly independent with toileting, needing assistance with buttoning up and some clean up.

Overall, Lupita is charming, social, and affectionate and seeks regular attention and affection from adults and children.

Jamal

Two-and-a-half-year-old Jamal is bright-eyed, active, and has a newly diagnosed hearing loss in the severe range. He needs full-time care now and will need half-day care in the fall when he will attend a special education preschool.

Jamal wears hearing aids that are new to him. He has had them for only two months. He needs help taking them off and on. He needs someone to be responsible for taking care of his aids when he is not wearing them, and replacing dead batteries when necessary. He also needs some extra understanding since hearing so many sounds is new to him and he sometimes becomes overstimulated and needs time without his hearing aids.

Jamal has unique language skills. He understands what is said to him by watching lips, faces, and body language and putting these together with what he can hear. With his hearing aids he hears some speech, but he will still use a combination of language tools. He is just being introduced to formal sign language (ASL), but because his parents aren't fluent in it, they would prefer he learn to vocalize. Jamal's language is difficult to understand but he has no difficulty letting you know what his needs are.

David

Six-year-old David has epilepsy and is developmentally delayed. He attends a half-day special education program where he has received services since two years of age. Because David's parents both work, he needs child care for half of his day.

David uses a cup and is able to feed himself with an occasional prompt from an adult, e.g. help him scoop. David's special education teachers are working with him on a toileting program that requires adult assistance five minutes every two hours.

David does not use words but communicates using objects and pictures. For example, his teachers help David with transitions by showing him a pump soap container when it is time for him to wash his hands; showing a tennis ball before going to the playground; and stomping feet before going for a walk. Additionally, David has a series of pictures of commonly used items that he carries with him.

David's epilepsy requires that he receive medication three times daily. However, David occasionally has seizures that cause him to drop to the floor. He wears a protective helmet to prevent injury. David is able to walk on his own. David's parents are knowledgeable about his disability and want very much for him to be around typically developing children of a similar age.

Kyle

Kyle is an extremely active and somewhat aggressive four-year-old. In the classroom he is always on the go and moving fast. He enjoys outside activities and playing in the gym.

Kyle understands everything that is said to him, even if he doesn't always respond. He definitely can make his needs known, although not always appropriately. He often needs help in using words instead of physical actions.

Any activity that requires Kyle to sit still, such as listening to a story or other teacher directed activities, is interrupted by Kyle's outburst of sheer physical energy. But his remarks at group time, though sometimes inappropriately timed, are intelligent and thoughtful.

When frustrated Kyle becomes angry. He may throw blocks at a child who is not building the way he wants or he may grab toys from other children. Kyle needs a lot of attention and patience. On good days, his exuberance is quite lovable.

Tanika

Meet five-year-old Tanika. She has a special florescent pink chair with wheels that helps her get around, and get around she does! She is active and friendly and loves to play outdoors with other children. She needs child care before and after her half-day kindergarten class. Tanika has a little sister, age three and a half, who also needs full-time child care. The family wants the girls to be in the same setting.

Tanika has a type of cerebral palsy called spastic diplegia, which means that primarily her legs are affected. Her legs don't move smoothly. They are still and jerky so that she is unable to walk without much assistance.

Tanika is intelligent, loves to read, and has good communication skills. Her jerky movements sometimes frighten people and this makes her sad.

Tanika has strong arms from working her wheelchair and from pulling herself along on the floor. She can get out of her chair without help but needs help to get back in. She needs help with transferring to the toilet but is getting closer to being independent all the time. Tanika needs someone to understand how her chair works, including how to adjust it and how to fold it up to put in a car. She wants to go on the field trips too.

In training for anti-bias practices, our task is to address attitudes, practices, and structures of power. No one training will bring about change in these areas, but a consistent focus that provides a safe and trusting climate encourages people to move along in this journey. While we work to integrate aspects of addressing diversity in all of our training, we also urge teachers to seek out ongoing opportunities to specifically focus on different forms of bias. In this way, dispositions as well as skills are developed in embracing diversity.

Chapter 15
What to do about Holidays

Perhaps one of the most agonizing aspects of doing an anti-bias curriculum is determining what to do about holidays. We receive continual requests for consultation and training on holiday policies and curriculum practices. Some programs have gone the route of trying to include the major holidays of all cultures and religions, while others have decided to banish all holiday celebrations from their programs.

Over the years of extensive reading and working with hundreds of teachers on this topic, we've put together a set of principles to guide teachers in discussions and planning. Particularly useful to us in this process has been the unpublished thesis of Julie Bisson done as part of her Masters degree work with Pacific Oaks College.[19] Bisson interviewed respected early childhood specialists with a commitment to anti-bias practices around the country and discovered a range of approaches, each striving to honor diversity while avoiding a tourist or holiday centered approach to curriculum planning. The principles we offer draw on ideas from a number of such sources, alongside our own convictions about what humans need across all cultures and spiritual practices—seasonal rhythms, wonder, reverence, ritual, tradition, celebration, and community.

Principles for including holiday celebrations

Principle 1: Cultivate a sense of time, seasonal rhythm, and wonder
• provide multiple opportunities to mark time
• offer experiences with deeper rhythms related to seasons
• cultivate a sense of wonder and mystery

Principle 2: Develop connections and classroom culture
• provide opportunities for meaningful connections between children and adults; and children, family, home, and the program
• invent rituals and celebrations as part of shared life together in classroom

Principle 3: Continually celebrate similarities and differences
• validate experiences of children, family, and staff
• enhance understandings of differences
• stretch thinking away from egocentrism
• teach critical thinking and activism regarding bias

Principle 4: Provide sensory experiences with cultural symbols and values
• enhance understandings of symbolic representations
• further ability to represent own experience

We believe celebrations are central to our humanity and therefore the emotions around holiday practices can be intense. We use a number of strategies to alert teachers to the roots of these strong feelings and to help them think through their goals and decision making about holiday practices. As with many of the other sections in this book, this topic could fill the pages of another whole book. What follows are some examples of strategies that have been particularly

useful to get teachers started in approaching holidays with cultural sensitivity and anti-bias principles.

AWARENESS TOOLS

Strategy: The Best and the Worst of Times

As we approach the holiday season or begin a training on the topic, we often begin with a childhood memory activity. As described earlier, we remind participants that they will be asked to recall experiences from their younger years, but if those memories are too painful, they are welcome to choose something from their adult life. This statement is usually helpful to those who struggle with unpleasant associations regarding their childhoods, and it can also be an eye-opener for those who are unaware that many have this experience.

We ask people to work in pairs, each taking a turn to describe one of their favorite holiday celebrations while growing up. After six or eight minutes, ask participants to bring their discussion to a close. On chart paper with two columns, write "best" as the heading over one. Considering what they heard, ask pairs to call out, not the details of the story, but the elements of what made a holiday so special. After these are listed, ask participants to again talk with their partner, this time discussing one of their worst holiday memories. Debrief these stories similarly by listing the elements in the second column with the heading of "worst."

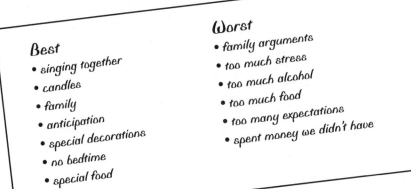

Best
- singing together
- candles
- family
- anticipation
- special decorations
- no bedtime
- special food

Worst
- family arguments
- too much stress
- too much alcohol
- too much food
- too many expectations
- spent money we didn't have

Often the same element, such as "family time" may turn up listed in both columns. A simple review of what is in each column illuminates why people have such strong, and sometimes conflicting, emotions around holiday plans. This awareness of the very different feelings people may have often enables participants to more thoughtfully consider curriculum built around holidays. End by circling the elements everyone would like to see included and noting the ones all want to avoid.

Strategy: Why We Do It

Another simple way to begin raising awareness concerning holiday practices is to ask the group to brainstorm. On chart paper develop a list of all the reasons why teachers build curriculum around holidays. This usually results in a mixture of things that are thoughtful and appropriate, and those that are out of habit and of some questionable value or problematic. For instance, a typical list that is generated includes such things as:

- it's fun
- it's easy
- a break from the daily routine
- easy to find curriculum activities
- teach traditions
- everyone does it
- pressure from parents
- way to teach about diversity
- important to me as a child
- the kids are all talking about the holiday

Sometimes we have to coax teachers to be honest in this brainstorming. Many feel hesitant to admit that they might do something because it's easy, fun, or offers a break from the routine. Even when they include something we feel is problematic, we add it to the list without initially commenting on it. Next we ask the group to brainstorm the problems they run into in doing holiday curriculum. As is often the case, issues brought up here are the ones we want to see discussed.

Teachers almost always have had some difficulties in doing holiday curriculum. Some agonize over the validity of doing a few holidays and not all, while others feel totally overwhelmed at the thought of having to create activities for holidays with which they are not familiar. Teachers tell stories of children being excluded from classroom holiday celebrations, either unintentionally due to lack of awareness or intentionally due to religious beliefs.

During this discussion we add our concerns if they haven't already been addressed. We especially want teachers to examine the dangers of relying on holiday curriculum activities to teach about cultures, reviewing some of the points previously discussed about the limitations of a tourist approach. Here we also summarize the different levels of culture *Alerta* outlines, noting that holiday curriculum usually emphasizes the *what* and sometimes the *how* of cultural practices, but rarely gives children insight into the *why*.

In many cases the *why* of a holiday practice is too abstract for young children and thus developmentally out of reach for them. For instance, what do children understand about wearing green and making shamrocks for St. Patrick's Day? Do the teachers even know the significance—or *why*— behind this or the tradition of leprechauns and pinching those not wearing green?

Most holidays are based on religious traditions or a particular political perspective on an historical event, yet in many cases teachers aren't clear about the origins, symbols, or values implied. Some try to sidestep the religious aspect, representing only the commercial or "Hallmark" elements of a holiday. This, in turn, is offensive to those for whom the holiday has special religious significance.

Some children get unwittingly singled out, either as examples of or exceptions to the culture the holiday is said to represent. For example, we heard a teacher say, "Saul's not like us. He's Jewish and he celebrates Passover instead of Easter. Jewish people eat matzo instead of bread." These incidents happen, not because teachers intend to isolate a child, but usually because they have only a superficial understanding of both the holiday and the cultural traditions from which it comes. Intended or not, the result is that the child, the holiday, and the culture easily become misrepresented and trivialized.

There are teachers who recognize that their holiday curriculum activities often go against the philosophy or curriculum practices of their program. Children are often asked to sit together as a group, all making the same art project modeled after the teacher's example. There is usually an emphasis on a product, rather than process, with expectations that each child should participate and conform.

Recognizing the range of possible problems and biases that easily get reinforced through holiday curriculum activities can leave teachers confused and overwhelmed. This activity is intended to alert teachers to these concerns, but not to leave them in the lurch. We often follow up this activity with at least one of the other strategies listed in this chapter, allowing time for them to talk through their feelings and concerns, as well as problem solve an approach to take.

We like to end this activity by asking teachers to list the aspects they do want to retain in their classroom holiday celebrations. This can become a springboard for developing an agreed-upon approach to holidays, and an opportunity to introduce the principles we suggest they consider.

Strategy: Images, Messages, and Meaning

We find that most teachers have not really examined the religious or historical origins and perspectives that most holidays represent. To provide awareness and discussion of this, and of specific holidays, we ask them to work in small groups to fill out the chart below. With four people in a group, each group can choose a holiday to discuss and make notations on the chart. When this is completed a whole group debriefing can be held.

	Holiday	Holiday	Holiday
Images:			
Prevailing Messages (consider historical origins, religious values, commercial, or economic interests):			
Why celebrated?			
Does this celebration reflect cultures of children enrolled?			
How is cultural awareness and sensitivity increased?			

During the debriefing we ask if anyone has holes in their chart, things no one in the group knew about the holiday. In that case we solicit information the rest of the group may have. We see which holidays have been considered and, with each, consider what various groups may have put on their charts. Each box on the chart gets to the heart of the discussion we want to have with teachers as they plan holiday curriculum.

ACTIVE TOOLS

Strategy: Analyzing the Curriculum

This activity works well following most any one listed above under awareness tools. It is based on analyzing holiday curriculum developed by two different teachers. We first give small groups of teachers "Holiday Curriculum 1" to examine with the discussion questions and when they have finished, we hand out "Holiday Curriculum 2" to analyze in the same manner.

The debriefing discussion allows teachers to identify the things they already know about how children learn best, as well as to integrate some new thinking about messages inherent in each of these monthly plans. This usually leads to introducing the principles that we think are useful to guide teachers in their planning.

Questions for analyzing the curriculum

- What does this teacher want children to learn from this curriculum?
- How does the teacher think the children learn?
- What are the sensory aspects of this curriculum?
- What are the values promoted? (consider religious, commercial, and diversity/divergent thinking)
- How do these curriculum plans draw on the children's daily lives and experiences?

Holiday Curriculum 1
Themes: scary things (witches, bats, black cats, spiders), trick-or-treat, costumes, party.

Art Projects:

Paper plate pumpkins: children paint plates orange and paste on black cutout shapes for face.

Construction paper spiders: children cut pieces of construction paper and attach them together for legs and body of spider. Hang with string around room.

Scary night: use crayons to draw a scary Halloween picture. Use sponge to wash over the picture with diluted black tempera paint.

Ghost print: use white tempera on black construction paper.

Stand-up pumpkins: use stiff cardboard to make construction paper pumpkins and use them for name tags or table places for Halloween party.

Trick-or-treat bags: children glue Halloween shape cutouts onto a painted paper bag.

Pumpkin accordion people: children accordion-pleat strips of black construction paper. Glue to a cutout jack-o-lantern shape. Hang with string around room.

Egg carton witch: using the egg section of the carton for the head, make a witch face by decorating it and attaching to cutout construction paper body.

Games and Movement Activities:

The old witch and the cat: one child is the witch; the others sit in a circle and are cats. The witch hobbles around the circle with a blindfold. One of the cats meow. The witch tries to guess who that child is.

Spiders and flies: three or four children are the spiders. The rest are flies. The spiders try to run after and catch the flies. When they catch them, they tag them.

Ghost, ghost, witch: a variation of duck, duck, goose.

Jack-o-lantern bean bag throw: make a cardboard jack-o-lantern. Have the children throw bean bags through the eyes, nose, and mouth.

Poems and songs: Halloween Time; Five Little Ghosts; Five Little Jack-o-lanterns; How Does a Goblin Go; Cackle, Cackle, Ugly Witch.

Cooking projects: spooky gelatin spiders; monster toast; witches brew; jack-o-lantern fruit cup.

Books: Little Witches Halloween Book; The Tooth Witch; The Halloween Party; Scary, Scary Halloween; Ghost's Hour, Spook Hour.

Room environment: commercial cutouts of jack-o-lanterns, cats, bats, spiders, witches, skeletons; spider webs hanging on wall with creepy bugs on it; children's completed Halloween art projects.

Special Activities:

Carving pumpkin: children help teacher decide what kind of jack-o-lantern face to have on a pumpkin and watch while it is carved.

Halloween party: children wear costumes from home (such as Native Americans, Batman, Ninja turtles, Barbie, Princess, and Bride); trick-or-treat within program classrooms; jack-o-lantern cupcakes, witches brew, and Halloween candy as party treats.

Holiday Curriculum 2

Themes: fall, harvest, end of the growing season (death); surprise, transforming materials, masks, dress up, role play.

Special Activities/Field Trips: go to pumpkin patch and apple orchard; children harvest their own pumpkins and apples to take back to classroom.

Sensory/Cooking Activities:

Pumpkin cutting: children each help cut their own pumpkin; explore the seeds, texture, smell, taste, etc.

Roasting and tasting pumpkin seeds.

Baking pumpkin pie, custard.

Peeling, coring, and washing apples.

Making applesauce.

Tasting, comparing different kinds of apples.

Harvesting, drying apples, herbs, and flowers.

Making and drinking teas (mint, chamomile).

Grinding and tasting spices (cinnamon, nutmeg, cloves).

Making and eating soups (pumpkin, squash, potato, vegetable).

Making and mixing potions (food color and water, oil and water, cornstarch and water, baking soda and vinegar).

Sensory table to include pinecones, leaves, cinnamon sticks, dried flowers, mint, nuts.

Cracking and eating nuts.

Black playdough scented with spices: cloves, cinnamon, vanilla, almond, peppermint extracts; some with glitter.

Classification and sorting:

Variety of apples, squashes, seeds, nuts, leaves, pinecones, herbs, and flowers to sort and classify.

Dramatic play/dress up:

Prop boxes with a variety of fabrics, scarves, hats, jewelry, shoes, capes, wands, and pouches. Children create their own costumes and dramatic play with the props.

Face painting: use nontoxic face paints; have mirrors, camera, related books about fiestas, carnivals.

Warm clothes: mittens, scarves, hats, quilts, afghans, boots in house corner.

Art Activities:

Collage materials including glitter, feathers, fabric, paper scraps; full range of paint colors; drawing and cutting implements and a variety of ways to attach things together, including glue, stapler, tape, hole punches, brads, yarn, and rings; papier-mâché to make masks.

Sample masks, pictures, and books displayed in area.

Music and movement:

classical music, blues and jazz, nature sounds, harvest and fall songs
move like animals, the weather, leaves, trees, etc.

Room Environment:

Objects from outdoors displayed for children to observe: dead vines, pinecones, gourds, pumpkins, nuts, seeds, dead plants, skeletons, bones, leaves.

Rotting and molding pumpkin; magnifying glass; small container for composting to watch decaying process.

Photographs of children on field trips to pumpkin farm and apple orchard with children's dictated stories of their experience.

Display table honoring people, pets who have died: photographs from home, dictated stories.

Books: *The Pumpkin Seed; The Little Old Lady Who Was Not Afraid of Anything; The Barn Dance; Rain Makes Applesauce; All For Fall; Frederick; Life-*

times; Tenth Good Thing About Barney; Pablo Remembers; To Hell With Dying; science and nature books about seasons, changing weather, harvest, bones, herbs; children's dictated stories.

Strategy: Worksheet for Decision Making

After teachers have done some self-reflection and examination of holiday curriculum practices, they are usually eager to have some guidelines to return to their program and use. We stress that these guidelines must be developed by each program and that the process of arriving at them is probably as important as the end product. Whereas we don't offer specific guidelines ourselves, we do give teachers some considerations to keep in mind and a worksheet for this undertaking.

Guidelines should give direction to what role holidays will have in the overall curriculum. They need to help teachers choose what is important to celebrate and what to avoid. Fitting holidays to the children and families in the program is key. Programs that are homogeneous may find ways to bring aspects of diversity through holidays, *if* holidays are not the only way they are trying to do this.

In our minds, guidelines can alert teachers to think in terms of contributing to the development of their classroom culture. They should enable all staff and family members who wish to be involved to do so. Guidelines should also make provisions for those who choose not to celebrate. It is important that no one be marginalized or stigmatized. And finally, effective guidelines will anticipate conflicts and tensions over holiday practices and indicate how these will be addressed.

With these considerations as a backdrop, teachers can work with parents to develop specifics for a particular program. To help them decide whether to include a given holiday, we review the four principles outlined at the beginning of this chapter and walk participants through the first round of a worksheet in indicating how any holiday curriculum might incorporate the four principles.

This worksheet might look like the example below, or any other form that clarifies thinking and promotes discussion.

	Principle 1	Principle 2	Principle 3	Principle 4
Holiday				
Holiday				
Holiday				

We conclude this by suggesting that for each holiday activity under consideration teachers ask:

• What do I want the children, families, and program adults to know?
• Why?
• What activities will contribute to this understanding?

STORY TOOLS

Strategy: A Book of Celebrations

Two of our favorite resources for sparking new thoughts about holiday celebrations are Byrd Baylor's book, *I'm in Charge of Celebrations* (Macmillan, 1986) and Bonnie Neugebauer's article, "Going One Step Further—No Traditional Holidays" (in *Child Care Information Exchange,* 1990, no. 74). These inspired us with the idea of having teachers work with children to create individual books of celebrations that stay in the classroom and get added to throughout the year. To convey the idea of how affirming this might feel for a child, we spend a training session having the teachers make a book of personalized celebrations for themselves.

Begin by asking teachers to talk in pairs to recall something significant they feel they have learned to do as an adult. As they talk, they should consider the feeling they had during this process, how they first recognized they had learned this, and the significance this accomplishment has meant to them in their lives. If they were to place it on a calendar, what date would it fall on? If they were to commemorate it each year, what might they do?

With book-making supplies, which include a variety of art materials, ask teachers to create a page for a book that describes this accomplishment as a holiday to be celebrated each year. Time permitting, they can recall another significant event or two from their childhood or adult life to add as pages to this book. Or this can be a follow-up assignment to bring back to the next meeting.

This activity can be concluded with a reading of *I'm in Charge of Celebrations* and a discussion on how this activity might be adapted for use in their classroom. And, of course, we remind them to keep adding to their own book and make these celebrations real in their lives.

PLANTING THE SEED

Early childhood education holds tremendous promise for raising a new generation with each child not only proud of their own heritage and identity, but committed to standing up against bias in all its many forms. With each teacher steadily moving forward in their own journey, children will be influenced to do so as well.

Our deepest personal passions move into our professional goals in the arena of cultural sensitivity and anti-bias practices. We want to impact not only those in our training and the children they care for, but the system of education and overall socio-economic and cultural conditions of our country. Our goal is not solely to see more diversity reflected in classrooms, but to get teachers to examine institutions and power structures, to raise questions about who gets to be in charge, and why, and to explore the roles we each play in upholding or undermining this structure in society.

Section 5
Training in Different Settings

*I*n recent years the early childhood profession has been acknowledging that, despite isolated efforts of good teacher education, the overall professional development picture is uneven in quality, haphazard in its conceptual framework, and uncoordinated in its delivery systems. This situation is highly problematic given the combined factors of an ever-shrinking pool of qualified teachers, the inaccessibility of early childhood education college programs, and the continuing low regard and compensation child care professionals receive.

Whether pre-service or in-service, teacher training typically occurs in three arenas:

• course work or classes
• on-site program settings through field coaching and during staff meetings
• workshops, seminars, or conferences

Gaining in popularity is teacher training through telecommunications. While we applaud efforts to use available technology in an effort to make training more accessible, we are eager to see it include more opportunities for active learning and practice, rather than just passing along information. Otherwise, this approach to teacher training will perpetuate the shortcomings of all the other arenas.

In most college settings, course work is isolated from field work. Classes tend to be taught in a vacuum of real experience, covering theory or methods that students have difficulty applying. When lab schools are part of a college program, students often comment that they are too ideal and foster unrealistic expectations for what a typical classroom of children is like. On the other hand, out in the real world of child care and preschool programs, the everyday demands of working with children leave little time, energy, or opportunities for exploration of theoretical ideas to enhance one's ongoing professional development. The design of the remaining settings—workshops, seminars, and conferences—offers no possibility to pursue teacher development with a consistent theoretical framework or body of ideas.

These problems have given impetus to the establishment of the National Institute for Early Childhood Professional Development, a laudable effort

launched by NAEYC to achieve an articulated professional development system for early childhood education.[1] While the institute is making reference to what constitutes good teacher training, its primary focus is on coordinating the delivery mechanisms towards a system of articulation. Our primary work complements this effort by focusing on the pedagogy of the training process, wherever it takes place.

Chapter 16
A Methodology
for All Settings

In any given month we typically work with teachers in each of the main settings —college classrooms, program sites, and conferences—using the same basic principles in all of our training. It was heartening to discover that what we've learned about successful training is substantiated in the findings of the High/Scope Foundation.[2]

The results of the High/Scope study suggest the key elements for the delivery of effective in-service training to be the following:

- Provide a focus over time, where knowledge is cumulative and follows a consistent theoretical framework.
- Actively involve participants through interaction with the trainer and each other.
- Allow time for reflection.
- Provide hands-on practice to try out new ideas and strategies.
- Follow up with observation and feedback and more opportunities for peer exchanges.

These are the basic elements we incorporate into most of our training. We draw our content from the body of identified core knowledge that defines our profession.[3] To narrow the focus of the topic for a training, we choose one or two big ideas to explore. As we plan training in any setting, we first refine the big ideas we have selected, perhaps by making a mental list of what we hope to see and hope not to see in a teacher's practice related to this consideration. This list is our version of a set of competencies or standards akin to the format found in Sue Bredekamp's *Developmentally Appropriate Practice in Early Childhood Programs Serving Children from Birth through Age 8* (NAEYC, 1987).

Our specific training plan or agenda for a session is influenced by the setting, but it always includes time for consideration of the ideas, activities to reflect on the participants' experiences and understandings to date, and opportunities to practice applying the ideas in collaboration with others. Our goal is to help teachers acquire a mind-set and methodology with which to pursue their understandings and skill development. In fact, the way we plan a training reflects the framework we want teachers themselves to be using as they construct their knowledge.

In Chapter 3 we outlined a framework we developed to explore any early childhood topic, involving a set of five examinations. By continually using this framework, we help teachers find a way to consider most any aspect of their work with children. Stated again, the five examinations framework includes:

5 Examinations Framework

- Examining our own filters
- Examining the environment
- Examining child development
- Examining issues of diversity
- Examining teacher roles and strategies

- *Examining our own filters*
  What experiences and conditioning do we bring to this teaching situation?

- *Examining the environment*
  How is it influencing or prescribing the context?

- *Examining child development*
  What indicators are operating here?

- *Examining issues of diversity*
  What assumptions, biases, or limiting factors are at work?

- *Examining teacher roles and strategies*
  How can we be more responsive and skillful?

This framework not only underlies our planning process, but is also explicitly shared with teachers. We suggest that they begin to practice using these five examinations to approach problems they encounter and discussions they undertake with coworkers and parents. If they are taking ECE classes or attending conferences or workshops, we recommend teachers try approaching the content with this methodology as well.

The early childhood field now has a vast amount of literature, information, and deliberations. Instead of trying to find a specialized package or standardized system for our teacher training, we prefer to use open-ended frameworks to guide our thinking. Between the two of us we most often employ the hope to see and hope not to see guidelines and the five examinations framework because we are interested in a methodology that encourages an ongoing process of exploration, rather than a more closed, tightly defined system. We ourselves move back and forth between these two frameworks to define a focus for the big ideas and activities of a given training. It is our hope that you will experiment with using these yourselves, developing a consistent approach as a trainer and a methodology for teachers to build on over time. This practice will reinforce useful dispositions for you and the teachers with whom you work.

Chapter 17
Workshop Settings

In today's reality most early childhood teacher training occurs not as a pre-service but rather as an in-service program. Usually, it is delivered in a one-session workshop format, at a conference, resource and referral agency, or staff meeting of child care programs.

In most cases a "something for everyone" offering of workshops means it's a smorgasbord, hit-or-miss approach to training, lacking the critical elements of a sustained focus and consistent theoretical framework over time. Understanding this, we've wrestled with ways to frame our approach and practice of leading workshops to be compatible with what we believe constitutes effective staff training.

Our method of five examinations creates a consistent framework woven throughout all of our training. We explain to teachers that if they attend more than one of our trainings, they will get repeated exposure to a body of ideas, reinforcement of certain dispositions, and opportunities to practice the same methodology with a variety of topics.

GOALS AND FORMAT

Any workshop we offer is introduced with an explanation of the larger context of which it is a part. For instance, a workshop on some aspect of behavior management begins with an overview of considerations involved in child guidance, and an explanation that we will be taking up but one particular aspect.

Though it may not be obvious from the agenda, our goals for one-session workshops are focused more on reinforcing dispositions than they are on teaching particular content. We want to spark enthusiasm in teachers to see some new roles for themselves in their work with children. We want them to experience what a particular idea or method might taste or look like in action. We want our workshops to ignite a renewed motivation for teachers to continue their professional development and a sense of what they might want to try next. We try to connect them with available resources to do this, including reading, places to visit, and questions to pursue in classroom observations.

To meet these general goals, we use a workshop format adapted from the High/Scope Training of Teacher Trainers model. The sample format (pg. 156) is based on a one-hour time frame, our least favorite, but one we are frequently faced with. In the case of such a short workshop, it is tempting to feel we should use the precious moments to convey all the information we can. In fact, we've found the opposite better meets our goals.

Workshop participants become motivated to learn when their appetite has been whetted through active engagement with ideas that relate to their real-life experience. Thus, even for an hour-long training, we devote at least half of the time to exercises that have participants actively involved. In longer workshops

Sample workshop format
- Welcome, introductions, work-shop overview (5-10 min.)
- Opening activity to reflect on topic (10 min.)
- Presentation of core ideas (10-15 min.)
- Practice applying ideas (15-20 min.)
- Next steps and follow-up (5 min.)
- Summary and evaluation (5 min.)

the sample time frames can be expanded, but the bulk of the additional time should still be spent in the practice of applying the workshop ideas.

PLANNING PROCESS

As previously mentioned, we start the planning process for a training by brain-storming an overview of the core ideas on the topic, often in a hope to see and hope not to see format. We narrow our workshop to the big ideas that fit the particular goals and time frame we've been given. From there, we design an opening activity to spark initial thinking on the topic. This is similar to what some call an icebreaker. However, it is designed to not only loosen up the group, but also give them a common experience to reflect on and discuss together.

Our next step in the workshop planning process is to design one or more activities for practice in applying the core ideas to be explored. Examples of these are woven throughout this book. Time permitting, we sometimes set up self-directed learning stations for workshop participants to choose from or rotate through.

As the workshop comes to an end, we solicit next step thoughts from partici-pants, offer follow-up suggestions, and alert them to relevant resources. If the group has been together for several hours or more, we usually summarize what has happened during the workshop as they move into completing evaluation forms. This helps in the reflection process and brings closure to our time to-gether as a group.

PRESENTING AND FACILITATING

Our approach to leading workshops relies more heavily on observing, listening, and group facilitation skills than it does on lecturing or public speaking. Apart from the opening and summary, the only presentation aspect of this workshop format is in introducing the big ideas. This can be done in a mini-lecture or informal talk with the use of visual aids.

Another approach is to shape the presentation by first soliciting what partic-ipants know about the big ideas, writing this on flip chart paper, adding any missing pieces yourself, and then talking about how all this fits into the larger body of ideas under consideration. We increasingly use this latter method because it helps us build from where the participants are in their current think-ing and practice. A more in-depth description of this process is described in Chapter 3, "Landscaping for Constructivism." Less experienced workshop lead-ers, or those more comfortable with a linear progression of presenting ideas, may choose the more structured approach. Either way, this presentation section of the agenda should be brief, with the majority of the time devoted to active par-ticipation rather than passive listening on the part of those present.

Apart from designing activities and setting up the environment, the primary skills required of a workshop leader are those of facilitating discussions and debriefing experiences. For readers less familiar with practical group process skills, most libraries and bookstores stock any number of resource books to choose from. Early childhood management journals such as *Child Care Information Exchange*, along with those of other professions frequently feature useful articles on this topic. One of the most comprehensive resource books we've found for ideas on training exercises and skills for group dynamics is Julius E. Eitington's *The Winning Trainer* (Gulf Publishing, 1989).

Beyond general facilitation skills, we strive for workshop leader roles that reflect constructivist theory, parallel the ones we suggest teachers play with children, and reinforce valuable teaching dispositions. We watch and listen and build on participants' ideas and stories; help interpret and connect people, their experiences, and ideas to each other; pose questions that may uncover contradictions; and expose further complexity to be explored. Again, a full description of the elements of this debriefing process are described in Chapter 3.

For all the limitations workshops present a trainer, they are usually affordable, accessible, and fit with the real-life constraints of teachers. Conducted with the principles of constructivist theory, where participants are active and given the opportunity to reflect on what they know, this form of training can become significantly more useful to teachers. Furthermore, we can encourage them to become advocates for a more useful approach to workshop offerings, lobbying their local and national professional organizations for longer workshop time blocks and extended "tracks" to pursue a training focus with a consistent theoretical framework over time.

Chapter 18

Courses and Ongoing Classes

Traditionally, early childhood education courses have been offered in vocational, two- or four-year college programs. Some are part of a degree program, while others are available through a continuing education program. With our profession's goal of developing a teacher training articulation system, ongoing classes are now sometimes offered through child care resource and referral agencies. Large agencies, such as Head Start or corporate child care programs, have begun contracting with training institutions for courses to be offered on-site to teachers during work hours. Many of these classes are structured around the new Child Development Associate (CDA) credential competency areas.

There are some obvious advantages to working with teachers in an ongoing class setting. Repeated contact with teachers allows a trainer to better understand their learning process. There is time to build relationships; a sense of community often develops among those in the class. By its nature, course work provides a consistent focus over time and repeated experiences with a methodology.

OBJECTIVES AND REQUIREMENTS

Though there are disadvantages to training in college classes, we have found ways to work around them. Usually the instructor is required to submit a course outline, along with learning objectives. While we agree with some aspects of the outline's and objective's intent, the requirement usually results in language, if not an approach, that is contrary to our view of how learning takes place.

We shape our learning objectives in the language of our five examinations framework. For example, rather than say "students will learn such and such," we say, "students will have the opportunity to examine their own filters . . . the environment . . . issues of diversity" and so on. We develop an overview for the course outline, but to be responsive to our students, we fill in the actual agendas for each session as we go along. Examples of course learning objectives are found in Chapter 20.

Knowing the limitations of discussing teaching concepts outside of real settings, we make extensive use of stories and video clips of actual children and classrooms. Reading assignments of authors who observe and write accounts of children are useful as well (see the Recommended Resources section). We also give assignments that require students to do their own observations in classrooms. During our actual time together in a course, we provide the kinds of activities and props found throughout this book to give students real-life experiences to reflect upon.

Most instructors are required to grade students in their classes. Because we believe students can do the best assessment of their learning, we structure a self-evaluation process for them linked to a self-grading system. A list of other

options and extra credit projects expands the choices students in our classes have to pursue their own interests and goals, as well as the grade they want for the class.

In the early years of teaching classes, we drew upon the books of Betty Jones for creative inspiration.[4] We continue to invent ways to meet institutional requirements without undermining our beliefs about teaching and learning. Central to this process is creating an open, inclusive atmosphere, with agreed upon guidelines that foster trust and risk taking. In fact, we begin many classes with a brainstorming session on ways we want to behave together and then go through them to develop a list everyone agrees to.

Because we want teachers of young children to give thoughtful attention to the physical environment, we do so as well. This usually requires rearranging rooms that are set up with rows of desks or tables facing the front of the room. Because a good deal of time is spent in small group activities and because we want students to turn to their classmates as resources, people need to be seated so as to interact with each other. We've found it's worth the time to soften up and beautify the often hard and sterile elements of typical college classrooms, so we add different ethnic textiles to a wall or table here and there. Students repeatedly tell us this makes them feel more immediately relaxed and curious. We've also played music as students arrive or when we bring the group back together after a break or small group project.

Equally time consuming and valuable are reflective writing assignments for our students. Because this is so different from the writing assignments they are used to, we initially have to prompt them with an explanation, example or two, and question to ponder in their writing. (For examples, see Chapter 4.) Our goal is to get to know the students as individuals, their ways of thinking, the questions they are wrestling with, and how our topic relates to experiences they've had. Rather than grade these papers for the student's mastery of *our* goals and agenda, we prefer to play the role of pen pal, responding to their concerns, sharing our experience, and placing all this in the context of the body of ideas under consideration.

Teaching ongoing classes in other delivery settings can be done in a similar manner. In fact, we've found it helpful to work with training agencies in designing their workshop offerings to be more like classes. A series of workshops on a topic offsets the fragmentation and lack of context that comes with a one session workshop or seminar.

By the year 2000 the demand for child care workers will grow by 20% and the demand for preschool teachers by 36%.

U.S. Bureau of Labor Statistics[5]

It is the responsibility of the pedagogista to work with teachers to identify new themes and experiences for continuous professional development and in-service training. This is a delicate task because of the insufficient basic preparation of many of our teachers. But we believe that the highest level of teaching is best achieved through work experience, supported by continuous reflection and enrichment.

Tiziana Filippini, *The Hundred Languages of Children*[8]

Chapter 19
On-Site Training

There is no training setting more pertinent, yet more problematic, than on-site in programs where teachers work on a daily basis. Here we find them agonizing over curriculum plans, inadequate supplies, children's behaviors, parent requests, conflicts with coworkers, their paychecks, and sense of self-worth. If not obviously eager to learn, they are longing to be heard, understood, and recognized. And, they have many things to teach those of us who are trainers.

STAFF DEVELOPMENT MODELS

Our profession has several models for on-site training that are useful reference points. With the CDA credentialing program, we have a rich history of on-site training, primarily found in Head Start settings. Supervisors and trainers have a great deal to learn from this model and the role of the CDA field advisor. But while the need for on-site early childhood training has expanded exponentially, the new CDA process diminishes the official role of the field advisor.

Less frequently noted in our profession's experience with on-site training is the early Perry Preschool Project. Its continuing longitudinal study emphasizes the benefits of a program with self-selected, active learning experiences for children, neglecting to mention the role of this same form of education in the ongoing staff development for teachers in the program.[6] Finally, along with acknowledging the important role of ongoing staff development in the quality of the Perry Preschool Project, the High/Scope Foundation has released a study on the effectiveness of their ten-year training of trainers program in which they comprehensively looked at the process and outcomes of their in-service training.[7] As mentioned earlier, the findings of this study substantiates our own experience of what constitutes effective training.

Finally, the Reggio Emilia model of early childhood education offers important insights for on-site staff development through the role of a "pedagogista," a pedagogical coordinator who acts as a consultant and resource person for the teachers. Though the pedagogisti have a variety of coordinating responsibilities that parallel those of program supervisors in the United States, their role of coaching teachers in the application of educational theory is stronger than what we commonly see in this country.

THE SUPERVISOR AS COACH

For the most part, it is only Head Start or large corporate child care programs that employ education coordinators whose primary responsibilities are supervision and maintenance of performance standards. Their job does not include the multitude of other tasks a child care director is responsible for, but in the balance, education coordinators are besieged with regulations and paperwork that leave them little time for the coaching and staff development needed.

In the majority of child care programs across the country, the director is a one-woman show when it comes to administrative responsibilities. It is up to her to squeeze in teacher training, which she rarely has the time or budget for, let alone the needed expertise. Staff meetings get used for announcements, reminders of rules and requirements, and, if the teachers are lucky, for a bit of problem solving. As a result, unless there is an obvious problem, teacher training gets short changed. Family home providers are even more isolated and strapped for time and funds to pursue professional development for themselves or assistants.

With constant staff turnover, we find directors in a variety of settings calling out for help with staff training. This cry is heard in orientation meetings with state licensing agencies, child care management organizations and seminars, and at local and national conferences. As with the teachers they supervise, directors are typically looking for a "quick fix." They want strategies that will immediately improve behaviors, neglecting to explore the larger questions of how learning and change take place. Taking the long view seems like a luxury they can't afford.

Continually encountering this dilemma of directors, along with examining our own on-site training practices as director, education coordinator, and private consultant, led us to develop a training of early childhood trainers class, and ultimately to write this book. We believe on-site coaching, especially in conjunction with in-house workshops or ongoing classes, holds the greatest potential for effective teacher development. It is our contention that with a promising set of dispositions and a rewarding methodology, supervisors can find the time to regularly coach their teachers.

COACHING BEHAVIORS

Being a coach is different than being a supervisor. Supervisors are the boss, responsible for upholding standards and evaluating job performance. They have the power to hire and fire and issue directives. While it is true that standards must be upheld and marginal performers closely supervised, most of the significant learning that will improve teaching behaviors will not come about because the supervisor willed it or issued an ultimatum. Rather, real professional development occurs as a result of teachers setting goals for themselves and getting the support they need to translate theory into practice.

If supervisors and directors are to play the role of coach, steadily promoting staff development, they will need to wear different hats at different times. Sometimes they will need to play the role of enforcer, requiring that basic standards of quality be met in prescribed ways—for instance, following certain health and safety procedures, talking to rather than yelling at a child needing discipline, and never leaving children unattended. There needs to be plenty of other times, however, when supervisors are in classrooms with teachers modeling, rather than monitoring, acknowledging the positive things that are happening and collaborating on approaches to problem areas.

When supervisors are playing the role of coach, they are focused on dispositions, rather than rules. As they set up systems to meet requirements, they do it such that teachers are supported in their continued development. For instance, to meet the requirement of documenting curriculum plans, supervisors can offer teachers optional formats, rather than a prescribed form or lesson plan. If they require individual plans for children, they can pose questions for teachers to explore, rather than just boxes to check.

The pedagogista works to promote within herself and among teachers an attitude of "learning to learn," an openness to change, and a willingness to discuss opposing points of view.

Tiziana Filippini, *The Hundred Languages of Children*[9]

Given the complexity of their roles, there must be a diversity of meetings that touch on issues of educational theory, teaching techniques, and sound social relations and communication. We help teachers improve their skills of observing and listening to children, documenting projects, and conducting their own research.

Tiziana Filippini, *The Hundred Languages of Children*[10]

Although lack of knowledge of what is developmentally appropriate practice is often seen as the major issue facing teachers and caregivers, we would argue that this is not the case. . .the real issue, as we see it, is whether teachers and caregivers are supported in their efforts to translate language and concepts into everyday practices.

David Weikart and Clay Shouse, *High/Scope Resource*[11]

When teachers make choices some will grow more than others. They may become more different rather than more alike, directing their energies in varied ways, setting their own priorities, and developing a unique style of teaching as well as of professional growth. The organic development fostered in a growth model produces variety, not predictable sameness. It is more fruitful, more fun, and more risky.

Elizabeth Jones, *Growing Teachers: Partnerships in Staff Development*[12]

I could imagine a director saying to a staff (who probably wouldn't believe her at first): "I'm going to take some time each week to observe children's play. I'd like to collect and share notes about what our children are playing and learning. I'll plan to rotate through the classrooms unless you'd rather I left you alone. Please don't do anything different because I'm coming. This is not an evaluation; when I'm evaluating you, I will let you know and schedule that time differently."

Margie Carter and Elizabeth Jones, "The Teacher as Observer: The Director as Role Model"[13]

A coach provides a framework and a vision for mastering needed skills. In early childhood programs this means devoting meetings to pedagogical considerations with activities related to teacher needs—time to reflect and discuss happenings with children and to hear and learn from each other. Coaches encourage teachers struggling with new skills by highlighting the growth they've seen and recognizing appropriate risk taking and whistle-blowing. Staff evaluations are primarily framed as self-evaluations, a chance to assess and reflect with feedback from an observer. Training plans grow from these as teachers' self-selected goals for professional development, rather than receiving a mandate or schedule from the boss.

A supervisor who wants to coach more than command is faced with some challenging choices and time management struggles. This is not unlike other aspects of the job, but when an investment is made in helping teachers give birth to a set of dispositions, roles, and skills with children, the outcomes are far reaching.

ASSESSING TRAINING NEEDS

When program directors or education coordinators develop staff training plans, they typically project a range of topics within a short time frame, casting about for interesting speakers or workshop leaders. As mentioned earlier, the elements of effective training suggest a very different approach. Rather than structuring staff training around a variety of topics, it is more effective to conduct a training needs assessment and choose one or two topics to focus on over a year. Supervisors initially balk at this idea, feeling their teachers need training in a number of areas. We understand this concern, but know that learning happens effectively when content is integrated and cumulative. Asking staff to shift gears each month and focus on a new topic undermines the key elements for meaningful learning.

There are a number of ready made tools for assessing early childhood programs and individual teacher performance. An informal adaptation of something like the NAEYC Accreditation Criteria or CDA competencies can serve as a useful starting place. Time permitting, a supervisor can develop a training needs assessment tool tailored to the specific program philosophy, such as the example found in Appendix C. Assessment tools can become the basis for some individual and program wide training plans.

Whatever assessment process is used, it is important to involve all staff in determining the focus of your training. When teachers define their interests and needs for training, they have a bigger investment in applying new understandings and skills to their work. A program-wide topic for training unites a staff toward a common goal. Sustaining this focus for a period of time provides teachers the time and practice to construct their own knowledge and acquire skills. Within the chosen topic, they can set individual goals for themselves.

A COMPREHENSIVE TRAINING PLAN

Once a training focus is determined, staff can work together to clarify what they hope to see and hope not to see within the big idea that's been chosen. A training plan should provide time and multiple ways for staff to reflect on and practice the ideas under consideration. A comprehensive plan includes the following aspects:

Attending workshops

- Design a series of on-site workshops that relate to the topic. If led by more than one person, workshop leaders should approach the topic with a consistent framework so staff has an ongoing methodology to apply and evaluate new understandings on the job. It is vital that workshops offer not only content and resources, but also hands-on practice and group discussion.
- In the absence of in-house resources or expertise, look for college classes, workshops, and conference sessions that relate to the training focus. Choose those that describe practical strategies and active involvement by the participants. Have staff attend together or if funds are limited, have several attend and prepare a follow-up discussion for a staff meeting.
- Offer the following questions for reflective writing or group discussion to help teachers reflect on the workshop content and its use for their work.

    - What do I already know about this topic? What knowledge or skills do I still need?
    - Does the framework seem consistent with my ideas? If I sense any discomfort, what is it related to?
    - How inclusive, flexible, and respectful of diverse cultural and ethnic backgrounds is this content or strategy?
    - What changes might this imply for my classroom or work environment (for instance, in routines, schedule, equipment, organization)?
    - Do the techniques suggested foster such things as self-esteem, a positive group identity, self-reliance, critical thinking, and social interaction? Is success dependent on my initiative or someone else's?

Creating "thinking" systems

- Build into your systems of responsibilities and requirements, questions and forms that require teachers to observe, reflect, and practice consolidating their understandings, as opposed to checklists or mechanically filling in boxes.
- Provide space on lesson plans or record-keeping forms that addresses the focus area.

Broadcasting stories

- Use mechanisms such as an in-house newsletter, video, or bulletin board display to relate stories that highlight progress and changes in the program.

Arranging peer exchanges

- Encourage peer exchanges with time for staff to observe for things related to your focus area and share insights and difficulties.
- Provide time for staff to visit other programs, observe and talk with other teachers working towards the same expertise.

Organizing observation and feedback conferences

- Work with staff to create checklists and observation forms to heighten awareness of how the ideas look in practice in a classroom.
- Offer verbal and written feedback (specifically related to the training focus) in regular informal conferences.
- Regularly visit classrooms to show by example and when asked, offer suggestions.

• Ask for feedback on how you can further support teacher learning in this area.

Providing handouts and related resources

• Provide books, articles, videos, and other resources related to your focus in a staff lounge area or teachers' library.

Identifying barriers

• If there is limited progress toward meeting the hope to see goals, hold a discussion to identify barriers that might be in the way—ones external or internal to teacher or supervisor control.

Rewarding training with higher pay

• Develop specific budget and personnel policies that recognize the value of ongoing professional development with pay raises.

INDIVIDUAL TRAINING PLANS

Teachers may have individual needs and interests that are different from the program-wide training focus. For example, an individual training plan is useful for a staff member completing the requirements for a CDA credential. To address such needs, help teachers develop their own individual training plans, using a process similar to your program-wide plan. Starting places can include reviewing job descriptions and qualifications, a CDA related checklist, or your program's or the individual's staff evaluation form. A simple staff questionnaire or self-assessment form might also help them choose a training focus.

An individual plan may include attending workshops, conferences, or college classes related to the training focus, and the other aspects of a comprehensive training plan listed above. Sample staff evaluations and self-assessments are in Appendix C.

EFFECTIVE STRATEGIES

When doing on-site training with individuals, we first ask teachers to identify what aspect of their teaching they would like help with. As someone shares with us a goal for their learning, we can more readily identify the larger framework of ideas that would be helpful to them in meeting this goal. We then set about reinforcing desirable dispositions, designing strategies, and offering repeated experiences in applying the methodology we hope will become their own:

• Examining one's own filters
• Examining the environment
• Examining child development
• Examining issues of diversity
• Examining teacher roles and strategies

Strategy: Coaching with Examinations

Typically, a teacher approaches us wanting help with a perceived behavior problem or learning deficit in a child. For instance, David approached us with concerns about Crystal, a shy child who was not playing with anyone. Hoping to reinforce a disposition towards being reflective, we first tried to explore his views on shyness and how this relates to his understandings of child development. In the following weeks, we examined the environmental factors that might be affecting Crystal, discussing how the room organization and materials might or might not foster a sense of belonging and inclusiveness. Finally, we considered strategies David might use in helping Crystal interact with other children. Our conversation went something like this.

> *Coach:* What is Crystal doing that leads you to label her as shy?
>
> *Teacher:* She's always on the sidelines watching. She doesn't enter into any group play, even when I coax her to do so.
>
> *Coach:* Does she seem unhappy being alone? Tell me how you think she sees this. Would she like to get in the play and doesn't know how? Does she feel excluded by the other children?
>
> *Teacher:* I really feel sorry for her. She doesn't seem to have any friends. If she doesn't overcome this now, she'll really have trouble when she gets to a big kindergarten class.

Because David hadn't really answered the question about the child's perspective, it seemed important to pursue this.

> *Coach:* Let's do some observing and see if we can find out how she might be feeling in the classroom. Is there anything in the environment that she specifically is drawn to or typically avoids? Looking around, I wonder what seems familiar and comforting to her. What makes her feel like she belongs here?

Together we created an observation form to gather more data about Crystal. We used this information to brainstorm strategies David can use to help Crystal.

This method usually provokes insights for the teacher, both in terms of strategies to try and further information and knowledge needed. At the same time dispositions to be curious about children's development and to be reflective and a watchdog about inclusiveness are being nurtured. With repeated exposure to this approach, it becomes second nature for teachers to independently examine these considerations in addressing concerns that arise.

Strategy: Questions for a Coach

In beginning a coaching relationship, we have a set of mental questions to guide our observations of teachers. They help us clarify what we are seeing and want to offer as feedback to the teacher. We ask ourselves:

- What am I specifically seeing?
- What is my first reaction or judgment?
- How would I name the essence of this experience for this teacher?
- How can I account for what I am seeing? Why is the teacher behaving in this way?
- What does this teacher seem to understand about this situation?
- What is the teacher doing well?
- What big idea about child development would be helpful to this teacher?
- What could this teacher do differently to be more successful?

Strategy: Clarifying Toddler Curriculum

A team of teachers working with older toddlers approached us with extreme frustration. They felt their entire day was taken up with caretaking activities, such as toilet training, feeding, and redirecting behavior, and they never got to any curriculum activities. We heard questions and comments like the following:

> "There are so many wet clothes all the time, can't we just keep them in diapers?"

> "Those who do try to use the potty end up taking all their clothes off and then we have to spend all this time getting them dressed again."

> "Our director wants us to have them serve and feed themselves, but they just end up making a mess and playing in it."

Going through the questions for a coach on page 165, we identified our own judgments as well as those of this teaching team.

> They obviously don't understand this stage of development and what toddler curriculum is.

> They are frazzled and frustrated, feeling they're not real teachers and the children aren't learning the real things they need for preschool.

> If they understood the developmental theme of autonomy for this age child and the role it plays in an evolving positive identity and self-esteem, they could redefine this as their curriculum.

> Setting up the environments and routines to foster and value this self-help could make these teachers feel considerably more successful. They might even begin to value and delight in these fledgling efforts of autonomy.

With these thoughts in mind, we proposed engaging in some research together. We posted a large chart on the classroom wall with columns indicating children's initiative in self-help activities and teacher behaviors that support autonomy. As the children played we began documenting examples and in the coming days the teachers followed our example. This provided the basis for terrific informal discussions during our classroom visits and later in staff meetings without the children present. Our chart looked something like this.

Children initiating	Teachers acknowledging	Providing time and coaching	Arranging the environment
• Casey put shoes on wrong feet	• BJ: Casandra, you took your pants off!	• Melanie stayed behind with Sam and Janis who were trying to zip	• Stepping stool by sink
• Jerome insisted on carrying his own plate to sink	• Melanie: Look how Taiko is taking the stool to the sink.	• BJ: I'll wait while you pull up your pants.	• Small mirror by sink

The process of noticing to document, rather than to correct or change, helped these teachers see the children's behavior in a new light. Having concrete examples of their own behaviors that supported autonomy encouraged the teachers to become even more intentional in their language and actions. We increasingly heard comments like "Look at Jerome working on that zipper" and "Did you see how carefully Amanda poured her milk?"

The team began reorganizing the room, their routines, and schedule to provide more support for self-help activities. In staff meeting discussions, we redefined the meaning of curriculum themes for their group. The emphasis was now more on planning for independence than it was learning about animals and shamrocks. The enthusiasm of these teachers spread throughout the program. Soon we had requests to "come to our room and make those charts for us."

Strategy: Broadcasting Children's Play

Because we want teachers to regularly observe and focus on children's interests and development, we try to keep the focus on children during our classroom visits as well. There are numerous ways to model an interest in children's play and call attention to it:

• Talk with teachers on the sidelines, pointing out an example of sustained play.
• Share stories of children's play during staff meetings.
• Create bulletin board displays or newsletter articles with stories, sketches, and photos of "Master Players."[15]

This idea can lead to discussions and further broadcasting of the way in which room arrangements and teacher behaviors encourage sustained play. Annotated sketches, photographs, samples of work, audiotapes, and videotapes are all useful tools for broadcasting.

Spreading the news of things that reflect an awareness of and provision for children's play is contagious. It tends to generate an ever increasing delight and curiosity over what is happening in a program.

Strategy: Marketing Developmentally Appropriate Literacy

Because many early childhood teachers are intent on teaching reading and writing skills, we worked with colleague Marilyn Jacobson to develop "Hot for Literacy," a comprehensive on-site training program to promote developmentally appropriate literacy activities with preschoolers. We developed five approaches to highlight appropriate environments and activities for teachers and parents to consider.

1. Points and prizes

We developed a list of appropriate activities teachers might do and presented them as a tracking system of literacy activities for teachers to document. The list included materials to put in the classroom, teacher behaviors and activities, classes to take, and parent education projects, each rated on a point system for teachers to tally, accumulate points, and turn in for prizes. Prizes themselves were related to literacy, including adult and children's books, cassette tapes and players, camera and film, release time to visit another program, and a visiting storyteller or puppeteer. See Appendix B for examples of "Hot for Literacy" strategy.

2. Preschool reading and writing readiness assessment tool

This form was developed primarily as a training tool to alert teachers to children's activities that they may not have previously understood as literacy related. They were encouraged to use this tool as part of their portfolio collection of data to aid in parent conferences and the formulation of individual plans for a child. A sample is in Appendix A.

3. Monthly workshops on literacy

We planned a series of literacy related workshops, but left participation optional. Topics included creating literacy environments with props, storytelling, stages of literacy development, and whole language strategies.

4. Observation/feedback conference

In our visits to classrooms, we observed and documented examples of appropriate literacy strategies and broadcast these throughout the program. In completing staff conferences, evaluations, and program monitoring, we placed special emphasis on accomplishments in developing appropriate literacy activities.

5. Parent newsletter articles

We emphasized appropriate literacy activities as part of our parent education program. In newsletters we duplicated a version of the preschool assessment tool and encouraged them to look for examples in their child's interests and activities at home. Periodic articles included ideas of literacy related activities to do at home, publishing of library hours and programs, and invitations to come share a favorite family book with the class.

Strategy: Making Rules to Construct Knowledge

Because many teachers are "rule" orientated, and indeed there are requirements to be met, we sometimes convert what we see as a means to constructing knowledge into a rule or regulation. For instance, in requiring teachers to document curriculum plans we included an evaluation form to be discussed in team meetings, with the goal of sparking closer observation and reflection on both teacher initiated and child initiated activities. This requires a significantly more important thinking process than just filling in the names of curriculum activities on a weekly calendar.

Evaluating curriculum plans and activities
As a team, discuss the following questions as you evaluate your curriculum plans and develop the next set.

Teacher Initiated Activities
• Which of your planned activities engaged the children the most? Be specific about circle time, small group time, materials provided, and so forth.
• Describe a few examples of what you saw children doing with your planned activities.
• Which activities would you repeat in the future?
• What changes would you make in the future?

Child Initiated Activities
• Describe the themes you observed in children's spontaneous play.
• How did you see children using materials (as individuals and in small groups)?
• Describe social interactions you observed.

- What role did the teachers play in these child initiated activities?
- How will you follow up on the interests that emerged?
- What areas of development or key experiences were the children gaining as a part of these activities?
- What entries will you make in individual children's portfolios (observations, photos and samples of children's work, drawings, and dictation)?

PLANTING THE SEED

Because pre-service and in-service training will continue to occur in a variety of settings, it is enormously helpful to have a theoretical framework and training methodology that can be applied wherever you are. This makes the planning process smoother for the trainer and the learning process more predictable for the teacher.

When working with a consistent group of teachers over time, a training cycle that moves through needs assessment, setting goals and a focus, training activities, practice, reflection, and evaluation can be very effective. For workshops and one-time trainings, the principles of this cycle can be condensed into parallel process, with activities designed for participants to self-reflect on their experience and needs, take in some new considerations, practice a bit, evaluate, and determine some next steps for themselves.

Once we figured this out for ourselves, our work life became considerably less stressful and our training more effective. Our preference is still to work with a group or coach individuals over time because we have seen significant changes happen in teachers' motivation and behavior when they come to value and focus on children's play.

We can't end this section, however, without an honest acknowledgment of the limitations of our training in producing high quality programs. Effective training is only half the equation. *The National Child Care Staffing Study* revealed that both a trained and an adequately paid staff are key to determining quality in early childhood programs.[16] Teachers can't live indefinitely on enthusiasm about children's play. They need respect for their work and decent salaries and working conditions.

Time and time again we have seen the fruits of our in-service training efforts slip away as teachers soon move on to other jobs that pay an equitable wage. The injustice of this situation, and the direct impact it has on our jobs, propelled us into active involvement with the Worthy Wage Campaign for child care workers. Here we work with teachers who are finding their voices, gaining strength in numbers, and bringing hope and staying power to us all. To help others see the Worthy Wage Campaign in action, we have produced two videos: "Worthy Work, Worthless Wages" and "Making News, Making History." Both are available from the National Center for the Early Childhood Work Force. See the Recommended Resources section for more information.

Section 6

A Course on Child-Centered Curriculum Practices

*P*erhaps the best snapshot of the theory and practice woven throughout this book is found in a course we've developed for our local community college. In effect, it uses a project approach to teacher training. This course conveys core knowledge and skills with activities designed to simultaneously encourage the dispositions we feel are critical for master teachers.

The chapters in this section detail the approach and strategies we've used for an eight-week course on child centered curriculum planning. We've taught this both as a community college class and as an ongoing in-service training program in child care centers. The activities and the project approach lend themselves well to involving an entire program staff in training with a sustained focus over time. Whatever the setting, each time we offer this course it generates new learning and renewed enthusiasm for teachers and builds a collaborate spirit towards learning among staff, children, and parents.

This class has been a great inspiration and affirmation for me. I really appreciated the process and structure in which it was presented. Thank you!

Anita, teacher

I'm grateful to both of you for teaching this class. This approach has freed me up to really look at the children and see what they think and know. It's been challenging to me and will continue to be—and I do think it's worth it!

Juanita, teacher

Since taking this class I've come to realize that if my activities are to succeed I must pay close attention to the children. Also I've learned that I can let the children take the lead on what we do, giving them the opportunity to be spontaneous and even repeat activities if they want to. I've discovered that it is difficult for me to free myself up enough to let this happen. I need to learn to be more flexible.

Kevin, teacher

Chapter 20
Designing a Course

With the goals of influencing dispositions and enhancing skills in curriculum planning for young children, we designed this course to have teachers practice child development research through informal classroom observations and documentation of children's interests, questions, and behaviors in response to materials made available. Working in research project groups, teachers compare notes and insights, following a set of focus questions we provide them each week. We support their research with workshop activities and discussions that provide the opportunity for further reflection on their experience, observations, and emerging questions. As a result, teachers begin to redefine their understanding of developmentally appropriate curriculum and formulate new roles and behaviors for themselves.

PLANNING PROCESS

To provide specific definition to the teacher dispositions and behaviors we want in planning curriculum, we brainstorm lists of hope to see and hope not to see. These become the big ideas around which we plan activities and discussions. Our initial lists look like this.

Child-Centered Planning

Hope to See

- Teachers understand that play is at the heart of children's learning and they provide for this with ample time and materials.
- Teachers recognize individual children's culture, stages, and themes in their physical, cognitive, social, and emotional development.
- Teachers understand that children are active, sensory learners and need multiple opportunities for self-chosen exploration, social interaction, and problem solving. Teachers are much more interested in this process than in final products.
- The environment is the foundation of the curriculum. It is child-centered with attractive, interesting materials provided in an organized and thoughtful fashion.
- Teachers observe children's play to uncover the children's themes, interests, questions, skills, and frustrations.
- Teachers use children's themes as the basis for curriculum planning. Planning involves an introduction of materials and interactions to stimulate the emergence of the children's ideas and understandings.
- Teachers anticipate avenues the children may pursue, preparing for this with enrichment materials and activity options to add.
- As the children engage with materials provided, teachers observe, documenting and guiding interactions and future planning.

- Teachers share their own passions, interests, and questions as another source of curriculum.
- Written curriculum plans primarily document what occurred with materials provided, rather than teacher directed activities.
- Individual planning for typically developing children is focused on children's strengths as a means to address their frustrations. The teacher seeks the child's point of view in addressing any readiness agenda.

Hope Not to See

- Teacher planning is focused only on group times, rather than continually creating an inviting environment with materials to spark curiosity and engagement.
- Curriculum activities are focused on dittos, art products, and abstract information "told" to children during group time.
- Teachers center their plans around dominant culture holidays and prepackaged curriculum theme books.
- Children's interests are overridden by teacher directed curriculum themes with look-alike products to be sent home.
- Cultural diversity and sensitivity are ignored in the environment planning and interactions with children.
- Teachers ignore child initiated play, doing housekeeping and record-keeping tasks during "free choice time."
- Teachers focus planning on children's academic deficiencies and school readiness lessons.

With these ideas to guide us, we go to our five examinations framework—examining oneself, the environment, child development, issues of diversity, and teacher roles and strategies—as we plan our weekly agendas. We find specific ideas in our toolshed of training activities.

COURSE SYLLABUS AND REQUIREMENTS

College courses address concerns about teacher accountability and student performance with required paperwork and regulations. Though the specific wording is taken seriously by some and not by others, we want to satisfy institutional requirements without implying we believe in the banking method of education. Thus, the course syllabus we develop reflects a constructivist approach to teaching, while using the language and format required by the institution.

Our course objectives are defined in terms of our five examinations framework emphasizing a process approach to learning we believe leads to desired outcomes. Stated expectations and assumptions for the course reinforce the notion that each student is in charge of their own learning, while at the same time being involved in the learning process of classmates and the teacher. Class assignments and our grading system provide choices and involve self-evaluation and reflection. This approach fosters the dispositions central to our goals in teaching, while meeting institutional requirements that could otherwise undermine them. Following is an example of a syllabus for a course on child-centered curriculum planning.

Course syllabus

Goals and Objectives

This course is designed to provide practical information and experiences for teachers to:

- Examine the impact of specific curriculum goals and practices on the behavior and learning of young children.
- Develop skills in observing and analyzing children's activities, ideas, and interests as sources for developmentally appropriate curriculum planning.
- Deepen understandings of child development through observation and practical research.
- Explore the role of the environment in developmentally appropriate curriculum for young children.
- Formulate new roles and behaviors for yourself as a teacher.

Course Expectations and Assumptions

The instructors' role in this class is to provide a theoretical framework, activities, and assignments for students to utilize in developing understandings, knowledge, and skills. We care very much about how and what you learn in our class, but we believe that you are responsible for participating in learning from the activities we provide. We will make ourselves accessible for discussion and feedback as often as needed, and we encourage you to see colleagues as equally valuable resources for your learning.

Requirements and assignments

- Observe a group of children over time as part of a practical research project that this course is based on. This involves individual investigation and data collection in a classroom of young children and group time during the class to discuss your findings and questions. Specific guidelines for the project will be provided.
- Pursue answers to the observation questions we pose, completing the forms provided. These will help you consolidate the ideas of this class with the real work you do with children.
- Do reading and written reflection on a book chosen from the course reading list. Using a form provided, write about your discoveries, reactions, and questions in reading. Make a copy of your report to share with each member of the class.
- Turn in a brief weekly evaluation of the class to give us feedback, as well as a snapshot of your own learning process. Try looking at school in a different way. Instead of asking," What does this teacher want from me?" ask yourself, "How can I use this opportunity to learn in a way that works best for me?" Offer suggestions that will help the class be more useful for your learning.
- Complete an initial self-assessment on the form provided at the beginning of the course and a final self-assessment at the end. The more thought you put into these assessments, the more powerful they will be as a tool for your own learning.

Grades

Because you are in the best position to determine what you have done and learned in this class, you will grade yourself using the following criteria.

Since taking this class I would now define the term developmentally appropriate curriculum as "observing the children, recognizing what they do, and then providing opportunities and materials for them to do it more!"

Rebecca, teacher

From now on I would like to plan my curriculum by watching the kids, drawing the curriculum from them with some assistance from myself (ideas, imagination, inspiration and passions). I will use curriculum plan books only after I know what the children are interested in.

David, teacher

This class has inspired me to think about planning in a new way. I'd like to allow more room for child self-directed activities. Currently, I do a monthly calendar with group activities laid out for the bulk of each day. I'd like to leave this more open and flexible for child-selected activities.

Geneva, teacher

Consider the amount and quality of the work you did for this class as you decide on the specific grade point for yourself. If we take issue with your decision, we will negotiate with you.

- 2.0 Active participation in group research project and presentation.
- 3.0 The above, plus completion of the initial and final self-assessments and the weekly class evaluations.
- 4.0 The above plus completion of the reading and reflection paper and assigned observations.

Strategy: Book Reflections

Rather than using a textbook for classes, we develop a bibliography of selected books, in this case related to child development and child-centered practices. Asking students to choose their own reading supports the idea that they are in charge of their learning. When they read something they are interested in, the information will be more meaningful for their learning. Having each student distribute written reflections on their reading to classmates exposes the class to a number of books, as well as reinforces the notion that participants are resource people for each other. Here's a sample book reflection form we've used for college classes and extended in-service training in programs. Books used for the reading list can be found in the Recommended Resources section at the end of this book.

Book Reflection Form

Teacher's Name_____

Book Title and Author _____

The main ideas in the book are:_____

_____

_____

Questions on my mind after reading this book:_____

_____

_____

I can use these ideas in my curriculum planning by:_____

_____

_____

Why I would or would not recommend this book to others:

_____

_____

Strategy: Initial and Final Self-Assessments

At the beginning of the course, we want students to name what they believe about child development and curriculum planning. This becomes a place for considering new information and understandings. It also serves as a reference point for assessing changes and new thinking that occur by the time of the final self-assessment. Asking students to complete self-assessments reinforces their disposition to be reflective and intentional in their learning process. Here are self-assessment questions we've used for this course.

Initial Self-Assessment
- How would you define the term Developmentally Appropriate Curriculum?
- How would you describe children's learning process?
- Describe your current approach to curriculum planning. What influenced you to use this approach?
- Describe one of your curriculum activities that held the children's interest for a while.
- Describe an activity that didn't seem to mean much to them.
- What kind of pressure do you receive from others about your curriculum planning?

Final Self-Assessment
- Since taking this class, are there any changes in your definition of Developmentally Appropriate Curriculum?
- How did your research project impact your thinking about children's learning process?
- Are there any changes you plan to make in your approach to curriculum planning?
- What response might you now make in the face of pressures from others?

I began providing woodworking materials for the kids on a daily basis. I wanted to find ways to work with them on building projects. Then I saw their primary interest was in exploring the mechanisms of how the tools worked.

Esther, teacher,
from her research journal

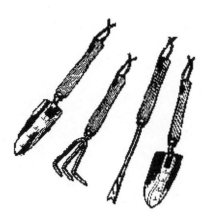

At first the children just seemed interested in the individual materials. They explored the different shapes of the wood pieces, experimented with the moving parts of the tools, pounded with the hammer, and so on. Then they began to see how things worked together. Some stacked the wood pieces, others tried pounding nails into the wood. Still another pounded the wood scrapes with the hammer to break and splinter them.

Esther, teacher,
from her research journal

Chapter 21
The Project Approach

As early childhood professional literature began referring to "the project approach" to curriculum planning, we realized that this was the approach we were developing in most of our teacher training.[1] Encompassing many of the elements of the effective teacher training discussed earlier, the project approach enables teachers to choose a focus to explore over time. They engage in direct observations and discover the delightful play of children. Together with colleagues, they analyze data and pursue questions, thereby constructing their own understandings of child development theory.

We introduce the research project idea by first asking teachers to form groups based on the developmental stages and ages of the children in their care. Their work sites or classrooms with children become their research laboratories. After several opportunities for open-ended observations at these sites, we ask them to consider a generic project theme to pursue over time with a group of children. We adapted the elements of an in-depth study project described by Debbie LeeKeenan and John Nimmo into a set of guidelines for our group research project assignment.[2]

The project theme should be:
• concrete
• keyed to the children's interests
• readily observable to children
• able to connect from one day to the next
• able to be carried out over a long period of time
• offer possibilities for variation

In the years we have taught this course, successful project themes that teachers choose include water, textures, sand, dirt, clay, wood, measuring time, and construction. Our guidelines remind teachers to choose themes that allow children to explore in their own way, rather than depend on teacher direction or close supervision. We emphasize that their focus should be on learning from the children, rather than teaching them. They are to be researchers, taking time to observe, document, and reflect.

RESEARCH PROJECT GUIDELINES
As the research groups determine their project themes, we distribute the following handout.

Research Project

Goals
• To learn about child development and developmentally appropriate curriculum through observing children with a project theme over time.

- To identify new roles for the teacher that support and extend children's "developmental themes" and interests.

Research Guidelines
- During the next six weeks, each person will provide daily opportunities for children to use materials and participate in activities related to the theme.
- Project group members are responsible for conducting their own research, bringing written observations and representations of what you discover for discussion with group members. Group discussions will pursue questions your findings raise and suggest enrichment strategies that follow the children's interest in the project.

Research Schedule and Elements
The focus of the project will build and shift as the children become more familiar and engaged with the theme materials. Use the following schedule and questions in data collection and come to your research group with observations, stories, and concrete representations of what you are discovering.

Weeks 1 and 2: Exploration
Provide the theme related materials and ample time for the children to explore your group's chosen theme. Observe, document, collect, and represent the children's activity using the following questions:

- What do the children do with the material provided?
- What do they find fun and pleasurable?
- What are the children inventing and understanding through their involvement with the material?
- How do they talk about and represent the project material in their play?
- What experiences, people, and other materials do they connect with this?

Weeks 3 and 4: Planning
During this stage of your research, continue to observe for the children's interest but begin to extend their interests and ideas with more props and related activities. Continue to document and collect representations of what occurs. Discuss the following questions with your research group:

- What new ideas, questions, and solutions are the children discovering as they use the project materials?
- How are the children building from one day's experience to the next?
- What other materials might extend their experience or represent their ideas and feelings?
- What other directions might the children's ideas and connections branch out to?

Weeks 5 and 6: Conclude and Represent
Using the following questions, analyze the documentation and representations you have been gathering.

- How are the children's ideas and actions different from their beginning ideas and actions?
- What can you conclude about the children's learning in the course of the project?
- What did you discover about child development and developmentally appro-

The kids were really attentive and remembered the work that they had done the day before. Sometimes they continued with this and sometimes they took the wood, nails, and screws off to begin something new. In either case they always used a wood base. They seem so pleased to be working on an ongoing project, adding more changes each day.

Esther, teacher,
from her research journal

I keep adding new shapes of wood and different tools. Each time I do they return to first exploring the aspects of the new materials before combining them with familiar ones. At one point I offered paint and it took them in an entirely different direction. Their attention shifted to naming what they were making.

Esther, teacher,
from her research journal

After working on something for weeks one child decided she had made a bird feeder. Another child liked that idea and joined in the discussion. They began describing what a bird feeder needed and explored ways to change the creation to make it "really a bird feeder."

Esther, teacher,
from her research journal

Every time they used the tools they seemed more confident, focusing more on what they could do and less on the tools themselves. They discovered what they were capable of doing by repeating actions and activities, and then by challenging themselves with some new task. They learned how to implement their ideas.

Esther, teacher,
from her research journal

They learned they could teach each other how to use tools, answer each other's questions, and share tools. I was amazed to watch this, as I had never thought of them as able to do this on their own.

Esther, teacher,
from her research journal

I mostly played the role of prop manager, cheerleader, and observer. I discovered that children learn by having materials and the opportunity to explore and come up with questions and answers from their own initiative. I now understand that my role is to provide the opportunities for them to do their learning.

Esther, teacher,
from her research journal

priate curriculum during the project?

• What role did you and other adults play throughout the project?

Research Presentation

Each research group will develop a presentation to represent what they observed and learned during the duration of the project. This should include concrete examples of project materials and observations. Representations could include the following:

• children's drawings, paintings, stories, dictations, and other creations.
• audio and video recordings, photographs, or slides of the children engaged in the project.
• anecdotal notes, observation stories, journal, or diary entries.
• demonstrations and role plays of what occurred.
• related activities for your colleagues to experience.

Chapter 22:
Weekly Class Sessions

WEEK 1: EXAMINING CURRENT PRACTICES

The first class session is designed to give students an overview of the non-traditional approach we use in teaching classes. The activities also set the stage for teachers to examine different approaches to early childhood curriculum and new roles they can play.

Strategy: What Do You Do Now?

We use a four corners kinesthetic activity for teachers to get to know each other and uncover their ideas and experiences regarding curriculum planning. We ask a question regarding an approach to curriculum planning and provide four answers, designating one corner of the room for each answer. Once participants have chosen a corner, they discuss the pros and cons of their approach to curriculum planning. For example, two of the questions we ask follow.

Is the basis for your planning
• daily?
• weekly?
• monthly?
• yearly?

Is your curriculum primarily developed around
• holidays and other themes?
• curriculum activity books?
• a prescribed curriculum model (such as High/Scope, Montessori, or the Creative Curriculum)?
• whatever is happening?

This activity acknowledges participant's current approach and reminds teachers that there are other options. The discussion provides practice in reflective thinking and suggests the need to become intentionally aware of how their planning impacts children.

Strategy: Analyzing Curriculum Plans

Most approaches to curriculum planning focus on teacher planned and directed activities related to a particular theme. Using descriptions of actual observations we've made, we designed this activity to get teachers to rethink this approach.

Form small groups based on the age of children teachers work with. Ask each group to examine the scenarios below, using the "evaluating curriculum plans" questions that follow.

Infant Room Scenario

Molly loves the babies in her class. She spends much time tickling and jabbering with them about how cute they are. She often has three or four of them placed on their backs or tummies around her so she can read them a story. This is one of the central activities of the curriculum plans she turns in each month to her director. Another activity is singing to the babies as they lie near her.

Molly watches out to keep her babies from getting frustrated. If they try to reach for something, she quickly helps them get it.

Conscious of health and disease control, Molly has developed some efficient systems for the classroom. She wears an apron with two pockets. She has one full of clean tissues and uses the other for dirty ones. The minute she spots a drool or runny nose, she makes a quick wipe before the baby even knows what happened.

In a similar manner she has a system of two baskets, one of clean toys and one for used ones. Molly watches for a baby who might mouth and then drop a toy. She scoops it into the appropriate basket. If another child goes for the dropped toy, she efficiently swoops it out of the baby's hand or mouth before it is even noticed. Diapers get changed in an equally swift and efficient manner.

Being so organized, Molly is able to have a story and music time for her curriculum twice a day.

Toddler Room Scenario

Jami knows that her toddler group loves art and has planned carefully this morning. She pulls all but two of the chairs away from the table and puts them in a row nearby, facing the table. She spreads newspaper on the table, puts a cup of red paint with two brushes in it, and in front of each chair puts a heart cut out of pink paper. With two paint aprons in hand, she calls to LaToya and Matthew, "Do you want to do art? I've got some hearts for you to paint. Come to the table and I will help you put your aprons on."

LaToya and Matthew come to the table, along with several other children. While putting the aprons on the children, Jami says, "Look how many chairs there are at the table. How many people can paint at one time? Everybody will get a turn. You can wait in one of those chairs." Several of the children push toward the table, picking up and squabbling over the hearts. Jami rescues the paint and brushes just as they are discovered.

She calmly puts all but LaToya and Matthew in the waiting chairs, returning to the table to give Matthew a brush. "See here's a valentine for you to paint. What color paint do we have for painting today?" Matthew says, "Paint," dabbing some on the heart. "What color is your paint, Matthew?" Jami asks again. He ignores her, drops the brush, and continues painting with his fingers.

"We use brushes for painting, Matthew," reminds Jami. "Let's wipe your hands off and then you can use the brush again." Meanwhile, LaToya has gone to the doll corner and returns to the table with a baby in hand. "LaToya, the baby needs to stay away from the table," says Jami. "Let's have Marisa hold the baby while you paint."

Jami turns to give the doll to Marisa and discovers several children have left their seats. Others have begun a game of pushing the chairs up to the art table or around the room in a train fashion. "This is art time. The chairs need to stay here. Everyone will get a turn to make valentines," Jamie says.

With steady patience, Jami eventually gets most of the children back in the waiting chairs and begins helping them with turns at the art table. When some start painting on their hands and on the newspaper on the table, Jami reminds them that the paint needs to stay on the hearts. "If you keep the paint on the heart, you'll have a pretty valentine to take home to Mommy and Daddy," she says.

Preschool Room Scenario

Fran is a new teacher and has tremendous enthusiasm. To start off her first month, she is planning curriculum activities to teach the children their colors. For each of the four weeks in September, she will have a " color of the week." Here are some of the activities she will do for each color:

• mix only that color for painting at the easel
• create a collage art project with different shapes of that color to use
• add food coloring of that color to the water table
• make playdough of that color each week
• paint milk cartons with the weekly colors, turning them into colored bricks for the block area
• label the colors in a bulletin board display
• dismiss the children by the colors they are wearing

School-Age Room Scenario

In anticipation of St. Patrick's Day, Peter has planned a week of activities for his after-school group, investing a fair amount of time in gathering materials.

Monday: He will bring in a video on Ireland that includes some footage on St. Patrick's Day celebrations. After the video he will have the kids gather around the globe and show them where Ireland is, asking them to compare its size and location with other European countries. During snack time he will play a tape of Irish music.

Tuesday: Peter plans to read *The Little Leprechaun*, giving all the kids paper and markers to draw their favorite part of the story. If they are calm, he will again let them hear the tape of Irish music.

Wednesday: Peter will tell the kids that there will be a party on Friday and that they will put on a program and serve snacks for the preschool-aged kids. They can choose between making shamrocks or leprechaun party invitations at the art table, or learning to dance the Irish jig down in the gym with the tape they've been listening to.

Thursday: Peter plans to make snacks for the party on Friday. The children can choose between making green shamrock cookies or green lemonade. He has gathered together all the supplies for both and has written up a chart with all of the ingredients and procedures. Before the kids leave, Peter will remind them to wear something green the next day. He has made a few shamrocks out of construction paper so if someone forgets to wear green they won't feel bad.

Friday: Peter's plans include making place mats for the party, setting the table, counting out the cookies and drinks and, for those who will perform, practicing the Irish jig. When all the preschoolers arrive after their naps for the party, Peter will have them sit on the rug while the school-agers tell them what they learned about Ireland and perform the Irish jig. They will then go to the tables for snacks while the tape continues to play. Anyone who isn't wearing green will be given a shamrock to wear.

Evaluating Curriculum Plans

• What does this adult want the children to learn in this plan?
• How does the adult think the children learn?
• How will the adult need to spend their time?
• What values and biases are conveyed in these plans?

We end this activity with a whole group discussion pursuing the following questions:

- What child development issues surfaced in the children's responses to the activities?
- What role did the teachers play in carrying out the curriculum? Were their curriculum goals met? What values, biases, and dispositions were reinforced through the activities?
- How did the teachers' behaviors impact these children? Do their behaviors reflect our goal for the children in curriculum planning?

At times this activity leaves teachers in disequilibrium and defensive because their approach to planning curriculum may have been called into question. We acknowledge these feelings and explain that we've experienced this disequilibrium ourselves. We encourage teachers to examine their discomfort for the possibility of new learning and insights.

This first week ends with an overview of the course assumptions, expectations, and requirements described in the course syllabus.

WEEK 2: OBSERVING FOR DEVELOPMENTAL THEMES

This session focuses on acquiring observation skills. First, we encourage teachers to suspend their own judgments in order to collect useful and important information about children. In addition to the in-class observation practice we do, there is a follow-up observation assignment to introduce the practice of uncovering the children's "developmental themes" they will use in the research project.

Strategy: Joys of Observing

We want to awaken teachers to the joys of observing the delightful and complex endeavors of young children. This session begins with an oral reading of a few descriptive observations of children done by master observers, such as authors Vivian Paley or Elizabeth Jones. Hearing observation stories of children at play usually evokes interest and pleasure for teachers. Here's an example from Jones.[3]

> Outdoors at Live Oak child care center, the teacher has filled a split-level water table—homemade, with cutout holes to insert plastic dish tubs—with cornstarch. Extra bowls, spoons, and trowels are at hand. Paula, Dena, and Megan are busy mixing; they have added leaves and dirt to the cornstarch.
>
> *Paula* (stirring competently): We're making chocolate.
>
> *Dena* (bringing more dirt): This is chocolate. Stir it up.
>
> *Paula:* We're making cookies and cream.
>
> *Dena:* Ice cream. Please can I have a cone?
>
> Dena presents a funnel to Paula, who fills it generously. Someone adds water to the mixture. "Don't," Paula yells, and the child, intimidated, retreats. Dena has finished her ice cream. Now she arrives with a cup of water to add to her friend's mixture.
>
> *Dena* (dumping water): Dumping. Lots of goosh.
>
> *Paula:* No more. It's getting too gooey, right? We have a magic. We're magic witches of the East, right? She's never gonna learn about us. She'll die.

Megan (arriving): We'll be the fairest one in the world. (She starts stirring in the other tub).

Dena: (running back and forth between the two tubs, with handfuls of mixture for each): We're gonna have our magic. This is our magic food for Snow White.

Megan: We don't blow hair out of our nose. The witch doesn't blow hair out of her nose. How about, we don't blow hair out of our nose, but our mother does?

Readings like this lead to wonderful discussions and motivations to observe children closely.

Strategy: Seeing Is Believing

A critical factor in the observation process is the ability to suspend one's own point of view to objectively see a situation. To consider how our own filters influence what we see, we use a simple strategy with a picture.

We ask for three volunteers to leave the room as we distribute a photograph depicting interactions between children and adults. We call the volunteers back into the room one at a time and ask each to study the photograph for a few minutes. Then we ask them to tell us what they saw.

The debriefing discussion focuses on the different perspectives people have and what influenced their interpretation of the photo. We emphasize the need to learn observation skills in order to get an objective picture of children and their behavior.

Strategy: Questions for Observing

To practice seeing with objectivity followed by the art of interpretation, we use short video clips of individual children of different ages. We watch an infant, toddler, and preschooler and discuss the following questions.

• What did you specifically see?
• How would you name the essence of this experience for this child?
• What does this child know how to do?
• What does this child find frustrating?
• How does this child feel about themselves?

We probe the first question in depth; formulating objective descriptions is a critical skill in the observation process. We write the descriptions teachers offer on chart paper and, when they make overly general statements, ask, "What did you specifically see that makes you say that?" We insist on statements that can be backed up with descriptive data.

For example, if someone says "the child was angry," we respond "What did you specifically see that made you think he was angry?" When they offer specifics, for example "I saw the child frown, stomp his feet, and yell out loud," we record those observations. Initially, we steer away from any inferences and conclusions because we want to stress the importance of objectively gathering clues and information before interpreting data.

As we move to the art of interpretation, we focus on what the experience might be from the child's point of view. Putting themselves in children's shoes is always an inspiring and insightful activity for teachers. It increases their sensitivity, enjoyment, and understanding of children and their development. They come away with a new respect for the complexity and importance of children's self-initiated activities.

We refer to the child's perspective as their "developmental theme." This term helps teachers begin to think about themes in a different way. It conveys the idea that, given the opportunity, children will choose to explore those tasks and skills that are optimal for their individual developmental level. Our hope is that teachers will become skilled observers of children's developmental themes and do their "theme" planning with this new perspective. A useful resource for developing observation skills is Warren Bentzen's *A Guide to Observing and Recording Behavior* (Delmar Publishing, 1993).

Strategy: Webbing with Themes

With the use of homemade video clips, we pursue the idea of developmental themes. A clip we like shows a child at an easel exploring paint in many ways. We encourage teachers to look below the surface for the themes imbedded in the child's behavior. For instance, is the child's theme really about painting or perhaps exploring how materials can be combined and transformed?

As ideas are offered about the child's developmental themes, we record them as the center of a curriculum web. In this case we might write "mixing and transforming," "sensory exploration," or "pride in discovery." We brainstorm all of the possible enrichment activities that could be provided to explore each of these themes and discuss this as a foundation for curriculum planning.

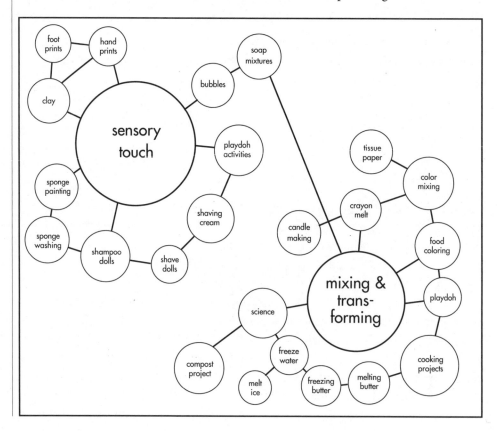

Strategy: Using Observations Skills

We practice observing and recording skills with teachers using the handout below (from an unknown source) and a set of photographs. After reviewing the directions together, we ask small groups to practice using each of the skills by studying the photos. This practice is followed by an observation assignment to continue developing this skill and begin their research on children's developmental themes.

Observation and Recording Skills

Directions: Practice using these skills when studying the photographs given to your group. Work together to write an objective and specific description of each scene.

Objectivity

To record objectively is to avoid making judgments or generalizations. Objective recording is non-interpretive. "The children were much too noisy while they were putting away the blocks," is a judgment about the level of sound. In contrast, "The children putting up the blocks laughed and called out across the room to those who were setting the table for snack time," describes exactly what happened.

Specificity

Specificity requires that the details of the situation be included. Give specific details as to numbers of children and adults involved in an activity, amount and kinds of materials, or other specific relevant information.

Directness

The skill of directness requires that notes include a person's direct quotes. Jason said, "I was playing with that doll first." This is a difficult skill to master, but it gives concrete information to work with when interpreting observation data.

Completeness

Completeness in recording means describing incidents from beginning to end. A complete recording would describe the setting, state who was involved, what action occurred, what the reaction was, and how the incident concluded.

Mood Clues

When mood clues are included in recording, the observer is helped to make inferences about the social-emotional climate of a situation. Mood clues are tones of voice, facial expressions, body posture, hand gestures, and other non-verbal clues.

Follow-Up Observation Assignment

Complete an observation of two or three children for a period of fifteen minutes each. Practice using the observations skills to collect data on what you specifically see. Reading over your notes of specific observations, answer the following questions.

• What does this child know how to do?
• What does this child find frustrating?
• How does this child feel about herself or himself?
• What developmental theme was the child engaged in?

Bring your observations to class next week as we will be using them to develop the research projects.

WEEK 3: THE RESEARCH PROJECT

Because the research project is the main component of the course, we spend a significant block of time helping the students understand its purpose and our expectations. They also need time to form research groups and choose a project theme.

Seeing themselves as researchers is a new concept for most teachers. We build towards this idea with the emphasis placed on acquiring observation skills and the process of having questions to be answered through observation. Discussing the research project guidelines described earlier further suggests new roles for teachers to consider as they plan and carry out curriculum activities.

Strategy: The Role of the Researcher

Because we formulate the concept of new roles for teachers in the language of metaphors, it's helpful to provide an initial activity for them to practice thinking in these terms. Many have not consciously explored the idea of symbolic representations and, through activities such as these, become aware of this aspect of children's play and its relationship to emotional and cognitive development.

Passing out markers and paper, we ask each teacher to create a representation of something that strongly influences their life right now. They can use pictures, words, or designs but they are not to show their representation to anyone. We collect the papers, placing them in a large bag. Teachers take turns choosing a paper and begin the task of researching to whom it belongs.

After quickly studying the papers and putting them aside, teachers engage in a group discussion along the following lines.

Discussion Questions

• Each person shares brief remarks on the kind of day they are having.
• After hearing everyone's initial remarks, each person can ask three questions of other group members. They can ask the same person all three questions, or the same questions to three different people. They may not directly ask someone if they made the representation.
• Each person has two guesses to name who they think the representation belongs to.

In debriefing this activity, we ask teachers about the strategies they used and the skills they needed to discover whose representation they had.

Typical teacher strategies and skills:

• careful observations and note keeping
• gathering clues
• asking the right questions
• pursuing a hunch
• observing body language and mood clues
• problem solving and the process of elimination
• creative associations
• avoiding initial assumptions

These research strategies and skills will serve teachers well in their project and generally in their work with children. We remind them of this as they begin their project work.

WEEK 4: ROLE OF THE TEACHER

As teachers begin to recognize the value of children's self-initiated activities, they are often confused about their role in the classroom. We hear comments like, "The children get so wrapped up in their own activities that I'm not sure how I can teach them anything."

Redefining their teaching role is made easier with some specific reference points. We find metaphors prove useful and fun in this process. The weekly questions offered in their research project guidelines also provoke different thinking about their roles. We use a number of training strategies to explore new roles for teachers, many of which are discussed in section 3. Here are a few additional ones. Further discussion and strategies on the role of the teacher can be found in chapter 10.

Strategy: Uncovering the Curriculum Theme

Rather than think their job is to present lessons on a topical theme, we hope teachers will see their role in terms of discovering the curriculum themes the children are already exploring. We've devised an activity using a "provision-sustain-enrich-represent" formulation developed by colleagues Betty Jones and Joan Newcomb.

Teachers form small groups to discuss themes they've recently seen in children's play. After five or ten minutes we distribute and review the handout below, asking them to choose a theme from their discussion to practice exploring the four teacher behaviors described.

Provision
Provide enough materials and space for children to explore. What props would help children explore a given theme? Consider props for the dress-up, block, art, and table areas. For example, if the theme seems to be "caring for babies," you might provide such props as baby dolls, blankets, and beds.

Sustain
Once children are absorbed in a play theme, you can do several things to sustain the activity. Teachers can provide more props—bottles, high chairs, car seats, bathing tubs, strollers, slings, snugglies, carriers, and an array of photographs. Try limiting your further participation to asking open-ended questions, making leading statements, and helping them to negotiate problem solving and conflict resolution to keep the play going.

Enrich
Continue to observe. If you discover interest waning or children needing a new level of complexity to sustain their interest, enrich with related props. For example, with the "caring for babies" theme, you might introduce doctor kits or books about the growth and development of babies; arrange for the children to bring in their baby pictures and develop a guessing game or display with them; ask a parent to bring in a real baby; take a field trip to a hospital nursery; explore where babies come from, how they grow, and come into the world, perhaps including examples of different kinds of animal babies. This may lead to classifications of how babies are born in different animal families—mammals, birds, reptiles, and so forth.

Represent
An important role for teachers is helping children represent their experiences. This provides a model for literacy and creative expression as well as the sym-

bolic thinking in their cognitive development. You might ask children if they could use blocks to create the nursery like the one they saw in the hospital. Working with clay, making drawings, and dictating stories are all ways you can represent the children's ideas.

Teachers themselves can make representations of the children's ideas. You can write down their words and read them back; or take photos and caption them together. Telling stories or creating finger plays about the children's activities are other forms of representations. Sketch creations like a block structure, make photocopies, and post one near the block area or put copies on the art table the next day. Children love the recognition they get when teachers represent what they've been doing. It gives further impetus for their own representations. This is a way to document the growing history of classroom activities and children's learning.

As teachers learn the behaviors of provisioning, sustaining, enriching, and representing, they gain insights into other ways they can carry out their teaching role.

Here is the result of one group of teachers who tried this strategy.

Theme observed: hiding

Provision

• bring in large boxes and sheets

Sustain

• notice what children are doing and affirm it
• add flashlights, pillows, clothespins and clothesline, pulley

Enrich

• descriptive language with words such as underneath, in between, enclosure, invisible, perspective, overview
• set up a tent and camping supplies
• extend to outside, build a fort, plan a tree house
• display pictures of different kinds of shelters
• explore concept of shelters for homeless people

Represent

• tell a story, create a song, record a video about the children's activities
• make blueprints or sketches of forts
• record the children's dictation about the activities; make a book
• take photographs and create a display
• make a video
• bring in related books from the library

Strategy: Supporting Children's Play

When teachers understand how their interventions impact children's play, they are usually eager to consider new behaviors. Short scenarios with choices of possible teacher responses are useful activities in this learning process. With the examples below, we discuss the role the teacher is playing and how this might influence the children.

Scenario

Jessica and Ryan are playing in the block area. They are balancing long blocks vertically in one corner and from the other side, rolling cylinder shaped blocks towards the long blocks, trying to knock them over. As blocks get knocked down, they remind each other of the score and whose turn is next.

How do these responses impact the children?

a) The teacher says, "Tell me about what you two are doing."

b) The teacher says, "That's not a safe way to use the blocks. Blocks are for building."

c) The teacher watches, smiles, and walks away. She jots down this quick note for her observation file: "Jessica and Ryan invented a bowling type game. They took turns and kept track of the score, counting how many each of them knocked down and who had more."

d) The teacher brings a pad of paper and marker to the block area and puts it on the shelf. She says, "Here's a score pad if you want to keep track of how many you knock down and whose turn it is."

e) The teacher takes a Polaroid picture of what Jessica and Ryan are doing. At circle time she shows the picture, along with others she has taken, and asks them to tell a story about Jessica and Ryan's play time.

Guidelines for further discussion:
- What role is the teacher playing in each response?
- How might the child feel or interpret this response?
- Does this response help the teacher learn more about the child's play and thinking?
- What response would you like to see happen?

WEEK 5: THE ENVIRONMENT AS CURRICULUM

During this session we want teachers to experience the influential role the environment and materials have in a developmentally appropriate curriculum. This furthers the notion of the teacher's role as provisioner and prop manager.

Strategy: Examining Curriculum Boxes

Assemble a selection of prop boxes representing various approaches to curriculum:

Toy curriculum box

An array of broken toys, including parts of toys; puzzles with missing pieces; cars with missing wheels; dolls with dirty faces or missing limbs, eyes, or clothes; used-up coloring books; broken crayons and dried up markers.

Kitchen drawer curriculum box

A collection of kitchen utensils, including ice cube trays, hand eggbeaters, sifters, grinders, steamers, ice cream scoopers, measuring cups and spoons, nutcrackers, and other kitchen equipment with interesting shapes, sizes, and moveable parts.

Mother nature curriculum box

Items gathered from the out of doors, including shells, pinecones, leaves, beach glass, driftwood, moss, herbs, nuts, rocks, dirt, clay, and sand, aesthetically arranged in see-through containers and baskets.

TV toys curriculum box

Toys related to TV shows and fast food franchises, including action figures of the Ninja Turtles, Barbie, GI Joe, Batman, and Jurassic Park.

Inventor's curriculum box

Collections of recycled materials, including toilet paper rolls, food packaging, buttons, different sizes of tubing, film canisters, telephone wire, corks, medicine bottle cotton, and twist ties, all sorted and organized in see-through containers and Ziploc resealable bags.

Texture curriculum box

An assortment of cloth and textures, including sandpaper, burlap, leather, fur and carpet scraps, ribbon, rope, cord, scarves, laces, netting, nylon stockings, and yarn, with a variety of fabrics, patterns, sizes, thicknesses, and weight.

Hardware curriculum box

Small wood or metal hardware, including locks, hinges, buckles, pulleys, gears, wedges, hole punches, and folding or retractable measuring tapes.

Ask teachers to work in small groups, moving to each box, investigating, discussing, and making notes on the following questions:

- How do the items look, feel, smell, taste, move, and respond to you? What is engaging about them? What is unpleasant?
- What can you do with the items? Explore possibilities for sensory experiences, building and inventions, dramatic play, and games.
- How does the organization, display, and condition of the items impact your response and interactions? Do you feel the material limits your interest or invites possibilities?
- What concepts and skills can children learn from playing with these items?

Teachers enjoy this activity and it generates useful discussion. We can generate a list such as "What makes a toy good for learning?" A major discovery that teachers have is the value of *loose parts*.[4] This concept refers to open-ended materials available for children to use, combine, and create their own inventions. Teachers come to understand the value of open-ended materials when they, themselves, have the opportunity to explore and create with them.

We believe a curriculum environment with loose parts is preferable to one with single-use commercial toys or so-called "learning materials." Loose parts are extremely engaging and promote curiosity, problem solving, and creativity. They provide for a range of cultural and developmental differences and enable teachers to get beyond the limited idea of topical curriculum themes to focusing on providing for the children's developmental themes.

Strategy: Tubes Video

We have made video clips that emphasize the loose parts approach to curriculum planning, and the developmental themes of different ages of children. This is easy for any trainer to do with access to a video camera and a child care program with different age groups. Simply rotate among the rooms, provisioning each with the same selection of open-ended materials. We like to use a large box of clear plastic tubing, all lengths and diameters, easily purchased at hardware stores. With no instructions, put the materials in a corner of the room and videotape what the children do with them.

Showing video clips of different aged children using the same material exposes developmental differences and reinforces the importance of observing children closely. The use of open-ended materials for this activity also emphasizes the value of children's self-initiated play.

As teachers watch these children in action, we discuss the following questions. (Teachers especially delight in giving each developmental theme a name.)

- What specifically did you see each group of children do with the material?
- What interactions among children did you observe?
- What do you think the children were trying to figure out as they used the material?
- How might you name the developmental theme of each age group?

WEEK 6: COGNITIVE DEVELOPMENT

Most teachers think of cognitive development as teaching "academics." Their curriculum plans for this area emphasize teaching the names of things, such as colors or calendar time, or rote memorization, such as naming numerals and alphabet letters. We want to deepen teachers' understandings of the complexity of children's cognitive development and help them recognize the limitations of a teacher-directed academic program for young children.

The "Kinds of Learning" training strategy discussed in chapter 4 is pertinent to understanding children's cognitive development. The following activities also help teachers deepen their understandings of the complex thinking that is often part of children's self-initiated exploration.

Strategy: Collections

For this strategy, ask teachers in advance to bring in any kind of collection they might have. As participants arrive, provide tables to display these collections and allow time for participants to look them over. Then, working in small groups, ask teachers to see how many ways they can sort, classify, arrange, and combine the objects in the collections.

Teachers typically bring remarkable collections for this activity, everything from nature items, such as shells, rocks, and butterflies to jewelry, postcards, socket wrenches, cookbooks, hats, music boxes, footballs, knitting needles, buttons, and family photos. These collections generate genuine interest and enthusiasm. This ultimately leads to a discussion of the complex learning inherent in investigating materials of interest and new understandings of children's need for curriculum materials that are special and meaningful in their lives.

Strategy: Replay Time with Collections

To explore the complexity of cognitive development, we draw on Bloom's Taxonomy[5] and the classification key experiences compiled by High/Scope.[6] After reviewing these with teachers, ask them to return to the collections (or a

Toddlers—Again and again, I do what I do with this stuff.

Threes—Hey! Look what this stuff can do!

Fours and Fives—What can I make this stuff be?

set of open-ended materials provided) to analyze their play with the materials in terms of the thinking skills described below.

Bloom's Taxonomy

Knowledge (lowest level of cognitive functioning): naming, remembering, gathering information

Comprehension: exploring, understanding, interpreting, seeing relationships

Application: using ideas, applying concepts and principles to new situations

Analysis: breaking things down into its parts; seeing relationships between parts; classifying, comparing, contrasting

Synthesis: forming a new whole; constructing own knowledge; making an original plan

Evaluation (highest level of cognitive functioning): judging based on criteria; solution finding and decision making

Key Experiences for Classification

• Investigating and labeling the attributes of things
• Noticing and describing how things are the same and how they are different
• Sorting and matching
• Using and describing something in several different ways
• Describing what characteristics something does not possess or what class it does not belong to
• Holding more than one attribute in mind at a time
• Distinguishing between "some" and "all"

It's often an eye-opener for teachers to discover that their curriculum plans for cognitive development usually address the lowest levels of cognitive functioning. They can cite numerous observations of children functioning at the higher levels, causing them to rethink the way they view and provide for cognitive development.

WEEK 7: LITERACY DEVELOPMENT

Teachers often plan a school readiness curriculum with limited understandings of the cognitive development that contributes to ongoing academic success. For instance, they concentrate on teaching children to memorize ABC's and letter-sound associations, thinking this will enable them to read. Most teachers aren't aware of the stages of literacy development and overlook the important activities that are vital to young children's emerging ability to read and write.

We use several activities to motivate teachers to learn more about this and begin providing appropriate literacy activities in their classrooms.

Strategy: Decoding Stories

Reading is a decoding and comprehension process that involves a number of skills. In our daily lives, adults and children decode and "read" many symbols beyond the written word.

To convey this idea, we distribute a variety of "stories" to be decoded in small groups: typical things include an X-ray, petroglyphs or cave drawings, a postcard in Braille, a reproduction of graffiti, a blueprint or technical drawing, photo illustrations of American Sign Language, and papers or books with words in languages other than English.

Each group is asked to "read" their story to the rest of the participants. There are usually many creative ideas and laughs. We then reflect on the strategies, skills, and information used to decode the story, brainstorming a list that nearly always reflects the research done on the literacy development process. In the discussion, teachers make immediate parallels between this experience and children's efforts to read and write. They are usually eager to digest the handout below.

Levels of Literacy Development

Knowledge of Function of Print
- understanding that print is a spoken word written down
- knowing that print represents things, people, and their ideas
- being aware that print has meaning and is useful in getting needs met

Knowledge of Form of Print
- knowing the names of alphabet letters or symbols
- knowing the sounds associated with letters or alphabet symbols

Knowledge of the Conventions of Print
- book handling and terminology
- oral reading competency
- rules governing grammar, spelling, and symbol formation

We conclude this strategy with a brief discussion on the importance of bilingual education, stressing that many of the same strategies are pertinent for children whose first language is not English. Teachers are fascinated to learn the difference between teaching English as a second language (ESL) and true bilingual education, which has the goal of keeping children developing in their home language, while they work to learn another one.

The research findings of Lily Wong Fillmore illuminate the relationship between the loss of one's home language and the loss of family bonds and cultural attachments.[7] This understanding is new to many teachers and encourages them to rethink their goals and practices when planning for language and literacy development in children who are learning English as their second language.

Strategy: Props for Literacy

To emphasize that learning the function of print is the goal of early literacy activities, ask teachers to work in small groups with the handout "Props in the Environment," found in Appendix B. This handout asks participants to generate ways to provision their classrooms with meaningful, contextual props—props that will enhance children's language and literacy development.

As a follow-up to this activity, we distribute the "Preschool Reading and Writing Skills" handout for participants to use in assessing their classrooms. This handout is also found in Appendix B.

Strategy: Responding to Clues

Because we want to reinforce teacher awareness and skills in responding to teachable moments for literacy, we have developed scenarios for small groups to discuss and share ideas. On occasions we have the small groups record their best answers to be copied and distributed to the entire group.

Every time they used the tools they seemed more confident, focusing more on what they could do and less on the tools themselves. They discovered what they were capable of doing by repeating actions and activities, and then by challenging themselves with some new task. They learned how to implement their ideas.

Esther, teacher,
from her research journal

They learned they could teach each other how to use tools, answer each other's questions, and share tools. I was amazed to watch this, as I had never thought of them as able to do this on their own.

Esther, teacher,
from her research journal

What I've learned from doing this project is that children can come up with the greatest ideas—their own discovery in the midst of play is so wonderful. It's important to watch for that and let children take the lead. Their ownership of an activity gives it great momentum, enthusiasm, and appeal.

Esther, evolving master teacher

Block Scenario

For about two weeks, the same four boys have been playing together in the block area making spaceships from small unit blocks. What could you do to introduce some literacy aspects to this play?

Work Crew Scenario

A crew of workers and machinery has been across the street from your classroom for the last three days, distracting the children from their work time. How could you take advantage of this situation to build some literacy activities?

Shy Artist Scenario

Taiko spends most of her work time in the art area making elaborate collages that she quietly puts in her cubby. She talks very little to other children, but is responsive to most adult initiation. What literacy strategies might you try that incorporate her interest in the art area?

Birthday Scenario

Rochelle, Katie, and Juan all have birthdays coming up and most of their play this month leads to pretend birthday cakes and blowing out candles. Today they made cakes and candles with the peg boards and announced these had to be saved for their party. What could you do to support this play with some literacy building activities?

Cooking Scenario

In the days following a cooking project, children frequently gravitate to the dress-up area pretending to cook and serve each other food. How would you enhance the literacy possibilities in this?

Field Trip Scenario

You are planning a field trip to the fire station. What literacy strategies would you use in field trip preparation, the actual excursion, and as a follow up?

WEEK 8: SHARING RESEARCH PROJECTS AND ENHANCING ADVOCACY SKILLS

Research project presentations are a wonderful culmination of this course and a highlight for us all. We provide time and space for groups to make displays of the representations they have made and collected. The room is suddenly filled with large charts, photographs, posters, actual toys, and materials used in the projects and excited teachers eager to share their new learning about the joys and intrigue of child development. Each group makes a presentation and answers questions.

The close look teachers have just had with children's learning processes leaves them impassioned about appropriate curriculum practices. We want them to leave with some advocacy skills and end our time together with some ceremony. The following three strategies were developed with this in mind.

Strategy: Responding to Pressures

Throughout this course, teachers continually remind us of the need for parent and, in some cases program supervisor, education on child-centered curriculum practices. We want to nurture their watchdog and whistle-blower dispositions, while assisting them with advocacy skills. A version of the TV game show activity described in chapter 9 is an effective strategy here.

Dividing teachers into small groups, we ask each to devise a sound to signal they have an answer. After learning to recognize every group's signal, the game begins. We read a question for each group to discuss. When they feel they have found the best response, they sound their signal and share it with the group.

Sample questions:

- A parent asks: Are you going to teach my child to read in this class?
- Another parent tells you: Isabel knows all the letters of the alphabet but can't seem to write her name. I want her to practice this every day.
- Your program director sends around a memo that says: Beginning in January we need to step up our kindergarten readiness program. Everyone should use our assessment tests to determine where children are deficient and need continual practice.
- From the education coordinator you hear: The NAEYC accreditation criteria requires that we have a yearly curriculum. Please turn in your plans for the year by August 30.

Strategy: Letter to Parents

Ask teachers to work as a group to develop an initial letter to parents regarding children and literacy. The letter should be no more than one page. Because group writing can be cumbersome, the following guidelines might prove useful.

> Directions for writing a parent a letter on literacy
> 1. Brainstorm a list of points to include.
> 2. Decide on priorities, grouping related points together.
> 3. Number the order in which you wish to cover the points.
> 4. Write a paragraph for each set of points.
> 5. Make a final copy to be read to the whole group.

Strategy: Children Were Not Born to . . .

To encourage teachers to carry their passion for child-centered practices on into their careers, we've developed a choral reading activity with an excerpt from Bev Bos' *Before the Basics: Creating Conversations with Children* (Turn the Page Press, 1983). Small groups of teachers read their assigned sections out loud together, adding their own rhythmic styles. Each time we've used this strategy, teachers have created expressive, playful performances, ranging from poetry to rap.

We distribute the excerpts below, along with rhythm instruments, scarves, and fabric, asking small groups to create dramatic readings. After the groups have planned their section, we ask one person to act as the director, calling the various parts together on cue.

> *Children were not born to wear name tags.* Imagine how you'd feel if your spouse or parent or child slapped a name tag on you each morning because it was too difficult or bothersome to remember your name.
>
> *Children were not born to sit still.* When I visit schools and I don't hear children asking questions, arguing, even interrupting, I suspect there's little learning going on. Children must be actively involved to learn.
>
> *Children were not born to stand in line.* Since most adults don't like to stand in line, we must understand, if we think about it, how awful standing in line is

for young children—all that energy and curiosity simply brought to a halt. Of course not!

Children were not born to speak with "inside voices." They can't shout all of the time, all at once, but when a young child—or even an enthusiastic older child—comes running in shouting, that raised voice is discovery—joy—wonder—and we need to listen before we ask for quiet.

Children were not born to walk. They were born to run—barefoot over rocks, through the water, through the mud. We need to give greater recognition to the energy and joy of children.

Children were not born to wear shoes. In our concern for hygiene and safety, we develop amnesia. Give children a break. Remember how good mud felt between the toes?

Children were not born to wear designer clothes. What an injustice to young children to mar their joy in discovering art, mud, building materials, sand, paint, or water by the sinking feeling that they have ruined their clothes. No wonder young children often prefer wearing no clothes at all.

Children were not born to be neat. I don't interrupt the new activity by insisting upon immediate cleanup of the old. The child's interest in discovery is more important than the cleanup. There's certainly more to life than putting away our belongings.

We have parallel sentiments when it comes to the teachers with whom we work. Teachers in training were not born to sit still, to work alone, be receptacles of information, memorize theories, pass tests, or go through someone else's motions and techniques.

Instead, teachers deserve engaging pursuits, where they use their minds, bodies, and experiences to find joy, success, and challenge in their learning and teaching. They need opportunities to collaborate with others, find their own voices and make meaningful contributions. Like everyone else, teachers are entitled to make mistakes and work through the disequilibrium that complex learning brings. They deserve the enrichment that comes with exposure to perspectives and experiences different from their own.

PLANTING THE SEED
We believe the project approach and other constructivist learning strategies described throughout this book offer a meaningful and effective pedagogy to teacher education. As we've come to consistently use these approaches in our work, our own joy and passion for teaching and learning have been enhanced. This, in turn, keeps us pursuing new ideas and strategies.

Hopefully, our stories have sparked your enthusiasm for this approach to training teachers, and you too will use and advocate for it in your own work and beyond. Teachers and children deserve no less.

Section 7
The Invisible Life of a Trainer

$\mathcal{N}$ot unlike the job of teaching young children, the most laborious aspect of being a trainer is behind the scenes, tending to the details of planning, preparing materials, mopping up, and evaluating. We find it fun, even exhilarating at times, to invent training agendas and strategies. However, preparing and gathering resources and then, afterwards, organizing and storing them for future use, eventually feels like less than a good time. Because we know that a hands-on training approach allows us to genuinely have fun and focus on participants and their needs, it feels definitely worth the effort. Besides, it's important to us to model and regularly experience the roles we continually advocate teachers play with young children.

We recognize that program directors and education coordinators have a multitude of responsibilities beyond staff training and many of these require extensive preparation and follow up. Still, when we held these jobs ourselves we found our staff training was effective only when we took the time for creative planning and resource collection. And, as we tell teachers struggling to plan their learning environments, once a system for planning and securing resources is in place, it will serve you well for years to come.

Though we have mobility, flexibility, and variety in our jobs, we who work as staff trainers can easily experience the same sense of isolation that teachers and directors speak of. Whether working in one city or crisscrossing the country, it is easy to get caught in one's own little bubble. And when the bubbles burst, who can we turn to? Building professional networks is not only important for staying current and connected in the early childhood field, but also serves as a mechanism for problem solving, collaboration, and creativity. This close association with colleagues and a continual return to self-care is what has sustained our enthusiasm and commitment over the twenty-some years of our work in the field.

Chapter 23
Training Resources and Supplies

A quick way to discover someone's approach to training is to observe what they carry as they walk in the door. If it's a "make and take" workshop, trainers come loaded down with supplies to make puzzles, lotto games, or other learning materials. Trainers with a banking pedagogy, wanting to convey all they know on a topic, typically arrive with a briefcase of handouts, beautifully written flip charts, overhead transparencies, or a forty-five minute videotape around which to build their presentation.

Adopting a constructivist approach and active learning strategies for adults means building an array of curriculum materials for training. When we enter the door for a training, we resemble some of the preschool teacher roles we advocate—prop manager, treasure hunter, and pack rat. Our large handbags always have an ample stash of certain things that might be needed; other supplies can typically be found in bins in our cars; and a rotating set of materials steadily move in and out of our office storage. Here are some of the strategies that keep us sane and prepared for nearly anything.

Strategy: Never Leave Home Without It

Because most of our training involves an "uncovering process" to explore teacher needs and understandings that relate to larger early childhood concepts, we carry supplies that support this approach, rather than an array of polished charts and overheads for presentations. Typically, you'll always find the following things in our traveling bags:

• large sheets of chart paper, sometimes folded for easy transport
• several boxes of markers
• rolls of masking tape and a package of fix-it gum, for hanging things on walls
• scissors
• index cards, scrap paper, and Post-it sticky pads

Strategy: Props for Active Learning

A centerpiece for many of our training strategies is material to explore, simulate, or represent experiences. Like teachers of young children, we continually scout out open-ended props for our adult learners to use in exploring ideas. This includes things with moveable parts, multiple textures, and aesthetics. Strategies throughout this book reveal how we use these materials. Our collections, ready for use in any given training, include the following:

For a "loose parts" catalog contact:

The Creation Station
7533 Olympic View Drive
Edmonds, WA 98026
(206) 775-7959
or
Creative Educational Surplus
9801 James Circle, Suite C
Bloomington, MN 55431
612-884-6427

After a few months of training I started to feel like a traveling road show. My car contained an incredible variety of "loose parts"— art materials, books, games, and just plain junk intended for different people in different situations at different centers.

Kristin, training colleague

Nature materials

shells, rocks, seed pods, pinecones, marble chips, driftwood, twigs, leaves, feathers, dried flowers.

Recycled materials

corks, buttons, yarn spools, fabric pieces, lids and bottle tops, tubes, film canisters, wood, cardboard, foam core and plastic scraps, various sizes of boxes, hair rollers.

Moving parts

clothespins, eggbeaters, jar openers, tongs, pizza cutting wheels, hand drills, metal steamers, pulleys, boxes with lids.

Things that hold things together

laces, twist ties, stickers and labels, nuts and bolts, telephone wire, yarn, string, rope.

Children's toys and materials

a supply of typical children's toys—puzzles, play props, and art materials for teachers to explore and critique; and more unusual and creative examples of discovery, multicultural, and inclusive materials, sometimes homemade to spark new thinking.

Pictures and photographs

pictures clipped from magazines, newspapers, calendars, and greeting cards to use in exploring concepts; photographs of harder to find images reflecting positive, inclusive images of the diversity of the human family.

Fabric and textiles

several yards of different ethnic fabrics that can be used as tablecloths or wall hangings to soften up and add an aesthetically pleasing aspect to training environments.

Rather than drudgery work, gathering resources can become a source of sensory delight and discovery. It's rejuvenating to take yourself outdoors to the woods, the beach, your own backyard or neighborhood, eyes and ears alert. Be kind to Mother Nature and conscientious about what you take. When outdoors, be alert for bottle tops and other discarded items. You can simultaneously help clean up the environment and add to your collections.

At home and in your office, keep a box or bag where you can toss in packaging, paper towel rolls, string, twist ties, and other found and recyclable materials. Neighbors, businesses, and friends are happy to save recyclable items. When our storage bins overflow, we take these items to early childhood programs that have discovered the value of open-ended materials. Regular visits to thrift stores and garage sales are preschool teacher behaviors we still carry with us.

A few cities are fortunate enough to have storefront businesses specifically aimed at supplying children and parents with unusual, terrific business and industrial castoffs. Search these out or consider securing such inexpensive training supplies through mail order.

Strategy: Print Resources

We always bring books with us to training sessions—favorite adult and children's titles related to the training topic. Bibliographies are useful, but seeing, touching, smelling, and browsing through books will more likely invite teachers to see them as resources. When building a training session around the ideas of a particular book, we purchase or make consignment arrangements with a bookstore or publishing company to have copies on hand to sell.

As with most educators, we use handouts and articles to support our training. However, unless they are part of a given training strategy, we seldom distribute them during a workshop; we usually wait until the conclusion. Whenever possible we limit handouts to those that specifically relate to the focus of our activities. Limited and focused handouts are useful in helping teachers revisit their training experience, consolidate their thinking, and internalize the concepts.

Several excellent early childhood professional journals permit reproduction of articles for in-service training. In cases where permission rights are not noted, a simple form letter can be used to request this from the author or publisher. We flag valuable articles as we come across them in journals and keep a topical filing system. Current favorites often travel with us to pass along to colleagues and teachers with whom we are in regular contact. We often make up our own packets of articles related to a particular topic for use in lieu of a book. To do this requires permission from publishers and sometimes a small fee. Teachers are usually happy to reimburse us for any costs associated with producing these packets. Periodicals we consistently draw on are listed below, with further annotations in the Recommended Resources section.

- *Young Children,* NAEYC
- *Child Care Information Exchange,* Exchange Press
- *Dimensions,* Southern Early Childhood Association (SECA)
- *High/Scope Resource and High/Scope Extensions,* High/Scope Foundation
- *Harvard Educational Review,* Harvard College
- *In Context,* New Horizons for Learning
- *Caring for the Little Ones,* Karen Miller
- *ERIC Digest,* ERIC
- *Report on Preschool Programs,* Business Publishers, Inc.
- *Rethinking Schools,* Rethinking Schools, Ltd.

Strategy: Using Technology

If we were rich, we'd probably buy stock in our local copy store. The incredible array of technology now available to support our work makes us feel like kids in a candy store. With the use of a computer we can make beautiful flyers, checklists, and observation forms and have them enlarged to any size. Photographs and pictures can be color copied and converted into puzzles, lacing cards, and stand-up props. These, along with a scroll saw, expand our options for creating low-cost learning materials for our training and the classrooms we visit.

Prices on camcorders and VCRs continue to come down, making them accessible for creating video clips of children for use as training tools in workshops. Teachers can benefit from watching videotapes of themselves or their rooms, a direct source of feedback that often leads to powerful insights. If you can't afford to buy one, consider forming a video equipment cooperative, with several people or programs purchasing and sharing the equipment.

The early childhood field is about as low-tech as they come, and because it is a predominantly female field, we have internalized the mistaken idea that technology is out of our reach. If you haven't already done so, invest some time in learning to use the technology that will enrich your training for a reasonable cost.

Strategy: Setting the Stage

As if our needs are less significant than those of children, little attention is paid to creating an inviting learning environment for adults. Most conference or classroom settings are sparse, dull, and rigid. On-site training typically happens on child-sized chairs in the classroom or hall. Though early childhood providers tend to be easy-going and flexible, doesn't our professional development deserve better than this? Is there a notion that if teachers are comfortable, they will be distracted and not absorb the training? We have found just the opposite. When they are relaxed and comfortable, participants become more engaged with our training.

The ideal training setup has comfortable furniture, natural light, and fresh air. The room is neither too sparse nor too cluttered. There is space for active, small group work, with rest rooms and snacks nearby. Because most training settings need some beautification and reorganization, we try to arrive forty-five minutes before the training begins. We need time to set up resources we have brought and rearrange furniture. We bring decorative fabric, posters, and pictures to brighten and soften the room.

As participants arrive, we try to speak with each individually, make name tags available and encourage people to get to know the resources and other people in the room.

Strategy: Assessments and Evaluations

We find evaluations critical in our work for two purposes. They provide us with direct feedback on the reaction to our activities. Also, when participants have thoughtful evaluation forms to complete, this is yet another activity for self-reflection and learning.

In evaluations we frame questions to help teachers reflect on the elements of effective learning. We design evaluations to encourage teachers to become more intentional in their approach to a training topic and see their power and responsibility for constructing their own knowledge. With one-time workshops, we begin an evaluation form with questions about the expectations teachers brought to the training—what they hoped to learn and if their expectations were met. We also ask them what new ideas they are considering and what questions they are leaving with.

Teachers find this emphasis useful and many spend a good amount of time completing evaluations. We have developed a variety of evaluation tools depending on the kind of training we are doing and the amount of time we spend with students. Some are brief, while others seem playful.

When a training is to continue over a period of time, we usually begin with a pre-assessment tool, asking questions about the teacher's current knowledge and experiences related to the topic. We also inquire as to the interests and expectations they have for our time together. Pre-assessments help us get to know the teachers and help them begin to focus on their current understandings and experiences as a basis for constructing new knowledge.

We are explicit with participants about the value of pre-assessments for our planning as well as for their own learning. Over the course of a class or extended in-service program, we use interim evaluations to check on how things are going. The final evaluation refers them back to their original expectations and asks them to reflect on what worked well for their learning and what would have improved the class or training. (See Section 6 for details of this pre-assessment/final evaluation process in a class. Sample evaluation forms are also in Appendix C.) Other assignments, such as the reflective writing observations described elsewhere in this book, provide ongoing feedback and information about how our approaches are impacting participants' learning. We try to stay alert to teachers' interests, questions, and responses during activities as a steady source of feedback.

We use a similar approach when working on-site with teachers in their classrooms. We have several meetings during the duration of the training to discuss how our work together is progressing and other ways we can offer assistance. The key is to continually help teachers see that they are in charge of their own learning and that the needs and interests they identify are being addressed.

When teachers reflect on their own experiences and learning during our trainings, we get much more feedback than if they just responded to questions about us and our presentation. Answers like "It was great," "I wouldn't change anything," or "I would rather have had less small group discussions" are not really useful for our egos or our future planning. We get more in-depth information and feedback about what has and hasn't worked in a training when we take a constructivist approach to evaluations and ask about the learning of participants. Here are evaluations that really have meaning for us.

> I came to class hoping to get ideas about discipline that would be effective and constructive with my two-year-old twins. I think I got a base I can work with. Hearing that it is okay to react humanly but try to be intentional and consistent was very reassuring. I was kind of hoping for some quick fix solutions, but I guess nothing this important is that easy!
>
> *Gina, parent*

> I came to class anticipating to learn just what the title of the series said: Guidance of Young Children, and I did.
>
> I believe I covered a lot of ground with myself tonight on looking at how I deal with situations and asking myself why am I dealing with it this way, and how can I have dealt with it better? I haven't ever really sat down and questioned what made me discipline or punish the way I do. I feel I am on my way to being more aware.
>
> *Trish, teacher*

I hoped to learn some strategies for conflict solving and did. What really helped me was realizing how much I do the "quick-fix" and now I see how the behavior just stops for the moment but continues to happen. I'm going to go to work tomorrow with a "discipline" attitude instead of a "punishment" attitude. I'm going to take the time to explain what children can do instead of hitting, etc. It should be a learning process instead of a punishment! See you next week!

Jody, teacher

I came hoping to find some new ways to develop discipline skills. I enjoyed the class because it reminded me of some of the things I already know and do, and gave me some new things to try. What worked for me was hearing other people discuss their situations and suggestions and give ideas. It made me stretch my definitions of things. I look forward to the other two classes I'm taking.

Jan, family provider

Chapter 24
Getting and Staying Organized

In gatherings of colleagues, we often swap jokes about trying to find our desks, kitchen tables, or beds under the piles of papers, books, and bags that forever grow there. Laughter only goes so far if locating agendas, handouts, and supplies for tomorrow's workshop becomes a reoccurring nightmare.

A prop- and resource-dependent approach to training can be overwhelming if one is not highly organized. Many program directors and trainers have developed an intentional style and system for organizing their work life while others remain "organizationally impaired." It took us awhile, but over time we've developed some systems that keep our life as trainers under control. You might find a way to adapt some of these to your needs.

Strategy: Storage and Transportation

Whether in an office, garage, or basement, having a central place to store supplies is essential. We use a mixture of cardboard boxes, baskets, see-through containers, and Ziploc resealable bags to keep our written materials and props organized, easily accessible, and aesthetically appealing to participants when they use them in a training activity. Whether organized by item or training topic, this allows for a quick gathering and return of materials as we move in and out of training sites. It is well worth the investment of time and money should you do training full-time or as only one aspect of your job.

As we've become full-timers, sometimes training at three sites a day, our cars have necessarily become a place for storing as well as transporting certain supplies. A hanging file box holds frequently used handouts, while another box stores similarly used books. Several stacking baskets contain the "never leave home without it" supplies and there's room for rotating prop storage. A folding luggage cart makes it easy to move things in and out of buildings. For trainings of large groups, we now use a big suitcase with wheels.

Strategy: Filing and Record-Keeping

Because we have no secretary or support staff, it's easy for paperwork and filing to get out of hand. We now carry a supply of file folders so we can immediately label and file new print resources. Two folders labeled "refile" and "photocopy" are our constant companions.

For our records and follow-up purposes, we have a sign-up list for training participants, using a mailing label format. This allows us to keep track of those attending and easily alert them to future trainings we offer. Because teachers

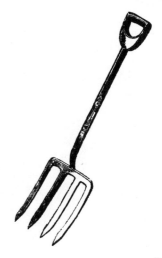

Filing is a pain but a really significant part of the work. My ability to build on previous training depends on being able to find what I did. Working on a computer has helped me think about how to file more efficiently.

Joan, training colleague

should have documentation of training they take, we have created a generic certificate of completion that we leave with participants at the end of a training. When a group is large, the person who arranged the training is usually willing to see these are filled out and distributed. A sample certificate is in Appendix C.

Chapter 25
Professional Collaboration

It's a lonely job in many ways. I've come to rely on regular get-to-gethers with other trainers to kvetch, problem solve, or just listen. Learning that I am not alone in many of my dilemmas about training has been very nurturing.

Kristin, training colleague

Much of our own learning and ideas for teacher training have come from exchanges with colleagues. Early on in our work, we started an informal support group for staff trainers, which quickly led to the development of a course on training early childhood trainers. Though we were the official instructors, our own professional development was greatly enhanced through the exchanges and consolidation of ideas during these courses.

While it is true that each of us must construct our own knowledge, there is no point in re-inventing a wheel that can make all of our work go more smoothly. Ongoing opportunities for sharing and discussion among colleagues are a vital part of our professional growth. Despite the fact that we may be competing for some training contracts, we never hesitate to share a strategy, handout, or workshop format with colleagues. Our profession needs all the help and good ideas available. Peer exchanges are stimulating and rejuvenating. If you don't have one in your area, we recommend making a few phone calls and starting a monthly meeting of early childhood trainers.

Strategy: Networking

In some early childhood education communities, supervisors and trainers are in regular contact with each other, while in other places they are working alone and in isolation. Professional affiliation and collaboration not only advance the overall quality of programs for young children, but they also lead to a valuable network of sources for training contracts. We keep a file of colleagues and their areas of expertise so that we can refer others to them or use them as resources for ourselves. We're strong believers in the notion that "when you come on something good, first thing to do is share it with whoever you can find."[1] We practice this and request it of others.

Strategy: Mentoring

We are committed to mentoring new people into trainer positions for several reasons. Our profession currently lacks an inviting career path, and people ready for a change often leave the field entirely or move into administrative positions for which they have little experience or expertise. We increasingly find our time spent coaching supervisors in staff training skills as often as working directly with teachers ourselves. Supervisors are in a much better position than we are to make a significant impact on teacher performance.

With the structure of power and privilege in our society favoring European Americans, there is a racial imbalance in our profession's leadership positions. We know we must be very intentional in addressing this inequity, and actively make room for and, where necessary, mentor people of color into supervisor and

trainer roles. Training with a diverse range of teachers has vitally enriched our own work. We've discovered our blind spots and biases, along with some wonderfully different ways of thinking about and being with children.

Mentor teacher programs are being piloted in a number of states as a method of giving master teachers recognition and compensation for training their peers.[2] Though we have no formal mentor teacher program in our area, we have seen teachers refine their own practice as they informally become involved in coaching someone else. Whenever possible we recruit master teachers to assist us in leading workshops. We encourage other teachers to visit their classrooms and see these masters at work. On occasion we have arranged with a program director to provide paid release time for a master teacher to visit, coach, and conference with another teacher seeking professional development. This model proved exciting to all involved.

Chapter 26
Minding Your Business

There are a variety of settings in which one can work as a teacher trainer. In the past we have directed child care programs and been Head Start education coordinators. Working as an employee of someone else means you can give minimal attention to details of business employment. There is initial paperwork to complete, payroll stubs to monitor, and annual income taxes to be filed. Currently, our employment has shifted and we combine a number of part-time options as college instructors and private consultants. This has both simplified and complicated our lives. The following strategies may seem obvious, but it took us awhile to learn them.

Strategy: Taxes and Licenses

As more of our training work moved to a contractual basis, we have had to learn the ropes of operating as a small, sole proprietor business. There are advantages and disadvantages of moving to this official status and it's worth a small fee to get some advice on the details of business licensing, insurance, taxes, and paperwork. Depending on the geographic range of your business, you may be obligated to city, county, and state regulations.

Libraries and bookstores stock numerous useful books on consulting and small business operations. Most states have materials that are free upon request. Small business associations in large cities often conduct seminars with pertinent information and technical assistance. Though this is not an area of high interest for us, we've found it useful to get some training in this area for ourselves. In addition to making us more savvy businesswomen, it further enhances our ability to offer technical assistance to child care directors who are struggling with running a business as well as providing quality care and education for young children.

Strategy: Promoting Yourself

Socialized as passive caring-for-others females and working in the early childhood profession makes it difficult for many women to actively promote themselves as professional experts. Furthermore, we see that many who claim this title are long out of touch with the daily life and working conditions of a child care provider or teacher, but that's not true for us. For many early childhood teachers and directors, it takes some "self-image adjustment" to assertively move into the self-employed training business.

Operating as a professional trainer requires business cards, a letterhead, and record-keeping and invoice systems. If you want to primarily work as an independent training consultant, it is useful to develop a brochure and promotional materials about specific trainings you offer. We've also discovered that the

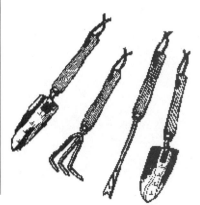

It's taken a long time for me to feel comfortable negotiating fees for my training services. I know too much about tight child care budgets and have often felt guilty making much more per hour than the teachers I work with.

Camilla, training colleague

certificates of completion forms described above become an indirect means of promoting your work.

Offering workshops at conferences and local professional meetings is a good way for people to become familiar with your approach to training. When we worked as program directors and education coordinators, we often exchanged workshop trainings with colleagues in parallel positions. This gave us more experience and exposure and clarified what further knowledge and skill we needed to become full-time trainers.

Strategy: Setting Fees

For us the most agonizing aspect of doing early childhood training is negotiating a fee. Budgets are thin and no one makes much money in this field. When we discovered what most private sector professional consultants and trainers earn, we realized our own self-esteem was suffering. Still, the discrepancy between the worthless wages of a child care provider and the fees charged by a corporate trainer have been a real challenge to our conscience.

In setting fees for our work, we want to be reasonable and fair while acknowledging our experience, expertise, and value to programs. We need to keep a roof over our heads and pay our own health insurance and social security taxes while looking ahead to possible lean times and retirement. Ultimately, this dilemma has led us to Robin Hood economics.

We have set a basic fee structure that builds in the cost of planning, travel time, materials, and a portion of the above mentioned costs. A guiding rule of thumb is that we spend two to three hours in planning, preparation, and follow-up for every actual contact hour of training. We explain this to those requesting training and negotiate from there according to the agency's budget, our time, and current financial needs. There are some trainings we are willing to do for free and some that cost agencies top dollar.

We became involved in the Worthy Wage Campaign because we found that continual staff turnover was undermining our work as staff trainers. No sooner would we train someone than they would leave the field. As we coached teachers to advocate for themselves and demand worthy wages, we realized that we had to do that for ourselves as well.

Chapter 27
Tending Your Own Garden

Just like teachers of young children, teacher trainers are subject to burnout. The pervasive lack of value and resources for children in our society impacts all of our lives. The lack of a national child care policy, along with little understanding outside our profession about the need for a trained early childhood workforce, continually plagues us. Even close to home where we continually tell stories of our work, friends and family members will wrinkle their brows and ask, "So what is it you do anyway?"

In the early years of our profession, most on-site trainers were teachers who, because they were effective with children, were informally asked to help new teachers learn the ropes. Until fairly recently, becoming a teacher trainer hasn't been viewed as a goal in a career path. Now, with the expansion of care and education programs for young children, and the concurrent lack of qualified teachers for these programs, there are more and more job opportunities with responsibilities that include staff development and training. The training of trainers component of our profession is struggling to catch up, both conceptually and practically.

Early childhood teacher trainers need knowledge and strategies for adult education. We need expertise on a variety of early childhood topics, including issues of management and supervision such as business and finance, strategic planning, team building, and conflict management. Being good in classrooms with children hardly prepared us for this. To be effective, our own education and skills must be upgraded.

The work of training early childhood teachers and directors offers many challenges. In child care programs where the need is the greatest, there are limited resources and time blocks for staff training. Head Start programs, on the other hand, have time and money designated for staff training, but it is rarely focused on individual training needs assessment. If we aren't directors or education coordinators, those of us trying to earn a living as an ECE trainer paste together a variety of part-time contracts in these settings, often working under less than desirable conditions, with paychecks somewhat unpredictable and intermittent. So why do we keep at it?

For us the answer lies in the opportunity to help create and influence the direction of programs for teachers, parents, and children. We can work at a level of systems design or direct instruction to bring about important changes in the quality of life for people. Moving between time with adults and classrooms with children, we have the delight of observing and participating in the span of human development. Significant new learning can be life changing for adults and when it happens before our eyes, there is no more satisfying work we can imagine.

Our schedules may be unpredictable, but they are also extremely flexible and varied. To keep ourselves fresh and eager to continue our work, we build in time

to pursue our own educational interests. We regularly spend time in conversation with colleagues, stay involved in professional activities, and actively advocate for change in the status, compensation, and working conditions of child care providers and teachers. Above all, we remain playful in our own learning pursuits as well as in our efforts to educate and advocate for others.

If you find yourself continually stressed, struggling against burnout, or in a rut repeating the same things over and over again, we recommend building in regular time for your own nourishment, both personally and professionally. Put it on your calendar and treat the task of self-care as seriously as you do any other demand or deadline breathing down your neck. We emphasize this for teachers and we must do the same for ourselves as well.

Sometimes it's as simple as taking a long walk or having tea with a colleague to get away from the gridlock of people and papers needing your attention. Getting a stress reduction plan built into your life is a critical part of the equation. But equally important is the task of continuing to feed your creativity and vision. If we are to stay in this work and contribute not only to our own advancement but also to the uplifting of the profession as a whole, we will need stamina, courage, and an active imagination.

We conclude with a couple of examples of how we stretch our eyes and brains to see and invent new things. Finally, there's an exercise for you to try which, hopefully, will reap some insight as to what your next step is as this book draws to a close.

Strategy: Thinking in Things

We have great fun using metaphors to push our thinking about concepts we are exploring. For instance, once when we felt stuck in writing a section of this book, we left the computer and took a walk through Deb's house, challenging each other to explain how an object we saw could be a metaphor for constructivism or the banking method of education.

Soon our creative juices were flowing again. We decided that a blanket could represent the banking method of education if we wanted to "cover the curriculum"; or it could stand for constructivism, reminding teachers of the need to "uncover the curriculum." When the washing machine was on "the soak cycle," that stood for the banking method, but "the spin cycle" represented constructivism.

Playful, goofy activities remind us that training is not about developing the perfect presentation, but about finding new ways to understand our experiences and the bigger picture they are connected to.

Strategy: All the World's a Possible Training Strategy

Training strategies come to us in the most unexpected moments and places. This is what makes our work seem like play. Out and about during our daily lives—paying bills, waiting in line, watching a movie, attending an art exhibit, riding on the bus, shopping at the grocery store—we continually find displays and activities that beg to become strategies for active learners. For example, when visiting a wonderful exhibition entitled *La Frontera/The Border* at a local art museum, we were moved by many of the ways artists depicted the Mexico/United States border experience.

One of the pieces was an alphabet book where the artist used each letter of the alphabet to list an English and Spanish word to evoke an idea or feeling related to living on the border of these two cultures. These simple words powerfully captured the conflicting experiences of being proud and rejected; doing real and meaningful work, yet being marginalized, misrepresented, and exploited. We immediately saw parallels for the work of child care in this country and in our next workshop had participants develop similar alphabet books to identify the issues surrounding their inadequate wages and working conditions.

Strategy: This One's for You

You've probably not read this book in one setting or from cover to cover. No doubt you've scanned the table of contents or flipped to various sections that seemed of interest to you. The question is, do you have a clear picture of the big ideas that relate to effective teacher training? Are there some outstanding questions you want to pursue before trying some of these ideas? Or are you ready to jump in and approach your teacher training with some new tools?

Perhaps the ideas in this book are familiar to you and you are just seeking some fine tuning in your understandings or training strategies. This is a good time to take stock of where you are and what you want to do next. Get a pencil and paper and try these exercises, alone or, better yet, with a colleague.

1. Think of a recent observation of a teacher that left you uneasy. Recall as much detail as you can to get yourself mentally back in that scene. Now, draw a line down the middle of your paper. On the left side, make a list of five things that you had the urge to say to this teacher. On the right side, list five questions that would help you gain more insight into this teacher's behavior. Is there a significant difference between what you have on each side of the paper? Which side of the paper seems closest to your practice? Therein lies some clue as to a goal you might have for this next period of your professional development.

2. Go through the contents of your purse, fanny pack, or desk and choose several objects that represent the role you currently play with most of the teachers you train. Name and describe these on your paper. Are you satisfied with these roles or is there another trainer role you would like to develop for yourself? What might represent that role? Develop this object as a totem for yourself and, in the coming weeks, pursue more insight into how this might help you move toward developing this role for yourself.

3. Using circles, arrows, or other symbols that make sense to you, develop a diagram of your personal and professional circles, noting influences and constraints on you, and influences and constraints you might have on them. Where do you feel the most powerful? the least? What sustains you and what drains you? How do these circles inhibit or enhance your learning to work better with diversity? List a few steps toward change that you want to make.

4. Make an alphabet chart, book, or cards capturing the ideas that you most want to remember about effective teacher training. Choose one or two at a time and learn more about them by rereading sections of this book, reading other

A is for:
A living wage
Advocacy for ourselves as well as children
Ain't I a woman? And why is this women's work?

B is for:
Baby-sitters, NOT!
Broke, always
Bigger budgets for child care programs

C is for:
Caring staff
Costs reflect reality of salary needs
Come on in to the worthy wage movement!

resources listed in the Recommended Resources section, instigating discussions with colleagues, practicing, and continuing self-reflection.

PLANTING THE SEED

We've come to the end of this year's harvest, recognizing, of course, that it represents years of gathering seeds and tilling the ground by those who have come before us. We are grateful to our elders across this profession and commit ourselves to carrying their contributions forward. Our colleagues, friends, and family, beside whom we work, have fertilized our thinking and keep us going season after season. We thank you.

Each year our garden is full of annuals, new crops of teachers just getting started, and, of course, favorite perennials, those who return each year to masterfully bloom. These teachers sustain us through our bouts with slugs and pests. We thank you, thank you, again and again.

We will continue to sharpen and share tools, and trust our paths will cross with many of you who till the same soil. The earth's been good to us. We want to walk with care and with ever deeper understandings as we seek to conserve and redistribute its bounty. Thanks to you, the reader, for plowing through this with us, for your interest, and for your feedback, which we'd love to hear.

Glossary

active learning: the act of involving the learner in activities that may include manipulation of materials, investigation, dialogue with others, and physically moving.

banking method: an approach to teaching first described by Paulo Freire, a Brazilian educator, as one in which the teacher attempts to "deposit" knowledge in students, assuming they will later be called upon to make "withdrawals."

bias: a preconceived attitude or way of thinking based on particular perspectives influencing perceptions and behaviors; often associated with exclusivity, prejudice, or negative views of those who are different; may be personal or tied to institutional structures of power.

big ideas: the larger body of ideas or conceptual framework of which a particular topic is a part; in training teaching our activities are built around big ideas drawn from the core knowledge developed by the early childhood profession.

broadcasting: spreading the news of something we hope others will pay attention to, thereby spreading the seeds of some possible change in behavior, attitudes, or thinking.

CDA: Child Development Associate; a credentialing process that formally certifies entry level competency in working with young children; administered by the Council for Early Childhood Professional Recognition in Washington, D.C.

child-centered curriculum: an approach to planning learning activities that focus on children's culture, interests, physical, cognitive, social, and emotional development.

constructivism: the process of putting together one's own understandings and advancing one's own knowledge by connecting new ideas to what is already known.

core knowledge: the body of knowledge that defines a discipline or professional expertise.

critical thinking: the process of analyzing and probing for complexities, perspectives and patterns, in contrast to rote memorization or recitation.

cultural relevancy: the formulation of experiences, ideas, language, behavior patterns, and programs that reflect the culture of those for whom they are intended.

culture of power: the standards, rules, ways of talking and doing things as set by those who control the institutions and resources that govern our lives.

curriculum box: a collection of materials to be used in activities for children, often focused around a particular theme; interchangeable with the term prop box.

DAP (see developmentally appropriate practice)

debriefing: the discussion that follows an activity or experience with the goal of developing individual and collective insights into what otherwise might be abstract ideas or incidental personal experience.

developmental education: an approach to teaching which acknowledges that learning is a dynamic process, involving stages of growth, a cultural context, and a continuous process of change.

developmental stages: a concept early childhood educators derived from Jean Piaget and Erik Erickson stressing that there are physical, cognitive, social, and emotional sequences to how humans develop, with patterns that can be recognized, understood, and built on for the next stage.

developmentally appropriate practice (DAP): a term coined by the early childhood profession and popularized by an NAEYC publication of this title outlining specific practices that build on developmental theory espoused by Piaget and Erickson (two European men of the mid-twentieth century); we often use this term interchangeably with child-centered practices, acknowledging that "appropriate" is defined within a cultural and social-political context.

disposition: typically used to refer to temperamental make-up, our understanding of this term, thanks to Lilian Katz, has broadened to mean a habit of mind or inclination towards a person, thing, or activity; patterns of behavior that deserve as much attention as acquiring skills or knowledge.

ECE: the field of Early Childhood Education, usually including children from birth through age eight.

emergent curriculum: an approach to providing and extending learning activities that arise out of student interests, actions, or serendipitous events.

five examinations framework: a term we invented to describe the methodology that guides our training on any topic—examine yourself, the environment, child development principles, issues of diversity and inclusion, and teacher roles and strategies.

hope to see/not to see: the mental or written checklist we generate to clarify the standard of quality, model, or big ideas we're pursuing on any early childhood topic.

kinds of intelligence: a term brought to us by Howard Gardner referring to the ways people understand and learn, including verbal/linguistic, logical/mathematical, intrapersonal, interpersonal, musical, spatial, and kinesthetic intelligences.

learning styles: a reference to the multiple ways people learn, including visually, auditorily, kinesthetically; we loosely interchange the terms learning styles, kinds of intelligence, and ways of knowing, each useful formulations in their own right, but all related to the need to provide for diversity.

loose parts: a term Simon Nicholson coined that we use to refer to any open-ended materials that can be transported and transformed in any number of ways by creative hands and minds.

master teacher: a teacher who is reflective, skilled, and wise in his/her thinking and communication.

mentor teacher: a master teacher who assumes the role of guiding and coaching others who are less experienced and knowledgeable; mentor teachers can be an informal arrangement or one for which training and compensation is provided.

metacognition: as a prefix "meta" means after, beyond, or transcending; we use this term to mean thinking about thinking and learning.

NAEYC: National Education for the Education of Young Children, a professional organization for those concerned with the education of young children; oversees the Academy, which coordinates the voluntary accreditation system, the Professional Development Institute, and membership services, including a national conference, publications, and advocacy for public policy related to children and families.

open-ended materials (see loose parts)

pedagogy: the teaching methods used for children or adults, with an implicit, if not explicit philosophy, perspective, and theory of learning.

play-debrief-replay: a term from Selma Wasserman that describes the process we use to apply constructivist theory—provide an activity to engage in, discuss people's experiences with it, relating these to the ideas under consideration, and then practice using these ideas with yet another activity; also see constructivism and debriefing.

politically correct (p.c.): a term reflecting different definitions of political depending on the community one represents; "p.c." is used to describe those who threaten the status quo, to discredit or attack efforts of inclusion, characterizing them as trivial or representing "special interest groups"; those who analyze the world with understandings of the dynamics of power, privilege, and injustice, advocate for equal and fair representation, using the preferred terms, language, and images of marginalized groups.

project approach: a reference to a curriculum centered around an in-depth investigation of a topic by a small group of learners/researchers; this approach is gaining in popularity thanks to Lilian Katz, Sylvia Chard, and the educators and ambassadors of Reggio Emilia.

R&R: resource and referral (unlike the "rest and recreation" meaning), describes the agencies around the country that provide a variety of information services and training to families, employers, and child care providers.

reframing: meaning to cast in a new light or consider within a different framework, we use this as a thinking and discussion process for analyzing experiences to acquire new insight and knowledge.

Reggio Emilia: a city in northern Italy with a highly acclaimed system of early childhood education; their approach has captured the attention of North American educators with its strong community involvement and valuing of young children, and the careful attention to fostering children's development through projects of active exploration and symbolic representation.

representation: a symbol or object used to stand for something else; finding or creating something to express an idea or experience stretches one's imagination and thinking.

teacher roles: rejecting the traditional teacher roles of depositing information, herding and disciplining children, our formulation of other roles for teachers was sparked in playful conversations with Betty Jones—the teacher as archaeologist, interpreter, historian, prop manager; these metaphors spark new thinking and behaviors.

tourist curriculum: a multicultural program approach that has children in the role of foreign visitor or sightseer during certain times of year, rather than experiencing the diverse ways of living in everyday life; a tourist approach often reinforces stereotypes.

ways of knowing: the developmental stages women experience as they become competent learners as identified by the research of Mary Belenky and her colleagues; these stages include silence, received, subjective, and procedural and constructed knowledge.

worthy wages: a term evolved from the first public statements of child care providers describing the "worthy work and worthless wages" of their condition; the exposure of the child care staffing crisis has grown to a national effort taking up the name of the Worthy Wage Campaign.

Recommended Resources

The following is by no means a comprehensive list, but rather a selection of resources we regularly draw on to enrich our thinking and spark new ideas for training strategies.

Books with Applications for Adult Education

Empowering Education: Critical Teaching for Social Change, Ira Shor (University of Chicago Press, 1992)
> A wonderful look at empowerment theory in action in community college settings. Has much usefulness in thinking about training child care teachers. Some specific ideas that can be applied.

Frames of Mind: The Theory of Multiple Intelligences, Howard Gardner (Basic Books, 1983)
> A new way of thinking about the different ways people learn and understand things with implications for children and the adults we train.

The Having of Wonderful Ideas and Other Essays on Teaching and Learning, Eleanor Duckworth (Teachers College Press, 1987)
> Detailed description of college instructor's work in teaching child development by applying the Piagetian concept of constructivism to work with adults studying to be teachers. An early picture for us about what this concept looks like in action.

The Tao of Leadership, John Heider (Humanics New Age, 1985)
> A clever and actually very useful little book on applying the Chinese classic by Lao Tzu, Tao Te Ching, to the stressful work of leadership in the 1990s. Certain sections are particularly useful to quote in workshops, while others help us get new perspective on our lives and work.

Teaching Adults, Elizabeth Jones (NAEYC, 1986)
> Jones describes a class she teaches on child development as a way of explaining how she applies adult learning theory in concrete settings. Many usable ideas as well as an understandable presentation of developmental theory for adults.

We Did the Best We Could: How to Create Healing Between the Generations, Lorie Dwinell and Ruth Baetz (Health Communications, Inc., 1993)
> Written for parents of adult children, we found this book an excellent primer on family of origin theory. It is chock full of self-reflection exercises, some of which are not unlike our childhood memory training strategies. If they would be willing to read it, this book could help many a child care provider and parent better understand the relationship between their own childhoods and how they are currently relating to children.

Women's Ways of Knowing: The Development of Self, Voice, and Mind, Mary Field Belenky, Blythe McVicker Clinchy, Nancy Rule Goldberger, Jill Mattuck Tarule (Basic Books, 1986)
> Because most child care providers are female, there is much food for thought in the research findings of the stages of knowing that women tend to go through.

Books Specifically on Staff Training

Beginnings and Beyond, Ann Gordon and Kathryn Browne (Delmar Publishing, 1989)
> Though this is written as a child development textbook, we would never use it as such. Instead, we find it a great quick reference book for gathering thoughts about the ideas to include in training on a given child development topic. We often make charts, handouts, or activities from information in this book.

Essentials for Child Development Associates Working with Young Children, Carol Brunson Phillips (Council for Early Childhood Professional Recognition, 1991)
> A detailed, readable guidebook outlining core knowledge needed for CDA. A good reference book, whether one is doing CDA advising or not in that it specifically covers basic ECE content teachers need.

Getting Involved: *Workshops for Parents*, Ellen Frede (High/Scope Press, 1984)
> An incredibly practical book on planning, leading, and evaluating parent workshops on a number of early childhood topics. Full of active learning strategies; applicable to teachers as well.

Growing Teachers: Partnerships in Staff Development, Elizabeth Jones (NAEYC, 1993)
> Readable review of adult learning theory with a number of specific stories of on-site staff development strategies, including using CDA as a tool, collaborative staff projects, and multicultural bilingual concerns; includes a chapter by Margie charting her journey of becoming a staff trainer.

A Guide for Supervisors and Trainers on Implementing the Creative Curriculum, Diane Trister Dodge (Teaching Strategies, 1988)
> One of the best recipe type books available on teacher training strategies. Whether using the creative curriculum or not, this book has a great set of concrete approaches and charts to use with teachers. Very readable.

A Guide to Observing and Recording Behavior, Warren Bentzen (Delmar Publishing, 1993)
> Because training involves close observation and in many cases assisting teachers with this skill, this is a useful book that provides an overview of developmental theories in underlying observations and a detailed set of guidelines on doing observations, documenting strategies, etc. Intended as a textbook, but readable and useful.

The Nesa Activities Handbook for Native and Multicultural Classrooms, Volumes 1 and 2, Don Sawyer and Art Napoleon (Tillacum Library, 1984 and 1991)
> A handy little set of books loaded with specific training strategies to deepen insights about working with different cultures. We periodically review these for new ideas.

The What, Why, and How of High Quality Early Childhood Education: A Guide for On-Site Supervision, Derry G. Koralek, Laura J. Colker, and Diane Trister Dodge (NAEYC, 1993)

> As with the other books by Diane Trister Dodge, what we find especially useful about this book are the clearly laid out pages with columns of what you should see and why and warning signs, reasons why this might be happening, and ways you can help. Though this prescriptive approach is significantly different from ours, we find this a useful resource to incorporate into some of our activities.

White Awareness: A Handbook for Anti-Racism Training, Judith Katz (University of Oklahoma Press, 1978)

> Specific ideas on how to do training with European Americans to awaken self-awareness and make a commitment to unlearning racism.

The Winning Trainer, Julius E. Eitington (Gulf Publishing, 1989)

> This book is almost overwhelming with its hundreds of pages of training activities (and its price!), but we periodically dip into it and find useful activities. In our Training of Trainer classes, we sometimes copy a page from this book and ask trainers to adapt one of the activities for an ECE setting. It's a good resource for those who don't find it easy to create workshop training strategies.

Books with Stories and Strategies from Teachers

Finding Our Own Way: Teachers Exploring their Assumptions, Judith Newman (Ed.) (Iteineman, 1989)

> Wonderful stories from teachers of school-aged children struggling to change from rigid, structured teaching to a more open, child sensitive, and holistic approach to teaching. Their stories inform us about how to understand the real world for teachers, their aspirations, barriers, dilemmas, and avenues for change.

The Good Preschool Teacher, William Ayers (Teachers College Press, 1989)

> Interviews with teachers provide a clear picture of what effective teaching looks like. Useful to hear stories from teachers and to relate to people you work with.

I Felt Like I Was From Another Planet: Writing From Personal Experience, Norine Dresser (Addison-Wesley, 1994)

> Full of specific stories and strategies of helping students find their authentic voices and gain the confidence and skill to express themselves in writing. Instructive in terms of better understanding diversity and useful in terms of strategies that can be easily adapted for teacher training activities.

I Won't Learn from You! The Role of Assent in Learning, Herbert Kohl (Milkweed Editions, 1991)

> A 47-page little gem with stories providing significant insight into why a student, child or adult, might choose, consciously or unconsciously, to not learn what is being taught. Offers very useful food for thought about the political and social context for learning.

Kindergartens: Four Success Stories, S. G. Goffin and D. A. Stegelin (Eds.) (NAEYC, 1992)

> Like *Finding Our Own Way,* these stories are great for a concrete look at how teachers have worked to change kindergartens to be more developmentally appropriate.

Lives on the Boundary: The Struggles and Achievements of America's Underprepared, Mike Rose (The Free Press, 1989)

> Part autobiographical and part stories of teaching, this beautifully written book details how schools fail children and adults who aren't from the mainstream culture. Very pertinent to working with children and teachers in the early childhood field.

Talks with Teachers, Lilian Katz (NAEYC, 1977) and *More Talks with Teachers*, (Eric Clearinghouse on Elementary and Early Childhood Education, 1984)

> Short, readable chapters discussing teachers learning to be teachers and teacher stages of development. Good theoretical framework in a practical context.

Teacher, Sylvia Ashton Warner (Simon & Schuster, 1963)

> By now a classic, this book details an Australian teacher's work with Maori children, with heartwarming stories and concrete ideas that can be translated to developmentally and culturally appropriate strategies for teaching academics to preschoolers.

Teaching Stories, Judy Logan (Minnesota Inclusiveness Program, 1993)

> Here is a middle school master teacher playing the role of researcher, scribe, storyteller, and broadcaster. This book gives us a clear taste of what teaching and learning could and should be about. Ripe with stores to retell and teaching activities to adapt.

Telling Your Stories, Donald Davis (August House, 1993)

> Great resource for specific strategies on drawing out people's stories and using them for education and community building.

To Teach: The Journey of a Teacher, William Ayers (Teachers College Press, 1993)

> A beautiful look at the art of teaching and policies that could make a difference. A good picture of teaching issues for school-aged students, with specific implications for the kind of teacher training needed.

White Teacher, Mollie Is Three, Bad Guys Don't Have Birthdays, The Boy Who Would be a Helicopter, Super Heroes in the Doll Corner, You Can't Say I Can't Play, Vivian Paley (Harvard University)

> Wonderful accounts of work with children that have greatly deepened our insights. We often extract excerpts from Paley's books for use in workshops. In one center where we consult, we discussed *Molly Is Three* chapter by chapter during staff meetings and generated tremendous new enthusiasm and insight into this age. *White Teacher* is extremely valuable as an account of a preschool teacher coming to terms with her own and children's racism.

Books on Specific Early Childhood Topics

Alike and Different: Exploring Our Humanity with Young Children, Bonnie Neugebauer (Ed.) (NAEYC, 1992, revised edition)

> A range of articles related to various aspects of diversity including the needs of children, parents, and staff. Margie has a chapter in this book on working with diversity in child care programs. In addition to a checklist to use in evaluating children's books, there is a wonderful listing of resources.

Caring Spaces, Learning Places, Jim Greenman (Exchange Press, 1988)
    One of the most valuable resources we have on considerations for designing environments that preserve childhoods. Particularly good chapters on infants and toddlers; many detailed drawings, poetry, and excerpts from other authors. Includes tips on working with architects.

Constructivist Early Education: Overview and Comparison with Other Programs, Rheta DeVries and Lawrence Kohlberg (NAEYC, 1990)
    An incredibly meaty, heady book, but one of the most valuable we've found in really understanding the concept of constructivism and the educational implications of Piaget's research and theory. Examines in great detail three approaches to translating Piaget's theory into preschool settings—High/Scope, Montessori, and Bank Street.

Engaging Children's Minds: The Project Approach, Lilian Katz and Sylvia Chard (Ablex Publishing, 1989)
    More matter of fact and written prior to *The Hundred Languages of Children*, this book provides a great set of ideas about how to use the project approach with school-aged kids. We use a variation of the project approach in some of our teacher training classes.

The Hundred Languages of Children: The Reggio Emilia Approach to Education, Carolyn Edwards, Lella Gandini, and George Forman (Eds.) (Ablex Publishing, 1993)
    U.S. interest in this approach to ECE programs is quickly matching the Italian influence of Montessori. The NAEYC conference now has a whole track on Reggio Emilia and there are regular group excursions, seminars, and newsletters on Reggio. We find this book and Reggio's approach to ECE one of the most inspiring ever. Many specific ideas to incorporate into training.

Learning by Heart: Teaching to Free the Creative Spirit, Corita Kent and Jan Steward (Bantam, 1992)
    A useful book in helping guide the reader to stop looking at things in habitual ways. Lovely stories and specific exercises to jog you to re-animate your observing skills and curiosity. Great for dispositions we want to encourage.

Looking at Children's Play: A Bridge Between Theory and Practice, Patricia Monighan-Nourot, Barbara Scales, Judith Van Itoorn (Teachers College Press, 1987)
    The authors describe the processes through which they, as teachers, observed children's play, listened to parents, raised questions, and sought answers. Detailed discussion on the meaning of play in particular situations.

The Piaget Handbook for Teachers and Parents, Rosemary Peterson and Victoria Felton-Collins (Teachers College Press, 1986)
    One of the most readable books on Piaget with easy to use explanations and charts that can be adapted for activity handouts.

The Play's the Thing: Teachers' Roles in Children's Play, Elizabeth Jones and Gretchen Reynolds (Teachers College Press, 1992)
    A wonderfully detailed book about how teachers can support or undermine children's play. Good, readable theoretical overview on role of play in children's learning and developmental stages of children's play. This book has influenced so many of the ideas we've discussed.

The Portfolio and its Use: Developmentally Appropriate Assessment of Young Children, Cathy Grace and Elizabeth Shores (Southern Association on Children Under Six, 1992)
    An invaluable discussion on why the assessment portfolio should be used with specific information on how to gather and analyze children's work for evaluation and communication with parents. Our favorite expression in the book is the assessment portfolio as "an attitude." We continually use this book with on-site training.

The Private Eye: Looking/Thinking by Analogy, Kerry Ruef (The Private Eye Project, 1992)
    An elementary curriculum approach about the drama and wonder of close observation, thinking by analogy, and theorizing. It's ripe for translating into teacher training strategies, given our practice of using metaphors, observation assignments, and developing good questions.

Reaching Potentials: Developmentally Appropriate Curriculum and Assessment for Young Children, Sue Bredekamp and Teresa Rosegrant (NAEYC, 1992)
    A meaty book, perhaps the sequel to the famous green DAP book; many chapters on issues related to theoretical considerations and applications of DAP in screening, assessing, and designing curriculum. Includes multicultural, anti-bias, and bilingual issues. All chapters are worth thoughtful study.

Serious Players in the Primary Classroom, Selma Wasserman (Teachers College Press, 1992)
    Another great complementary book to the Reggio approach, but definitely more left brained and sequential. Useful in school-aged training; includes adaptations that can be applied to preschool. As mentioned earlier, the methodology is akin to what we use in teacher training.

Speaking Out: Early Childhood Advocacy, Stacie G. Goffin and Joan Lombardi (NAEYC, 1988)
    A terrific guide for the how and why of advocacy work in the early childhood field. We use it as a reference for child welfare, school reform, and worthy wages advocacy efforts.

Teaching as Story Telling: An Alternative Approach to Teaching and Curriculum in the Elementary School, Kieran Egan (University of Chicago, 1986)
    Great formulations on how to apply the elements of good storytelling into all aspects of needed curriculum. Aimed at elementary education, but again, the story form ideas are easily translated into training strategies for adults.

Books on the Dynamics of Culture

Alerta: A Multicultural, Bilingual Approach to Teaching Young Children, Leslie Williams and Yvonne De Gaetano (Addison-Wesley, 1985)
    An extremely useful book in programming for bilingual, bicultural education. There are concrete ideas, forms, and handouts. Informs readers about concepts of cultural relevancy. We've adapted many things from this book in training on multicultural issues.

Anti-Bias Curriculum: Tools for Empowering Young Children, Louise Derman-Sparks (NAEYC, 1989)

The revised edition of this book will be out soon with new chapters on teaching about families, holidays, updated examples, and resources. An important reference book for all trainers. Many valuable materials to incorporate into training approaches and specific practices.

Black and White Styles in Conflict, Thomas Kochman (University of Chicago Press, 1983)

The specific descriptions of things we have encountered in our lives made this a very clarifying book. With this as a base, we could recognize further examples as they began to occur as well as create scenarios to use in training settings.

Black Children: Their Roots, Culture and Learning Styles, Janice Hale (Johns Hopkins University Press, 1986)

A landmark book with strong implications for programming for African American children. A challenge to traditional European American based formulations of ECE.

Cultural Etiquette: A Guide for the Well-Intentioned, Amoja Three Rivers (Market Wimmin, 1991)

A wonderful little primer on recognizing the pitfalls of unwitting racism and anti-Semitism. There is a mixture of humorous anger and touching generosity on these pages offering definitions, information, and personal do's and don'ts, many of which people feel too awkward to ask about.

Culture and Power in the Classroom, Antonia Darder (Bergin & Garvey, 1991)

A meaty book looking at issues of power dynamics and disenfranchising of people of color in college classrooms. A book we found difficult to read, but very important.

Deepening Our Understanding of Anti-Bias Education for Children: An Anthology of Readings, Louise Derman-Sparks (Pacific Oaks Press, 1993)

A remarkable collection of articles that can be used as a companion to the first edition of the *Anti-Bias Curriculum* book. These cover a wide range of topics related to bias impacting young children. Useful to enhance our own understandings as trainers and in many cases, as handouts for teachers.

Dismantling Racism: The Continuing Challenge to White America, Joseph Barndt (Augsburg Fortress, 1991)

Written with a Christian audience in mind, the chapters are thoughtful and persuasive whether or not this is your religious faith. Of particular interest to us were the distinctive chapters on individual racism, white racism, and cultural racism.

Diversity and Developmentally Appropriate Practices, Bruce L. Mallory and Rebecca New (Eds.) (Teachers College Press, 1994)

By far the most extensive critique of the bias and cultural arrogance woven into our profession's definition of DAP. Useful, though somewhat academic, essays about universal developmental themes and culturally determined childhood issues.

Homophobia: How We All Pay the Price, Warren J. Blumenfeld (Ed.) (Beacon Press, 1992)

A collection of essays that further clarified and better enabled us to address the issue of homophobia in early childhood settings. We particularly like the emphasis on how it is not just lesbian and gay people who are damaged by this oppression, but how the humanity of all of us is stunted by this hatred, fear, and intolerance. Includes a section on children, families, and homophobia and one on how to run an anti-homophobia workshop.

Hunger of Memory, Richard Rodriguez (Bantam, 1983)

One of the first books that gave us a clear taste of the confusion and loss that occurs for children of color who become assimilated into the dominant culture without retaining a strong positive identity and connection to their home culture and language. Profoundly clarifies the meaning and necessity of bicultural development.

Multicultural Issues in Child Care, Janet Gonzalez-Mena (Mayfield Publishing, 1993)

One of the most valuable books recently found detailing different cultural approaches to child rearing and the potential conflict this presents child care providers. We've turned some of the stories in this book into training strategies.

Race, Class and Gender: An Anthology, Margaret L. Andersen and Patricia Hill Collins (Eds.) (Wadsworth Publishing, 1992)

A resource to return to again and again with articles on inclusive thinking, institutions, and the politics of empowerment. Well-known and previously published authors and folks like your next door neighbors make this an extremely diverse and readable collection.

Journals and Periodicals

Caring for the Little Ones. A practical newsletter put out by Karen Miller offering great insights and resources for working with toddlers.

Child Care Information Exchange. One of the most valuable resources for child care managers with regular articles on current issues and experiences of directors. Many of the strategies in this book first appeared in issues of *Exchange*.

ERIC Digest. The easiest way outside of on-line services to keep track of current issues in academic circles that ERIC tracks.

Harvard Educational Review. A journal from Harvard College with an academic flavor, but very relevant "cutting edge" issues researched and discussed. We find much food for thought and professional discussion here.

High/Scope Extensions. A quarterly newsletter of the High/Scope Foundation aimed at trainers. Many practical ideas and active learning workshop suggestions.

High/Scope Resource. A quarterly publication of the High/Scope Foundation containing a combination of High/Scope news including research on effective training of teacher trainers.

In Context. This journal from New Horizons for Learning in the Pacific Northwest often focuses on alternative, holistic approaches to learning and teaching. Guest writers make the work of less accessible theoreticians understandable.

Report on Preschool Programs. Synopsis of research pertinent to preschool programming and thus staff training. Often gives us data for advocacy and public policy efforts.

Rethinking Schools. A quarterly journal advocating the reform of elementary and secondary public schools. Emphasizes issues of equity, social justice, and activism in building quality public schools for all children. This journal is a lifeline to the people who teach the children after they leave our ECE programs.

Young Children. The journal of NAEYC with articles ranging from research to public policy to specific teaching experiences.

Videos We Frequently Use

Anti-Bias Curriculum, produced by Louise Derman-Sparks, Pacific Oaks College, 5 and 6 Westmoreland Place, Pasadena, CA 91103, (800) 831-1306

> An excellent introduction to the anti-bias curriculum with interviews and scenes offering the rationale and history behind the formation of curriculum strategies and support groups for teachers in addressing their own biases and professional development in this area.

Creative Curriculum, produced by Diane Trister Dodge, Teaching Strategies, Inc., P.O. Box 42243, Washington, DC 20015, (202) 362-7543

> Whether or not a program uses the Creative Curriculum, this video provides an excellent visual overview of good early childhood education.

Essential Connections: Ten Keys to Culturally Sensitive Child Care, produced by Far West Laboratory Center for Child & Family Studies and California Department of Education, P.O. Box 271, Sacramento, CA 95802, (916) 445-1260

> Excellent interviews with ECE specialists such as Carol Brunson Phillips, Louise Derman-Sparks, and Lily Wong Fillmore, along with specific infant and toddler caregiving scenes. Includes role plays for potential parent-caregiver cultural conflicts.

Making News, Making History, produced by Margie Carter and Deb Curtis, National Center for the Early Childhood Work Force, 733 15th NW, Suite 800, Washington, DC 20005, (202) 737-7700 or (800) U-R-WORTHY/(800) 879-6784

> Footage and interviews from around the country showing the growing understandings and activities early childhood advocates are employing to get on our country's agenda a national child care policy with affordability for parents and adequate compensation for providers.

Prejudice: A Big Word for Little Kids, produced by Patty Johnson, KSTP-TV, 3415 University Avenue, St. Paul, MN 55114, (612) 646-5555

> Includes interviews with researchers on the development of bias in young children, parents, and teachers. Useful for parent and staff training.

Room Arrangement as a Teaching Strategy, produced by Diane Trister Dodge, Teaching Strategies, Inc., P.O. Box 42243, Washington, DC 20015, (202) 362-7543

> Great footage and narration on the role room arrangement has in promoting learning and preventing problems in ECE classrooms.

Time with Toddlers, produced by Kidspace, 912 Elliot Avenue West, Seattle, WA 98119, (206) 282-3622

> With specific scenes of typical toddler behaviors and caregiving dilemmas, Margie Carter guides the viewers in understanding, delighting in, and providing group care for this age group. Useful for parent education as well as staff training.

Worthy Work, Worthless Wages, produced by Margie Carter, National Center for the Early Childhood Work Force, 733 15th NW, Suite 800, Washington, DC 20005, (202) 737-7700 or (800) U-R-WORTHY/(800) 879-6784

> A chronicle of the efforts of the child care community in one city to address the staffing crisis. Teachers, directors, and parents describe their efforts to get the public and policy makers to take this issue seriously.

Sources for Dolls

People of Every Stripe
P.O. Box 12505
Portland, OR 97212
(503) 282-0612

Global Village Books and Toys
P.O. Box 262
Santa Monica, CA 90403
(213) 459-5188

Clear Vision Dolls
212 Teague Drive
San Dimas, CA 91773
(818) 577-3922

Sources for "Loose Parts"

Creation Station
7533 Olympic View Drive
Edmonds, WA 98026
(206) 775-7959

Creative Educational Surplus
9801 James Circle, Suite C
Bloomington, MN 55431
(612) 884-6427

Appendix A

OBSERVATION FORM

Teacher Observed _____ Observer _____

Date _____ Time of Observation _____

Write down details of any examples you saw of the teacher promoting self-esteem:

A child was being valued, appreciated, or encouraged by the adult

The adult was encouraging independence, child self-direction

The adult referred one child to another for assistance or problem solving

OBSERVING FOR LANGUAGE DEVELOPMENT OPPORTUNITIES IN THE CLASSROOM

Observer _____ Site/Class _____ Staff_____ Date _____

Hope to See

☐ Signs of dictation in room
Observed: _____
_____
_____

Comment: _____
_____

☐ Displays at child eye level
Observed: _____
_____
_____

Comment: _____
_____

☐ Books available to children
Observed: _____
_____
_____

Comment: _____
_____

☐ Enough materials to encourage interaction and discussion among children
Observed: _____
_____
_____

Comment: _____
_____

☐ Balance between adult and child talk
Observed: _____
_____
_____

Comment: _____
_____

☐ Adults available to children/listening respectfully
Observed: _____
_____
_____

Comment: _____
_____

☐ Adults at eye level with children
Observed: _____
_____
_____

Comment: _____
_____

☐ Adults using individual children's names
Observed: _____
_____
_____

Comment: _____
_____

☐ Adult offering descriptive recognition of what children are doing
Observed: _____
_____
_____

Comment: _____
_____

☐ Adults picking up on body language and verbal cues from children
Observed: _____
_____
_____

Comment: _____
_____

☐ Adults interpreting and delivering messages with children
Observed: _____
_____
_____

Comment: _____
_____

☐ Adults using imitative language/repeating what child says/extending/substituting new words
Observed: _____
_____
_____

Comment: _____
_____

☐ Adult parallel and self talk
Observed: _____
_____
_____

Comment: _____
_____

☐ Adults using open-ended questions
Observed: _____
_____
_____

Comment: _____
_____

☐ Adults reading to children/encouraging participation in reading process
Observed: _____
_____
_____

Comment: _____
_____

☐ Adults responding to interest children demonstrate in language
Observed: _____
_____
_____

Comment: _____
_____

☐ Children having fun with language/rhymes/chants/ word games
Observed: _____
_____
_____

Comment: _____
_____

☐ Adults referring children to each other
Observed: _____
_____
_____

Comment: _____
_____

☐ Adults modeling good communication among selves
Observed: _____
_____
_____

Comment: _____
_____

☐ Adults encouraging active listening between children
Observed: _____
_____
_____

Comment: _____
_____

☐ Adults aware of children's home language/honoring/using where appropriate
Observed: _____
_____
_____

Comment: _____
_____

Hope Not to See

☐ Too much teacher talk
Observed: _____
_____

☐ Negative feedback to children
Observed : _____
_____

☐ Adults correcting language/grammar
Observed: _____
_____

☐ Adult language with kids focused on manners
Observed: _____
_____

☐ Adults changing the subject in response to child-initiated talk
Observed: _____
_____

☐ Inappropriate techniques
Observed: _____
_____

© 1994 *Training Teachers,* Redleaf Press, 450 North Syndicate, Suite 5, St. Paul, MN 55104, 1-800-423-8309

use back for additional comments if needed

OBSERVING IN TODDLER ROOMS

The toddler age is one of great transition, filled with the themes of dependence and independence, limit testing and separation anxiety. The primary learning modes for toddlers are mobility, especially climbing, carrying, dumping, and sensory experiences. Adults play a key role in addressing the primary toddler developmental tasks of trust and autonomy. In group care there are specific adult actions that will either enhance or defeat trust and autonomy.

Hope to See

☐ Adults playful, warm, affectionate, and gentle, providing a consistent presence and guidelines.

_____

_____

_____

☐ Adults at child's eye level, modeling, supporting, interacting, using self talk, parallel talk, extending language.

_____

_____

_____

☐ Adults using toddler "swarming" to develop social skills/group activities.

_____

_____

_____

☐ Adults minimizing waiting by providing multiple materials and choices and activities for transitions.

_____

_____

_____

☐ Adults using observations before intervention.

_____

_____

_____

☐ Adults redirecting rather than punishing.

_____

_____

_____

☐ Adults saying what they want the child to do, rather than not to do.

_____

_____

_____

Hope Not To See

☐ Adult interactions are stern, harsh, rough, inconsistent in availability and rules followed.

_____

_____

_____

☐ Adults standing on the sidelines, calling across the room, tending to chores, not children.

_____

_____

_____

☐ Adults expecting toddlers to do planned activities in groups.

_____

_____

_____

☐ Adults requiring long waiting for turns, waiting until all children are ready before beginning the next activity.

_____

_____

_____

☐ Adults intervening before observing and strategizing.

_____

_____

_____

☐ Adults punishing rather than redirecting.

_____

_____

_____

☐ Adults emphasizing what they don't want to see and "wrong" behavior.

_____

_____

_____

Other Comments:

_____

_____

_____

Classroom/Teachers Observed: _____

Observer: _____

Date: _____

SMALL GROUP TIME OBSERVATION

Teacher _____Observer _____

Date_____Time _____

Materials used:

Beginning: • How did the teacher start the group?

Middle: • How did different children use the materials?

              • What words/language did the children use?

              • What extensions of materials and language did the teacher offer?

End: • How were children alerted to the end of the group time?

              • What clean-up strategies were used?

              • What king of review took place?

              • What follow-up ideas did the teacher offer?

continued on back

Learning focus:

• What focus do you think the teacher had?

• Did you see another focus emerge from the children?

• How could this be built upon the coming days?

Other comments/questions:

OBSERVING SMALL GROUP TIME

Teacher _____ Observer _____

Date _____ Time _____

Write down examples of child-talk that indicate how this activity/time was experienced by the child.

Write examples of adult-talk that acknowledged or responded to child-initiated talk.

Tally the number of adult questions versus adult comments to children.

 # Adult questions   *# Adult Comments*

Whose voice is heard most of the time?

© 1994 *Training Teachers*, Redleaf Press, 450 North Syndicate, Suite 5, St. Paul, MN 55104, 1-800-423-8309

OBSERVING ADULT TALK

Teacher _____ Observer _____

Date_____Time _____

Write down examples of adult-talk heard that falls into these categories:

1.   Ignoring child-initiated talk

      Acknowledging child-initiated talk

2.   Correcting a child

      Praising a child

3.   Close-ended questions

      Open-ended questions

      Problem-posing questions

4.   Teacher solved a problem

      Teacher referred one child to another to solve problem

5.   Teacher was frustrated with a child

       Teacher showing concern for a child

       Teacher showing delight in a child

6.   Tally the number of times the teacher ended a sentence with the question "Okay?"

7.   Each time the teacher uses the question "Okay?" at the end of a sentence, note whether there was a real choice offered to the child

       # Times "Okay?" was real choice offered

       # Times "Okay?" was said when no real choice was offered

OBSERVING TEACHER BEHAVIORS/INTERVENTIONS

Teacher _____ Observer _____

Date_____ Time _____

	Sustained the Activity	Participated in the Activity	Extended the Activity	Changed the Activity
Children's Behaviors and Activities				

PROPS IN THE ENVIRONMENT

Keeping in mind that a whole language approach includes speaking, listening, reading and writing, as a group, brainstorm lists of props to include in the following room areas. To organize your lists, think in terms of initial props and then additions for later in the year as development progresses.

Area	Props listening, speaking, reading, writing	
	Initial	Later Additions
Block Area		
Dress-up Area		
Art Area (includes sensory and writing center options)		
Quiet Area (includes table, toys, puzzles, books, snacks)		
Other		

© 1994 *Training Teachers*, Redleaf Press, 450 North Syndicate, Suite 5, St. Paul, MN 55104, 1-800-423-8309

PRESCHOOL READING AND WRITING SKILLS

Oral Language:

- ☐ Responds to simple commands and conversational sentences.
- ☐ Usually understands the general flow of classroom conversation.
- ☐ Child uses a small number of words to communicate (i.e. single words and a few phrases).
- ☐ Child communicates clearly about experiences, interests and needs.
- ☐ Plays with language, rhymes, makes up verses and songs, creates preschool riddles and jokes.
- ☐ Participates in making up a story with a group.
- ☐ Recalls a sequence (a past experience, steps in a process, daily routine) without visual cues.
- ☐ Dictates own story to adult or tape recorder.

Comments and Examples

Reading:

- ☐ Enjoys books and seeks them out spontaneously.
- ☐ Handles books appropriately (turns pages from front to back, looks at and comments on pictures and cares for them properly).
- ☐ Attends when books are read by an adult.
- ☐ Follows along with a book while listening to a tape at listening center.
- ☐ Contributes relevant comments during story telling activities.
- ☐ Retells the text of familiar stories.
- ☐ Puts things in a sequence (pictures, patterns) and can describe it.
- ☐ Aware that print is talk written down.
- ☐ Knows that print has meaning and recognizes own inability to decode it.
- ☐ Aware of the function of print (asks what print says in books, signs, cereal boxes, T shirts).
- ☐ Recognizes and identifies alphabet letters (usually starts with first letter of own name).
- ☐ Reads environmental print such as road signs, fast food signs, classroom area labels.
- ☐ Has acquired some sight words vocabulary (i.e. recognizes own name, names of peers, and other personally meaningful words) independent of contextual cues.
- ☐ Attempts to sound out words by using knowledge of letter-sound correspondence (phonics) and contextual cues.

Comments and Examples

Writing:

☐ Draws and uses paints to explore the materials and how they work.

☐ Draws and paints to represent objects and ideas (may make up a name after the fact rather than intentionally starting out to represent).

☐ Child's representations are recognizable to adults after child has explained them.

☐ Child's representations are recognizable to adults without any explanation.

☐ Scribbles and pretends to read it (i.e., writes a letter, a sign, a phone message in the context of dramatic play).

☐ Makes letter-like marks, squiggles, and combinations of circles and lines.

☐ Asks adults to write what he/she says.

☐ Asks adults about the sound value of different letters (i.e., asks adults, "What did I write or what does this say?"

☐ Forms recognizable letters (some may be reversed).

☐ Intentionally combines letters to form words using invented spelling (i.e., frd = friend).

☐ Makes own books with collection of pages with drawings/pictures.

☐ Makes own books with drawings/pictures and words related to a single theme or story.

☐ Seeks out picture dictionaries and other printed word sources as models of conventional spelling for copying (name tags, asks adult to write a specific word or phrase).

Appendix B

HOW PEOPLE LEARN

People Generally Remember

Ways People Learn

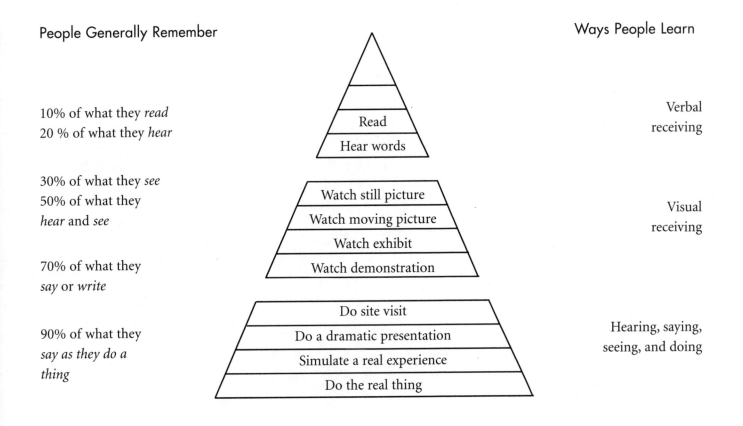

10% of what they *read*
20 % of what they *hear*

Verbal
receiving

30% of what they *see*
50% of what they
hear and *see*

Visual
receiving

70% of what they
say or *write*

90% of what they
*say as they do a
thing*

Hearing, saying,
seeing, and doing

Read

Hear words

Watch still picture

Watch moving picture

Watch exhibit

Watch demonstration

Do site visit

Do a dramatic presentation

Simulate a real experience

Do the real thing

Reprinted with permission from Diane Trister Dodge, *A Guide for Supervisors and Trainers on Implementing the Creative Curriculum for Early Childhood.* Washington, D.C.: Teaching Strategies, 1993.

PROFILE OF ADULT ABILITIES
by Jane Meade-Roberts

Cooking (I am able to . . .)

Boil water and heat frozen food	Make things from mixes	Prepare simple meals i.e. broil meat, bake potato	Follow recipes	Create gourmet meals and invent delicious dishes

Bowling (I am able to . . .)

Pick up the ball	Roll the ball and avoid the gutter	Pick up most spares	Regularly pick up 7-10 splits	Consistently bowl games of 290-300

Swimming (I am able to . . .)

Submerge entire body including face in water	Float for an extended period	Tread water	Perform particular strokes and lap the pool	Swim regularly for exercise and pleasure

Reading (I am able to read . . .)

Road signs and labels	Notes from kids' school and/or recipes when necessary	Newspapers and magazines in order to stay informed	For information and pleasure	Extensively on a specific topic

Tennis (I am able to . . .)

Recognize a tennis racket	Identify which end hits the ball	Successfully hit the ball against a backboard	Play only with close friends	Regularly play in matches for exercise and pleasure

Typing (I am able to . . .)

Position the paper correctly in the machine	Use 2 fingers and type a simple note	Position fingers correctly on the keyboard	Type 35-40 wpm with no errors	Type 60 wpm or higher including reports and tables and charts

Crafts (I am able to . . .)

Enjoy looking at other people's craft projects	Recognize good quality work done by someone else	Produce a product when walked through the process step by step	Follow another's written or verbal directions to produce a product	Create a recognizable product from a variety of material

Reprinted with permission from Jane Meade-Roberts, 1988.

IF THE SHOE FITS: A WORTHY WAGES FAIRY TALE

by Marcy Whitebook and Jim Morin

Once upon a time, not long after the last dragon was slain, there was a kingdom ruled by men. They controlled everything. The banks, businesses, government, industry, entertainment, medicine, education — even the family. Whenever the king gave speeches to his subjects he always spoke of how much he loved children and how important they were for the land. The king, as kings always had, spoke of the dignity of families, of justice and quality, and of the importance of learning. But it was all a charade. He was really the king for men.

During these times, the women of this kingdom learned their place. The few that were rich kept themselves beautiful and did the kind of things men liked. Most women stayed home, cooked, cleaned and raised babies. If women were poor, they did all the work at home and then worked outside as well. Things went on like this for a long, long time. But times changed. More and more of the women in the kingdom had to work outside the home if there was going to be enough food to feed their babies. And some of the women found that they liked the outside work. They said they felt fulfilled and challenged and satisfied as they made their way in what they used to call "a man's world."

Now, when the women went to work, or went to schools to train for their work, they needed a place for their children. Usually it was the women's job to find a place for their children. Women looked to other women, many of whom also needed jobs. For in this kingdom, only a few good men cared for children.

The king knew that women who took care of children were paid only a small pittance. But the king also knew the women of his kingdom were much too smart to accept this arrangement. They, like everyone in the land, agreed that children were the kingdom's most precious resource, so why would their caregivers earn only the minimum wage? The king knew that the only way to get a cheap pool of workers for these hard and stressful jobs was to trick them. So that is what he did. He called in his chief sorcerer, the OLD MAN who lived with the OLD WOMAN in the shoe. The OLD MAN remembered that his wife got through many a day because she loved the children, even when she was beside herself with exhaustion. So the OLD MAN cast a spell on the women of the kingdom, including his wife. From that day forward, any woman who chose to care for other people's children, whether in her home, the child's home or in a child care center or school, would ignore the working conditions and wages. She would only consider that she loved the children and that they needed her.

The spell was a powerful spell. It worked even in the most unexpected circumstances: Women believed the myth even when they didn't have enough money to care for their own children, had to work second jobs or take in more children than the rules permitted. This was the way things were supposed to be. Some of the women would even chant in public, "We love kids; we're not in it for the money!" "We love kids; we're not in it for the money!"

The spell was unbroken for a long, long time. (You might be able to see traces of it even now.) But gradually its grasp weakened. Some of the women caregivers had jobs that were so hard that even a magic spell couldn't smooth over everything. Many decided that, magic or not, they had to get out.

Almost every woman (and the few men) who took care of other people's children were dissatisfied with their wages. They were also unhappy because, even though the king said their work was important, nobody else seemed to think so, except a few of the parents and of course the children. When they went to festivals and tournaments people weren't interested in what they did. Most of the caregivers expressed their discontent by leaving child care work. Things got so bad in what came to be called the child care work force that nearly 50% of those who worked caring for young children left their jobs each year. Many of those who left were heartbroken, some were discouraged, and not a few were relieved. Some took teaching jobs with older children, which while not well paid, at least allowed them to make a decent living. But most went to work in the Royal burger parlors or horse stables where they could make more money.

This exodus of caregivers continued for many years, ignored by all but a few people in the kingdom. Young women setting out to find jobs avoided child care; the work was worthy but the wages were worthless. As you might expect, the king was not too happy. He reminded the women who took care of children that their work was too important to quit. Quality child care enables children to start school with a head start, it gets women off welfare, supports the family and is good for business. This convinced some women, but many continued to seek other jobs.

So the king called upon the sorcerer again. The king asked the OLD MAN in the shoe to cast an even stronger spell. This time the OLD MAN cast a "name game" spell: Just call yourself "professional," he told the caregivers, "and you'll be happy to stay on your job."

The OLD WOMAN who lived in the shoe heard her husband and the king plotting. She became so angry she didn't know what to do. (Or did she?) At the first opportunity she went to a meeting of caregivers in her community. "Do you know why we are paid so little for so much work?" she asked. To her surprise, most of the women had answers:

> *We are paid so little* because child care is considered women's work, and the king and his men (and even some of the women) don't believe it is skilled. They think anyone can do it.

We are paid so little because families aren't used to paying for child care, and they are reluctant to do so because rent, food and fuel costs keep going up.

We are paid so little because families think mothers' wages only should cover the cost of child care, and yet women in the kingdom earn less than two-thirds of what men earn.

We are paid so little because the king spends all our taxes on bombs and bankers, instead of babies.

Next the OLD WOMAN asked, "Do you realize what is happening to our land because we are willing to do so much for so little reward?" Once again, all the women knew:

We are hurting the children because we are underpaid. Children have to deal with too many caregivers, many of whom aren't trained and don't interact appropriately with them.

We are hurting families because we are underpaid. Each time a caregiver leaves, the children get so upset that parents are up with them at night or leave them each day sobbing in a stranger's arms.

We are hurting ourselves because we are underpaid. If we stay in child care we are so poor we cannot meet the needs of our own families. If we leave, all our experience and education goes to waste.

We are hurting businesses because we are underpaid. Parent workers can't concentrate because they are worrying about their children, or are missing work to cover for some child care arrangement that has just fallen apart.

The women went home that night thinking about things differently. They could hardly wait for their next meeting. When it began the OLD WOMAN, who was now a regular member of the group, asked, "Do you know why things don't change?" The women rushed to give reasons:

We can't complain. The economy is bad. Many people are losing their jobs, they don't want to hear our troubles.

We can't complain. Parents can't afford to pay more for child care. There's no place where the money can come from, unless of course, the king stops making bombs.

The OLD WOMAN smiled with pleasure as the women talked late into the night. She knew that her plan to break the spell was working. The women began to see how they themselves made the spell possible. They began to speak out:

"*We are too silent. How many of our parents know what we earn?*"

"*As long as we don't ask for more, we're saying that things are OK the way they are.*"

"*We act as if our work is worthless when we agree to accept such low wages for our work.*"

"*We are afraid of being told we are selfish. Why do we think so little of ourselves?*"

A few of the women were terrified by all these words and ran away. But most others nodded their heads in agreement. As the long night ended and the day began, the women knew the spell had lost its hold on them.

And that was it. The spell was broken. What seemed so reasonable only a few days before now seemed unacceptable. The more they looked at how willing they had been to sacrifice their own needs for the good of everyone else, the more stunned they became. How did it happen, they wondered, that so many of them had been acting as if getting dirt wages for hard and challenging work was the way things were supposed to be? Why were everyone else's needs more of a priority than their own? Why had they considered it "reasonable" that they work for poverty level wages, so that parents could continue to afford child care services? Why had they allowed themselves to suffer especially when they knew the toll it took on the children?

The relief when the spell was finally broken was enormous. Caregivers told each other how hard their jobs were, how much responsibility they had, and how much they had to give in order to do their jobs right. They told each other the bad things that they would never let happen again. No more hollow talk about children as the future of society. No more self-doubt about their skills or their rights as employees. No more despair that nothing they could do would make a difference. No more resignation in the face of a problem too big to do anything about. No more silence. No more magic.

The women decided to talk with every caregiver in the land about this problem. They also began talking with parents about the role they would have to play in creating a solution. The women created the Worthy Wage Campaign, which threw out the idea of a kingdom and began building a country that truly valued children and their caregivers. Many years after the terrible spell was broken, other women set aside one day a year to walk for Worthy Wages and to honor those who took the first steps.

The tradition continues...

DEVELOPMENTAL THEMES, TASKS, AND GOALS IN ANTI-BIAS WORK

Adapted from Louise Derman-Sparks, *Anti-Bias Curriculum:
Tools for Empowering Young Children* (NAEYC, 1989)

Gender Identity

Two's

- Curious about anatomy; notices differences in gender.
- Non-verbally explores differences (looking, pointing, touching).
- Learning names of body parts.
- Confused about anatomical differences; may think they have both types of genitals or that they can change their body parts.
- Learning attitudes of dominant culture toward gender; learning from different behaviors and messages towards boys and girls.
- *Developmental Goal:* To gain simple matter of fact information about anatomy. Acceptance regarding curiosity. Construct a healthy nonsexist identity based on anatomy as what determiner of gender, rather than looks, i.e., hair length or clothing.

Three's and Four's

- Know whether they are a boy or girl.
- Strongly influenced by dominant culture attitudes toward gender behavior; have definite ideas about how boys and girls are supposed to do things differently.
- Confused about gender constancy. Have questions about whether they will remain the same gender as they grow.
- *Developmental Goal:* To develop a clear, healthy gender identity through understanding that being a boy or a girl depends on anatomy, not on what they like to do; to expand understanding of gender anatomy and gender identity; to understand gender constancy so won't think that play preferences or roles will change one's gender.

Five's

- Have established gender identity constancy; know that they are and will remain a boy or girl.
- Have learned to be embarrassed about gender anatomy and show this through teasing, giggling and secret genital play.
- Curious about how babies are born.
- Defining own gender identity; acting out prevailing gender stereotypes.
- *Developmental Goal:* To expand ideas regarding gender roles and to counter prevailing biases; to acquire accurate information and terms about gender anatomy and differences; to be aware of a variety of role models that cross gender lines.

Learning about Physical Differences and Disabilities

Two's

- Notices the more obvious differences in physical abilities, such as a person using a wheel chair, a brace or crutches to move around.
- Uses non-verbal behavior to explore differences such as staring, imitating, pointing.
- Shows signs of "pre-prejudice," discomfort or fear with physical differences.
- *Developmental Goal:* To gain words for observations; to receive acceptance for curiosity; to develop comfort and familiarity with physical differences.

Three's, Four's and Five's

- Able to see shared abilities and similarities.
- Notices and asks questions about disabilities.
- Curious about equipment and devices people use to help with disability.
- Confusion about what a person with a disability can or can't do.
- Has anxiety and fear about being hurt or "catching" the disability through contact with the person or equipment.
- May reject, show fear or impatience with someone differently abled; lack skills for interacting with differently abled.

- *Developmental Goal:
  Children with disability*—to see themselves reflected in the world around them; to receive acceptance for who they are; to develop autonomy and independence. *Children not disabled*—to ask questions and express feelings about disabilities; to gain information about and comfort with those who are disabled.

Racial Differences and Similarities

Two's
- Notices differences in skin color; learning color names.
- Curious about differences in hair texture.
- Uses non-verbal cues to signal noticing differences; may react with curiosity or fear.
- Overgeneralized common characteristic such as skin color, i.e. "those are some of the Cosby people."
- *Developmental Goal:* To develop a positive awareness of own racial identity; to learn words for observations of differences to develop a comfortable awareness of others.

Three's and Fours
- Continued curiosity about racial differences; wonder where they fit in.
- Aware of and sensitive to attitudes toward skin color and other racial characteristics; becoming aware of societal bias against darker skin and other physical differences.
- Wants to know how they got their color, hair and eye characteristics.
- Aware that getting older brings changes; wonders if skin color, hair and eyes remain constant.
- Confusion about racial group names and actual color of their skin.
- *Developmental Goal:* To understand that racial identity does not change; to learn accurate information about racial identity to counter bias; to understand that one is part of a large group with similar characteristics (not "different") and to feel comfortable with exactly who one is.

Five's
- Can begin to understand scientific explanations for differences in skin color, hair texture and eye shape.
- Can understand more fully the range of racial differences and similarities.
- *Developmental Goal:* To understand and value the range of differences among racial groups.

Cultural Differences and Similarities

Two's
- Aware of cultural aspects of gender and ethnic identity.
- Can understand different words from different languages.
- *Developmental Goal:* To see self as a part of a family group.

Three's and Four's
- Understands cultural identity as it relates to their family; knows one has individuality and a group connection.
- Confused about criteria for ethnic/cultural group membership.
- Acquiring information and bias from the dominant culture's prevailing attitudes and images.
- Cultural understanding is based on concrete, daily living and family members through language, family stories, values, celebrations, spiritual life.
- Beginning to understand that everyone has a culture or group identity and that there are similarities and differences among children and adults.
- *Developmental Goal:*
  For white children—to counter the developing belief that the dominant white culture is superior to other ways of life.
  For children of color—to build a positive sense of person and group identity; to see themselves as of equal value to others.

Five's
- Begin to make connections between their individual and family cultural identity and the larger cultural/ethnic group.
- To begin to understand peoples' struggles for justice and a better quality of life.
- *Developmental Goal:* To understand the broader context of how individuals and families relate to the larger community; to begin to identify bias and find ways to take action to challenge and change injustice.

Adapted from Louise Denman Sparks and the A.B.C. Task Force (1989) *The Anti-Bias Curriculum.* Washington, D.C.: NAEYC.

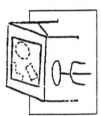

Teacher as Architect

- Evaluating space based on a child's eye view
- Adapting space to the children's play needs and interests
- Creating opportunities to explore light and shadow, sound, color and texture
- Integrating outdoor and natural world elements into the indoor environment
- Rearranging the environment to create new interest in each area

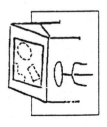

Teacher as Architect

- Evaluating space based on a child's eye view
- Adapting space to the children's play needs and interests
- Creating opportunities to explore light and shadow, sound, color and texture
- Integrating outdoor and natural world elements into the indoor environment
- Rearranging the environment to create new interest in each area

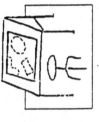

Teacher as Architect

- Evaluating space based on a child's eye view
- Adapting space to the children's play needs and interests
- Creating opportunities to explore light and shadow, sound, color and texture
- Integrating outdoor and natural world elements into the indoor environment
- Rearranging the environment to create new interest in each area

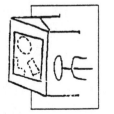

Teacher as Architect

- Evaluating space based on a child's eye view
- Adapting space to the children's play needs and interests
- Creating opportunities to explore light and shadow, sound, color and texture
- Integrating outdoor and natural world elements into the indoor environment
- Rearranging the environment to create new interest in each area

© 1994 *Training Teachers*, Redleaf Press, 450 North Syndicate, Suite 5, St. Paul, MN 55104, 1-800-423-8309

Teacher as Scribe
- Modeling that the spoken word can be written down and read
- Making written and pictorial representations of children's play and language
- Telling stories to children about their own play activities
- Taking dictation or transcribing children's language
- Supporting children's efforts to tell stories or write about their play or creations

Teacher as Scribe
- Modeling that the spoken word can be written down and read
- Making written and pictorial representations of children's play and language
- Telling stories to children about their own play activities
- Taking dictation or transcribing children's language
- Supporting children's efforts to tell stories or write about their play or creations

Teacher as Scribe
- Modeling that the spoken word can be written down and read
- Making written and pictorial representations of children's play and language
- Telling stories to children about their own play activities
- Taking dictation or transcribing children's language
- Supporting children's efforts to tell stories or write about their play or creations

Teacher as Scribe
- Modeling that the spoken word can be written down and read
- Making written and pictorial representations of children's play and language
- Telling stories to children about their own play activities
- Taking dictation or transcribing children's language
- Supporting children's efforts to tell stories or write about their play or creations

Teacher as Coach

- Recognizing strengths and providing opportunities to practice them
- Encouraging risk-taking with a supportive presence
- Teaching skills to support self-selected tasks
- Matching challenges to individual interests
- Creating teamwork with materials and activities that require group effort

Teacher as Coach

- Recognizing strengths and providing opportunities to practice them
- Encouraging risk-taking with a supportive presence
- Teaching skills to support self-selected tasks
- Matching challenges to individual interests
- Creating teamwork with materials and activities that require group effort

Teacher as Coach

- Recognizing strengths and providing opportunities to practice them
- Encouraging risk-taking with a supportive presence
- Teaching skills to support self-selected tasks
- Matching challenges to individual interests
- Creating teamwork with materials and activities that require group effort

Teacher as Coach

- Recognizing strengths and providing opportunities to practice them
- Encouraging risk-taking with a supportive presence
- Teaching skills to support self-selected tasks
- Matching challenges to individual interests
- Creating teamwork with materials and activities that require group effort

© 1994 *Training Teachers*, Redleaf Press, 450 North Syndicate, Suite 5, St. Paul, MN 55104, 1-800-423-8309

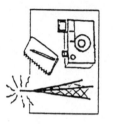

Teacher as Broadcaster

- Spreading the news of the play stories you observe in your group
- Collecting and displaying examples of children's activities and creations
- Representing a child's point of view about a significant event
- Sharing children's good ideas with others
- Educating parents about the learning embedded in their child's chosen play

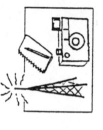

Teacher as Broadcaster

- Spreading the news of the play stories you observe in your group
- Collecting and displaying examples of children's activities and creations
- Representing a child's point of view about a significant event
- Sharing children's good ideas with others
- Educating parents about the learning embedded in their child's chosen play

Teacher as Broadcaster

- Spreading the news of the play stories you observe in your group
- Collecting and displaying examples of children's activities and creations
- Representing a child's point of view about a significant event
- Sharing children's good ideas with others
- Educating parents about the learning embedded in their child's chosen play

Teacher as Broadcaster

- Spreading the news of the play stories you observe in your group
- Collecting and displaying examples of children's activities and creations
- Representing a child's point of view about a significant event
- Sharing children's good ideas with others
- Educating parents about the learning embedded in their child's chosen play

© 1994 *Training Teachers*, Redleaf Press, 450 North Syndicate, Suite 5, St. Paul, MN 55104, 1-800-423-8309

Teacher as Observer

- Seeing self as a field researcher in child development
- Appreciating the details of children's complex play
- Making note of a child's likes, dislikes, accomplishments and frustrations
- Observing before intervening or reacting
- Planning curriculum projects from children's interests and ideas

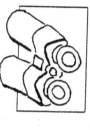

Teacher as Observer

- Seeing self as a field researcher in child development
- Appreciating the details of children's complex play
- Making note of a child's likes, dislikes, accomplishments and frustrations
- Observing before intervening or reacting
- Planning curriculum projects from children's interests and ideas

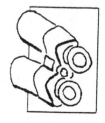

Teacher as Observer

- Seeing self as a field researcher in child development
- Appreciating the details of children's complex play
- Making note of a child's likes, dislikes, accomplishments and frustrations
- Observing before intervening or reacting
- Planning curriculum projects from children's interests and ideas

Teacher as Observer

- Seeing self as a field researcher in child development
- Appreciating the details of children's complex play
- Making note of a child's likes, dislikes, accomplishments and frustrations
- Observing before intervening or reacting
- Planning curriculum projects from children's interests and ideas

Teacher as Mediator
- Creating a climate of safety for children to speak their needs and feelings
- Seeing conflicts as opportunities to learn social skills
- Providing support and language for children to solve their own problems
- Focusing on the content of the play rather than on a violation of rules
- Interpreting the meaning of children's messages to each other

Teacher as Mediator
- Creating a climate of safety for children to speak their needs and feelings
- Seeing conflicts as opportunities to learn social skills
- Providing support and language for children to solve their own problems
- Focusing on the content of the play rather than on a violation of rules
- Interpreting the meaning of children's messages to each other

Teacher as Mediator
- Creating a climate of safety for children to speak their needs and feelings
- Seeing conflicts as opportunities to learn social skills
- Providing support and language for children to solve their own problems
- Focusing on the content of the play rather than on a violation of rules
- Interpreting the meaning of children's messages to each other

Teacher as Mediator
- Creating a climate of safety for children to speak their needs and feelings
- Seeing conflicts as opportunities to learn social skills
- Providing support and language for children to solve their own problems
- Focusing on the content of the play rather than on a violation of rules
- Interpreting the meaning of children's messages to each other

Teacher as Prop Manager

- Suggesting play possibilities through arrangement of materials
- Anticipating playscripts with a supply of related props
- Encouraging open-ended use and transformation of materials
- Creating order behind the play with casual picking up and putting away
- Providing additional materials without interrupting the play flow

Teacher as Prop Manager

- Suggesting play possibilities through arrangement of materials
- Anticipating playscripts with a supply of related props
- Encouraging open-ended use and transformation of materials
- Creating order behind the play with casual picking up and putting away
- Providing additional materials without interrupting the play flow

Teacher as Prop Manager

- Suggesting play possibilities through arrangement of materials
- Anticipating playscripts with a supply of related props
- Encouraging open-ended use and transformation of materials
- Creating order behind the play with casual picking up and putting away
- Providing additional materials without interrupting the play flow

Teacher as Prop Manager

- Suggesting play possibilities through arrangement of materials
- Anticipating playscripts with a supply of related props
- Encouraging open-ended use and transformation of materials
- Creating order behind the play with casual picking up and putting away
- Providing additional materials without interrupting the play flow

HOT FOR LITERACY

Introduction

Reading and writing are important lifetime skills that both teachers and parents value. Often in our attempt to insure that children gain these skills, we start formal teaching and drill too early. The approaches we use based on our experiences with older children, may undermine the learning process for preschoolers.

Current research points to the importance of fostering positive attitudes and the desire to read and write. There are also important skills that children need to master during their preschool years which are an essential part of the literacy process. (See preschool reading and writing skills.)

In response to the concern for the development of literacy in early childhood, the Hot For Literacy Program is designed to promote appropriate literacy environments and activities for preschool age children.

The goals of this program are to:

*Gain knowledge and understandings of how young children develop literacy
*Examine current practices and activities
*Develop and provide meaningful literacy experiences for young children
*Provide information and experience for parents to increase their awareness of how they contribute to their child's literacy development.

Prizes for points!!! Keep track of each of the activities and points earned on the calendar. Points are recorded for all classroom staff rather than one person. When you have reached one of the point levels contact your education coordinator to receive your prize.

50 points
____ Literacy props
____ Buttons
____ 1 children's book

100 points
____ 2 children's books

250 points
____ Children's cassette tape
____ Film and photo album

500 points
____ Teacher resource book

750 points
____ Puppets/other classroom materials

1000 points
____ Substitute for a day (to visit another program) or
____ show performance at your site

1 POINT for each day you . . .

____ Read to groups and individual children.

____ Encourage children to talk about pictures, photos and retell stories in their own words.

____ Check children's bookshelf for quality books and modify selection to meet children's interest.

____ Take dictation from children.

____ Model and comment on writing in presence of children (i.e. notes to parents and staff, reminders to self, etc.)

____ Introduce print within the context of pretend play (i.e. writing a shopping list, taking a phone message, making a sign for a block structure, etc.)

____ Provide opportunities for children to "write" in their own way (i.e. scribble name for attendance, a turn taking list, name on art work, etc.)

____ Assure that paper and writing tools are available for children's continuous use.

© 1994 *Training Teachers,* Redleaf Press, 450 North Syndicate, Suite 5, St. Paul, MN 55104, 1-800-423-8309

5 POINTS when you . . .

_____ Complete Preschool Reading and Writing Skills Checklist on 5 children.

_____ Add writing and literacy dramatic props to an area of your classroom (see Classroom Literacy Checklist for ideas).

_____ Set up writing/book making center (i.e. stapler, tape, hole punch, file folders, envelopes, stickers, paper clips, note pad, ink pad and rubber stamps, telephone, typewriter or keyboard, etc.)

_____ Make and use flannel board stories/stories with props and leave them in the classroom for children to retell/recreate.

_____ Provide creative dramatics experiences through story reenactment.

_____ Invite story tellers and puppeteers to classroom.

_____ Arrange field trip to library.

_____ Tape record yourself as you narrate, describe and label what children are doing or engaged in.

_____ Use picture sequence (to represent the daily routine, a weekly calendar, cooking recipe, directions for assembling).

_____ Set up a puppet theater for children to use.

_____ Share literacy examples with other teachers during site exchanges.

_____ Provide suggestions during a home visit on ways parents can support child's development of literacy, etc.

10 POINTS when you . . .

_____ Attend a workshop on language development, literacy, creative dramatics, story telling, children's literature.

_____ Organize a book lending library.

_____ Present a parent education meeting about supporting child's literacy at home and school.

_____ Be videotaped and analyze your skills in promoting language and literacy in the classroom.

25 POINTS when you . . .

_____ Complete a college course in whole language, children's literature, creative dramatics, emergent literacy, encouraging language development in the preschool.

_____ Carry out a library card drive for families in your program.

NAME: _____

MONTH:_____PREVIOUS TOTAL:_____

MONDAY_____
TUESDAY_____
WEDNESDAY_____
THURSDAY_____
FRIDAY_____
POINTS_____
THIS MONTH'S TOTAL_____

© 1994 *Training Teachers*, Redleaf Press, 450 North Syndicate, Suite 5, St. Paul, MN 55104, 1-800-423-8309

Appendix C

TRAINING EVALUATION

Workshop Topic _____ Date_____

I came to this workshop wanting....

The part I liked best was...

This workshop would have been more inclusive if...

I feel confident that...

I still don't understand...

Next time please...

And one more thing...

WORKSHOP EVALUATION

I came to this workshop hoping to:

I am leaving this workshop with a better idea about how to:

I'd like to give the workshop leaders this feedback:

WORKSHOP EVALUATION

Workshop_____Title _____

Workshop Leader(s)_____

1. What did you hope to learn in this workshop? Was this goal met?

2. What engaged you the most?

   the least?

3. What did you understand the main points of the workshop to be?

4. What ideas/activities from the workshop do you want to use?

5. Any outstanding questions or concerns on the topic that didn't get addressed?

6. Any suggestions for reorganizing how the time was spent?

7. What should the workshop leader(s) strive to improve in conducting this workshop?

8. Would you like a follow-up workshop on this topic?

9. Other comments? (use back of paper if necessary)

© 1994 *Training Teachers,* Redleaf Press, 450 North Syndicate, Suite 5, St. Paul, MN 55104, 1-800-423-8309

DEVELOPMENTALLY APPROPRIATE CURRICULUM

Initial Self Assessment

Name:_____

Date: _____

Use back of this page if necessary

Describe your current involvement with young children, the setting(s), and age group(s).

How would you define the term Developmentally Appropriate Curriculum?

What do you know about children and how they develop?

Describe how you think children learn best.

How do you go about planning curriculum for the children's learning?

Describe the activities that you now provide that you believe work best.

Describe the activities that you now provide that don't work as well as you would like.

Do you have people pressuring you to provide more "academic" instruction in your program? If so, who? How do they apply pressure?

© 1994 *Training Teachers*, Redleaf Press, 450 North Syndicate, Suite 5, St. Paul, MN 55104, 1-800-423-8309

DEVELOPMENTALLY APPROPRIATE CURRICULUM

Final Self Assessment

Name:_____

Date: _____

Use back of this page if necessary

Since taking this class do you have any changes in how you would define developmentally appropriate curriculum? If so, what are they?

From your group project, what new things have you learned about how children develop?

How has your thinking changed about how children learn best?

How has the class impacted your approach to planning curriculum for children's learning?

TRAINING SURVEY

Name_____ Class_____

Trainer_____ Date _____

Below is a list of teacher developmental stages. Please indicate which you feel you have mastered and which you need to work on.

	Mastered	Need to Work On
I know the principles of active play as a basis for determining learning objectives		
I find children and their play interesting		
I have basic knowledge of children's developmental themes and stages		
I know the principles of developmentally appropriate practice (DAP)		
I know how to arrange the room, provide materials and activities for		
physical growth		
social/emotional growth		
cognitive growth		
I know how to help children with		
self-help/self esteem		
negotiating/conflict resolution		
problem-solving		
I do observations of children and plan the environment and activities from these		
I am self-aware and intentional in my interventions with children		
I know how to perform these roles:		
documenting behaviors		
lead group time		
stage and prop manager for children's play		
scribe for modeling literacy skills		
coordinator of smooth transitions		
team player with other staff		
partnership with parents		

© 1994 *Training Teachers*, Redleaf Press, 450 North Syndicate, Suite 5, St. Paul, MN 55104, 1-800-423-8309

TRAINING QUESTIONNAIRE

To_____(Trainer)   Date _____

From_____(Teacher)

The following are my areas of strength and needs for improvement. Please arrange to meet with me to set up a training focus and plan.

	My Strength	Help Needed
Health and Safety Comments:		
Learning Environments Comments:		
Self-esteem and Child Guidance Comments:		
Language and Literacy Development Comments:		
Curriculum Planning Comments:		
Valuing Diversity and Anti-bias Practices Comments:		
Parent Involvement and Partnerships Comments:		
Staff Communication and Conflict Comments:		
Professional Self-esteem and Advocacy Comments		
Other:		

© 1994 *Training Teachers*, Redleaf Press, 450 North Syndicate, Suite 5, St. Paul, MN 55104, 1-800-423-8309

TRAINING NEEDS SURVEY

Name_____Class_____

Trainer_____Date _____

Please check the areas you would like your trainer to focus on with you.

Social/Emotional Development
- ☐ fostering self-help
- ☐ fostering self-esteem
- ☐ cultural identity
- ☐ separation anxiety
- ☐ problem solving/negotiating/turn taking
- ☐ promoting dramatic play

Cognitive Development
- ☐ language development
- ☐ representation and early literacy
- ☐ number and math learning
- ☐ classification experiences
- ☐ recognizing cognitive development in children's play

Learning Environment
- ☐ room arrangements
- ☐ materials for interest areas and key experiences
- ☐ multicultural/anti-bias images and materials
- ☐ provisions for self-help and independence in using the room

Curriculum Development
- ☐ the environment as curriculum
- ☐ curriculum webbing
- ☐ planning from observing children's interests and development
- ☐ weaving in multicultural perspectives and anti-bias themes

Building Parent-Teacher Partnerships
- ☐ verbal communications that work
- ☐ written communication systems
- ☐ cross cultural communications
- ☐ bonding and separation concerns
- ☐ parent education, resources and referrals
- ☐ parent conferences
- ☐ strategies for a child of special concern

Other:

INDIVIDUAL TRAINING PLAN

Staff Person_____ Supervisor _____

Date _____

A. Identify Problem (describe 2 examples of a behavior of concern)
    1.

    2.

B. Identify and describe how the new behavior should look (behavioral objective)

C.   Describe how change will be sought
    1. Identify strength to build from

    2. Possible action plan with time line

D. Describe how change/success will be measured

E. Delegation/Coaching Plan
    1) What

    2) Who

    3) When

Certificate of Training

Awarded to

In Recognition of

_Completion of _____ hours Training on_

_____

Date

Instructor

Notes and References

Introduction

1. Hawkins, David, in Edwards, C., Gandini, L., and Forman, G. (Eds.) (1993) *The Hundred Languages of Children: The Reggio Emilia Approach to Early Childhood Education.* Norwood, NJ: Ablex Publishing, p. xvi.

2. Carter, F. (1976) *The Education of Little Tree.* Albuquerque: University of New Mexico Press, p. 57. We acknowledge the controversy surrounding the author of this book, but found he offered us insight and a particularly relevant quote regarding our motivation to write this book.

3. Malaguzzi, Loris, in *The Hundred Languages of Children: The Reggio Emilia Approach to Early Childhood Education*, p. 82.

Section 1: Changing our Approach to Teacher Education

1. Freire, P. (1970) *Pedagogy of the Oppressed.* New York: Herder and Herder.

2. Jones, E. (1993) *Growing Teachers: Partnerships in Staff Development.* Washington, DC: NAEYC, p. xiii.

3. Duckworth, E. (1987) *The Having of Wonderful Ideas and Other Essays on Teaching and Learning.* New York: Teachers College Press.

4. Brooks, J. (February 1990) "Teachers and Students: Constructivists Forging New Connections." *Educational Leadership*, vol. 47, no. 5, p. 69.

5. Katz, L. (August 1979) *Helping Others Learn to Teach: Some Principles and Techniques for Inservice Educators.* Urbana, IL: ERIC Clearinghouse on Elementary and Early Childhood Education, p. 9.

6. Bredekamp, S. (Ed.) (1987) *Developmentally Appropriate Practice in Early Childhood Programs Serving Children from Birth through Age 8* and (1991) *Accreditation Criteria & Procedures of the National Academy of Early Childhood Programs.* Washington, DC: NAEYC.

7. Phillips, C. (Ed.) (1991) *Essentials for Child Development Associates Working with Young Children.* Washington, DC: Council for Early Childhood Professional Recognition.

8. Jones, p. 146.

9. Brooks, p. 69.

10. The educational implications of Piagetian research and theory are comprehensively explored in DeVries, R., and Kohlberg, L. (1990) *Constructivist Early Education: Overview and Comparison With Other Programs.* Washington, DC: NAEYC.

11. Duckworth, p. 26.

12. Ibid., p. 123.

13. Ibid.

14. Spodek, B. (March 1975) "Early Childhood Education and Teacher Education: A Search for Consistency." *Young Children*, vol. 30, no. 3, p. 171.

15. Ibid., p. 172.

16. Jones, E. "Constructing Professional Knowledge by Telling Our Stories" in Johnson, J., and McCracken, J. (Eds.) (in press) *An Early Childhood Professional Development System: From Concept to Reality.* Washington, DC: NAEYC, pp. 150-156.

Section 2: Tools for the Harvest

1. Brooks, Jacqueline Grennon, (1990) "Teachers and Students: Constructivists Forging New Connections." *Educational Leadership*, vol. 47, no. 5, p. 69.

2. The term "growing teachers" was brought to us by Elizabeth Jones and discussed in her book *Growing Teachers: Partnerships in Staff Development.*

3. Diane Trister Dodge is best known for *The Creative Curriculum for Early Childhood* (1992) and *A Guide for Supervisors and Trainers on Implementing the Creative Curriculum* (1988). She has also produced valuable audiovisual resources for trainers such as the video "The Creative Curriculum" and "Room Arrangement as a Teaching Strategy." These are all available from Teaching Strategies, Inc., P.O. Box 42243, Washington, DC 20016. A newer publication with a similar approach, *The What, Why and How of High-Quality Early Childhood Education: A Guide for On-Site Supervision,* is co-authored by Koralek, D., Colker, L., and Dodge, D. (NAEYC, 1993).

4. Wasserman, S. (1992) *Serious Players in the Primary Classroom.* New York: Teachers College Press, p. 102.

5. Ibid., p. 201.

6. For a summary of Piaget's formulation of the kinds of learning see Piaget, J., and Inhelder, B. (1969) *The Psychology of the Child.* New York: Basic Books, and more simply in Peterson, R., and Felton-Collins, V. (1986) *The Piaget Handbook for Teachers and Parents.* New York: Teachers College Press.

7. Dodge, Diane Trister (1993) *A Guide for Supervisors and Trainers on Implementing the Creative Curriculum for Early Childhood.* Washington, D.C.: Teaching Strategies.

8. This concept refers to information acquired by memorization or rote learning, learning by association rather than logic. It is explained in detail in *The Psychology of the Child* (Basic Books, 1969), and more simply in *The Piaget Handbook for Teachers and Parents* (Teachers College Press, 1986).

9. Our thoughts on this have been influenced by Sue Bredekamp (ED) (1987) Developmentally Appropriate Practice in Early Childhood Programs Serving Children from Birth through Age 8. Washington, D.C.: NAEYC.

10. Available from Jane Meade-Roberts, Adjunct Faculty, Pacific Oaks College, 815 Capistrano Drive, Salinas, CA 93901.

11. For copies of the big book version of the ABZ Child Care Center storybook and related activity props, contact the Worthy Wage Campaign, c/o National Center for the Early Childhood Work Force, 733 15th NW, Suite 800, Washington, DC 20005; (202) 737-7700 or (800) U-R-WORTHY/(800) 879-6784.

12. Derman-Sparks, L. (1989) *Anti-Bias Curriculum. Tools for Empowering Young Children.* Washington, DC: NAEYC, p. 16 and 146.

13. This idea is explored in depth in *The Having of Wonderful Ideas and Other Essays on Teaching and Learning.*

14. Prescott, E. (April 1979) "The Physical Environment—A Powerful Regulator of Experience." *Child Care Information Exchange.* Redmond, WA: Exchange Press.

15. Several valuable resources on the project approach include: *The Hundred Languages of Children: The Reggio Emilia Approach to Early Childhood Education*; Katz, L., and Chard, S. (1989) *Engaging Children's Minds: The Project Approach.* Norwood, NJ: Ablex Publishing; LeeKeenan, D., and Edwards, C. (1992) "Using the Project Approach With Toddlers." *Young Children*, vol. 47, no. 4; and Cassidy, D., and Lancaster, C. "The Grassroots Curriculum: A Dialogue Between Children and Teachers." *Young Children*, vol. 48, no. 6.

Section 3: Dispositions and Roles for Effective Teaching

1. Katz, p. 3.

2. June, 1993, Working Papers for National Institute for Early Childhood Professional Development. Washington, DC: NAEYC.

3. Katz, p. 3.

4. Duckworth, Eleanor in Schwebel, M. and Raph, J. (1973) *Piaget in the Classroom.* New York: HarperCollins.

5. This is a question we learned from Elizabeth Prescott in our graduate work at Pacific Oaks College. She taught us to capture the essence of an experience for a child by trying to give it a title.

6. Jones, E. (1990) "Playing Is My Job." *Thrust for Educational Leadership*, vol. 20, no. 2, p. 13.

7. Jones, E., and Reynolds, G. (1992) *The Play's the Thing: Teachers' Roles in Children's Play.* New York: Teachers College Press, p. xii.

8. Jones, E. (1980) "Creating Environments Where Teachers, Like Children, Learn Through Play." *Child Care Information Exchange*, vol. 13, pp. 9-13.

9. As with the upheavaling events of the late 1960s in major U.S. cities, we call the response to the 1992 not-guilty verdict in the trial of the police officers who brutally beat Rodney King in Los Angeles a "rebellion" rather than a "riot." A riot implies random, purposeless violence rather than an intentional uprising against racism.

10. For an in-depth look at the project approach, see *The Hundred Languages of Children: The Reggio Emilia Approach to Early Childhood Education* and *Engaging Children's Minds: The Project Approach.*

11. Katz, L. (1984) *More Talks with Teachers.* Urbana, IL: Eric Clearinghouse on Elementary and Early Childhood Education.

12. Ibid., p. 28.

13. Ibid., pp. 29-34.

14. Bateson, M. C. (1990) *Composing a Life.* New York: Penguin Books, pp. 2 and 4.

15. Katz, L. (1990) "On Teaching." *Child Care Information Exchange*, vol. 71.

16. Wasserman, p. 103.

17. Mentor teacher programs now exist in California, Massachusetts, North Carolina, and Wisconsin. For the most current listing, contact the National Center for the Early Childhood Work Force (202) 737-7700 or (800) U-R-WORTHY/(800) 879-6784.

18. Paulo Freire is author of numerous books, including *Pedagogy of the Oppressed, Education for Critical Consciousness*, and *The Politics of Education.* This concept is developed in nearly all of them, but especially in the book co-authored with Macedo, D. (1987) *Literacy: Reading the Word and the World.* South Hadley, MA: Bergin & Garvey.

19. Jones & Reynolds, p. 1.

20. Bateson, p. 6.

21. Crow, C. (Spring 1993) *Adult Learning and a Changing Economy.* Bainbridge Island, WA: New Horizons for Learning.

22. Jones & Reynolds, p. 1.

23. Ibid.

24. Malaguzzi, p. 85.

25. Ibid., p. 66.

Section 4: Training for Culturally Sensitive and Anti-Bias Practices

1. Information regarding the development of bias in children can be found in Clark, K. (1988) *Prejudice and Your Child.* Hanover, NH: Wesleyan University Press; Cross, W. (1989) *Shades of Black: Diversity in African-American Identity.* Philadelphia: Temple University Press; Dennis, R., in Bowser, B., and Hunt, R. (Eds.) (1981) "Socialization & Racism: The White Experience." *Impacts of Racism on White Americans.* Beverly Hills, CA: Sage Press; Goodman, M. (1970) *The Culture of Childhood: Child's Eye Views of Society and Culture.* New York: Teachers College Press; and Katz, P. (1993) "University Talk: Development of Racial Attitudes in Children." Unpublished paper presented at University of Delaware, May 6, 1993.

2. Delpit, L. (August 1988) "The Silenced Dialogue: Power and Pedagogy in Educating Other People's Children." *Harvard Educational Review*, vol. 58, no. 3, p. 297.

3. Our thoughts on this have been influenced by Sue Bredekamp (ED) (1987) Developmentally Appropriate Practice in Early Childhood Programs Serving Children from Birth through Age 8. Washington, D.C.: NAEYC.

4. The fullest explanation of the anti-bias curriculum approach is found in Derman-Sparks *The Anti-Bias Curriculum: Tools for Empowering Young Children.* Washington, D.C.: NAEYC.

5. Jones, E., and Derman-Sparks, L. (1992) "Meeting the Challenge of Diversity." *Young Children*, vol. 47, no. 2, p. 13.

6. Randall, M. (1991) *Walking to the Edge.* Boston: South End Press, p. 142.

7. A compelling explanation of the culture of power is found in "The Silenced Dialogue: Power and Pedagogy in Educating Other People's Children" and "A Conversation with Lisa Delpit." *Language Arts*, vol. 68, November 1991.

8. Delpit, p. 282.

9. Ibid.

10. Randall, p. 149.

11. Ibid.

12. Phillips, C. (1991) *Culture as a Process.* Unpublished paper, February 17, 1991.

13. There are several valuable resources with Wong Fillmore's work. Wong Fillmore, L. (1991) "Language and Cultural Issues in the Early Education of Language Minority Children" in Kagan, S. L. (Ed.) *The Care and Education of America's Young Children: Obstacles and Opportunities.* Chicago: University of Chicago Press; Wong Fillmore, L. (1991) "When Learning a Second Language Means Losing the First." *Early Childhood Research Quarterly*, vol. 6, no. 3.

14. *Essential Connections.*

15. Taken from a video produced by Far West Laboratory, Center for Child & Family Studies. (1993) *Essential Connections: Ten Keys to Culturally Sensitive Child Care.* Available from the Bureau of Publications, California Department of Education, P.O. Box 271, Sacramento, CA 95802-0271.

16. BAFA, BAFA is a copyrighted game that can be obtained from Simile II, P.O. Box 910, Del Mar, CA 92014.

17. Ginott, H. (1993) *Teacher & Child: A Book for Parents and Teachers.* New York: Macmillan Publishing, p. 245.

18. Derman-Sparks, L. (1991) *Goals of Anti-Bias Curriculum.* Pasadena, CA: Pacific Oaks College; unpublished paper.

19. Bisson, J. (1992) *Celebrating Holidays in the Anti-Bias Early Childhood Education Program.* Pasadena, CA: Pacific Oaks College, unpublished thesis.

Section 5: Training in Different Settings

1. You can find a fuller description of profession development predicament the institute is trying to address in the 1993 working papers of NAEYC entitled "Improving Professional Development in the Early Childhood Field."

2. You can find the results of the study that the High/Scope Educational Research Foundation conducted in Epstein, A. (1993) *Training for Quality.* Ypsilanti, MI: High/Scope Press.

3. For a summary of this, see Bredekamp, S., and Wille, B. (March 1992) "Of Ladders and Lattices, Cores and Cones: Conceptualizing an Early Childhood Professional Development System." *Young Children,* vol. 47, no. 3.

4. Jones, E. (Ed.) (1983) *On the Growing Edge: Notes From College Teachers Making Changes.* Pasadena, CA: Pacific Oaks College; and (1986) *Teaching Adults: An Active Learning Approach.* Washington, DC: NAEYC.

5. Bureau of Labor Statistics, cited in *High/Scope Resource* (Spring/Summer 1992) vol. 11, no. 2.

6. The High/Scope Foundation has several publications detailing the Perry Preschool longitudinal research study. The most recent is Berrueta-Clement, J., Schweinhart, L. J., Barnett, W. S., Epstein, A. S., and Weikart, D. P. (1985) *Changed Lives. The Effects of the Perry Preschool Program on Youths through Age 19.* Ypsilanti, MI: High/Scope Press.

7. Epstein, A. (1993) *Training for Quality.* Ypsilanti, MI: High/Scope Press.

8. Edwards, p. 115.

9. Ibid., p. 116.

10. Ibid.

11. Weikart, D., and Shouse, C. (Winter 1993) *High/Scope Resource,* vol. 12, no. 1.

12. Jones, *Growing Teachers: Partnerships in Staff Development,* p. xv.

13. Carter, M., and Jones, E. (October 1990) "The Teacher as Observer: The Director as Role Model." *Child Care Information Exchange,* vol. 75, pp. 29-30.

14. Whitebook, M., Phillips, D., and Howes, C. (1988) *National Child Care Staffing Study—Who Cares? Child Care Teachers and the Quality of Care in America.* Oakland, CA: Child Care Employee Project.

15. Creating this bulletin board display is an idea we originally learned from Betty Jones and is described by Carter, M. "Catching Teachings 'Being Good': Using Observation to Communicate" in Jones, *Growing Teachers: Partnerships in Staff Development* and in Jones, E., and Reynolds, G., *The Play's the Thing: Teachers' Roles in Children's Play.*

16. Our thoughts on this have influenced by M. Whitebook, D. Phillips and C. Howes (1988) *National Child Care Staffing Study—Who Cares? Child Care Teachers and the Quality of Care in America.*

Section 6: A Course on Child Centered Curriculum Practices

1. Some of the resources detailing the project approach include Edwards, *The Hundred Languages of Children: The Reggio Emilia Approach to Early Childhood Education* and Katz, *Engaging Children's Minds: The Project Approach.*

2. This outline from the University of Massachusetts laboratory school was first given to us by a colleague and later was developed for publication in LeeKeenan, D. "Using the Project Approach with Toddlers." *Young Children* and with Nimmo, J., as "Connections: Using the Project Approach with 2 and 3 Year Olds in a University Laboratory School" in Edwards, *The Hundred Languages of Children.* Though we have strong reservations about a formal project with toddlers, we found the ideas inspiring and easily adaptable.

3. Jones & Reynolds, p. 109.

4. The term "loose parts," an increasingly common phrase in early childhood programming, originated with Simon Nicholson and is aptly considered in Greenman, J. (1988) *Caring Places, Learning Spaces.* Redmond, WA: Exchange Press.

5. Adapted from Bloom, B. S. (1956) *Taxonomy of Educational Objectives: The Classification of Educational Goals,* Handbook 1. Cognitive Domain. New York: McKay.

6. Hohmann, M., Banet, B. Y., and Weikart, D. (1979) *Young Children in Action.* Ypsilanti, MI: High/Scope Press.

7. An overview can be found in Fillmore, "Language and Cultural Issues in Early Education" in *The Care and Education of American's Young Children: Obstacles and Opportunities.*

Section 7: The Invisible Life of a Trainer

1. Carter, F., p. v.

2. For an up-to-date list of these states (including California, Massachusetts, North Carolina, and Wisconsin) contact the National Center for the Early Childhood Work Force (formerly the Child Care Employee Project), 733 15th NW, Suite 800, Washington, DC 20005; (202) 737-7700 or (800) U-R-WORTHY/(800) 879-6784.

Index